The Chambers
Book of
Business Quotations

The Chambers Book of Business Quotations

Compiled by Martin H. Manser

Text © Martin H. Manser 1987
Illustrations © Dan Donovan 1987

Published by W & R Chambers Ltd, Edinburgh 1987

British Library Cataloguing in Publication Data

Manser, Martin H.
　The Chambers book of business quotations.
　1. Business — Quotations, maxims etc.
　I. Title
　338.6　　PN6084.B8

　ISBN 0 – 550 – 20488 – 1

Acknowledgements
The editor wishes to express his gratitude
to Rosalind Desmond for her research help
in compiling the text, and to the staff of
the Buckinghamshire County Library,
Aylesbury for their assistance in tracing
sources of references.

Designed by Tony Cantale Graphics
Typeset by Creative Editors and Writers Ltd, Watford
Printed by Martin's of Berwick

Contents

INTRODUCTION

This book of business quotations has been compiled with the aim of being both informative and entertaining. The selection will prove useful to those trying to find a quotation – serious or witty, contemporary or older – that will express a point of view for a report, article, or speech.

Quotations have been drawn from a wide variety of sources: not only businessmen, businesswomen, and economists, but also politicians, historians, philosophers, poets, etc., where their writings touch on business and topics related to the business world.

Approximately 2000 quotations have been selected. They are listed according to themes, which are arranged alphabetically within 9 major sections. The index includes the authors of quotations and themes in one single alphabetical listing.

It is hoped that this book will prove to be not only an instructive work of reference but also an entertaining – and at times amusing – guide through the world of business.

Martin H. Manser

SUCCESS & WEALTH

What are the secrets of becoming rich? How can you become prosperous and successful? Can money really buy anything . . . and everything? The quotations in this opening section reveal not only the great variety of ways of achieving success but also the extraordinary power exerted by money, wealth, and property. Alongside less familiar quotes such as 'The two most beautiful words in the English language are "Cheque Enclosed"'(Dorothy Parker) and the more well-known 'Time is money' (Benjamin Franklin), 'Man does not live by GNP alone' (Paul Samuelson), and 'The meek shall inherit the earth, but not the mineral rights' (attributed to J. Paul Getty).

MONEY

Money is better than poverty, if only for financial reasons.
WOODY ALLEN (Allen Stewart Konigsberg) (1935–), American film comedian, screenwriter, and director: *Without Feathers, 'The Early Essays'*

Money isn't everything: usually it isn't even enough.
Anon

What comes by nature costs no money.
Anon

Gold hath been the ruin of many.
The Apocrypha, Ecclesiasticus 21:6

Money, it turned out, was exactly like sex, you thought of nothing else if you didn't have it and thought of other things if you did.
JAMES (ARTHUR) BALDWIN (1924–), American novelist and essayist: *Nobody Knows My Name*

If you would know what the Lord God thinks of money, you have only to look at those to whom he gives it.
MAURICE BARING (1874–1945), English novelist, essayist, poet, and playwright, quoted in Dorothy Parker, *Writers at Work: First Series*

A man accustomed to think in millions – other people's millions.
ENOCH ARNOLD BENNETT (1867–1931), English novelist: *Journal, June 1929*

For the love of money is the root of all evil.
The Bible, Authorized (King James) Version, 1 Timothy 6:10

Money
A blessing that is of no advantage to us excepting when we part with it. An evidence of culture and a passport to polite society. Supportable property.
AMBROSE (GWINETT) BIERCE (1842–?1914), American journalist and humorist: *The Devil's Dictionary*

It has been said that the love of money is the root of all evil. The want of money is so quite as truly.
SAMUEL BUTLER (1835–1902), English author, painter, and musician: *Erewhon*

I consider in general that an increase of actual money causes in a State a corresponding increase of consumption which gradually brings about increased prices.
RICHARD CANTILLON (1680?–1734), British economist: *Essai sur la Nature du Commerce en Général*

And here I say to parents, especially wealthy parents, 'Don't give your son money. As far as you can afford it, give him horses.'
SIR WINSTON LEONARD SPENCER CHURCHILL (1874–1965), English statesman, writer, and prime minister: *My Early Life, 4*

How pleasant it is to have money.
ARTHUR HUGH CLOUGH (1819–61), English poet: *Dipsychus, I:4*

A fool and his money are soon parted. What I want to know is how they got together in the first place.
CYRIL FLETCHER (1913–), British comedian: *BBC radio programme, 8 May 1969*

Remember that time is money.
BENJAMIN FRANKLIN (1706–90), American statesman, scientist, and author: *Advice to a Young Tradesman*

Money is a singular thing. It ranks with love as a man's greatest source of joy. And with death as its greatest source of anxiety. Money differs from an automobile, a mistress or cancer in being equally important to those who have it and those who do not.
JOHN KENNETH GALBRAITH (1908–), Canadian-born American economist, diplomat, and writer: *The Age of Uncertainty*

If you can actually count your money then you are not a really rich man.
J(EAN) PAUL GETTY (1892–1976), American financier, quoted in Bernard Levin, *The Pendulum Years, chapter 1*

I find all this money a considerable burden.
J(EAN) PAUL GETTY, *Observer, 'Sayings of the Year', 29 December 1985*

Bad money drives out good money.
SIR THOMAS GRESHAM (?1519–79), English financier

Put not your trust in money, but put your money in trust.
OLIVER WENDELL HOLMES, SR (1809–94), American physician, professor, and author: *The Autocrat of the Breakfast Table*

Is this the sort of advice you're looking for? – 'Make money. Make it, if you can, fair and square. If not, make it anyway.'
HORACE (Quintus Horatius Flaccus) (65–8 BC), Roman poet and satirist: *Epistles*

Get money first; virtue comes afterward.
HORACE, *as above*

A man is usually more careful of his money than he is of his principles.
EDGAR WATSON HOWE (1853–1937), American journalist, novelist, and essayist: *Ventures in Common Sense*

When a man says money can do anything, that settles it: he hasn't any.
EDGAR WATSON HOWE, *Sinner Sermons*

IF YOU CAN ACTUALLY COUNT YOUR MONEY
THEN YOU ARE NOT A REALLY RICH MAN.

3

We all know how the size of sums of money appears to vary in a remarkable way according as they are being paid in or paid out.
JULIAN (SORELL) HUXLEY (1887–1975), English biologist: *Essays of a Biologist, 5*

Money, and not morality, is the principle of commercial nations.
THOMAS JEFFERSON (1743–1826), American statesman and U.S. president: *Letter to John Langdon, 1810*

There are few ways in which a man can be more innocently employed than in getting money.
SAMUEL JOHNSON (1709–84), English lexicographer, essayist, and poet: Boswell, *Life of Johnson*

The Owl and the Pussy-Cat went to sea
In a beautiful pea-green boat,
They took some honey, and plenty of money,
Wrapped up in a five-pound note.
EDWARD LEAR (1812–88), English humorist and painter: *The Owl and the Pussy-Cat*

For I don't care too much for money,
For money can't buy me love.
JOHN LENNON (1940–80), English rock musician and songwriter and PAUL McCARTNEY (1942–), English rock musician and songwriter: *Can't Buy Me Love, song*

Money
A good thing to have. It frees you from doing things you dislike. Since I dislike doing nearly everything, money is handy.
GROUCHO MARX (1895–1977), American film comedian, quoted in Herbert V. Prochnow and Herbert V. Prochnow Jr, *Quotations for All Occasions*

What's a thousand dollars? Mere chicken feed. A poultry matter.
GROUCHO MARX, *The Cocoanuts*, film, *1929*

Money is like a sixth sense without which you cannot make a complete use of the other five.
W(ILLIAM) SOMERSET MAUGHAM (1874–1965), English writer: *Of Human Bondage, 51*

The chief value of money lies in the fact that one lives in a world in which it is overestimated.
HENRY LOUIS MENCKEN (1880–1956), American philologist, editor, and satirist

Money brings honour, friends, conquest, and realms.
JOHN MILTON (1608–74), English poet: *Paradise Regained, II*

After a certain point money is meaningless. It ceases to be the goal. The game is what counts.
ARISTOTLE ONASSIS (1900–75), Greek millionaire, quoted in *Esquire, 1969*

Within certain limits it is actually true that the less money you have, the less you worry.
GEORGE ORWELL (Eric Arthur Blair) (1903–50), English novelist and essayist: *Down and Out in Paris and London, chapter 3*

The two most beautiful words in the English language are 'Cheque Enclosed'.
DOROTHY (ROTHSCHILD) PARKER (1893–1967), American writer

You must spend money, if you wish to make money.
TITUS MACCIUS PLAUTUS (?254–?184 BC), Roman comic dramatist: *Asinaria*

A fool and his money are soon parted.
Proverb

A man without money is like a wolf without teeth.
Proverb

If you have no money, be polite.
Proverb

Money brings money.
Proverb

Money is the best messenger.
Proverb

Money is the root of all evil.
Proverb

Money isn't everything.
Proverb

Money makes the man.
Proverb

Money talks.
Proverb

Money will do anything.
Proverb

'Tis money that begets money.
Proverb

Getting money is like digging with a needle; spending it is like water soaking into sand.
Japanese proverb

Money has no legs, but it runs.
Japanese proverb

Luxury either comes of riches or makes them necessary; it corrupts at once rich and poor, the rich by possession and the poor by covetousness.
JEAN-JACQUES ROUSSEAU (1712–78), Swiss-born French philosopher and writer: *The Social Contract*

My boy ... always try to rub up against money, for if you rub up against money long enough, some of it may rub off on you.
(ALFRED) DAMON RUNYON (1884–1946), American writer and journalist: *Furthermore*, 'A Very Honourable Guy'

Corin
He that wants money, means, and content, is without three good friends.
WILLIAM SHAKESPEARE (1564–1616), English dramatist and poet: *As You Like It, Act 3*

Money is the most important thing in the world. It represents health, strength, honour, generosity and beauty as conspicuously and undeniably as the want of it represents illness, weakness,

disgrace, meanness and ugliness.
GEORGE BERNARD SHAW (1856–1950), Irish dramatist and critic: *Major Barbara*

Money is indeed the most important thing in the world; and all sound and successful personal and national morality should have this fact for its basis.
GEORGE BERNARD SHAW, *The Irrational Knot*

When declining to sell Samuel Goldwyn screen rights to his plays
The trouble, Mr Goldwyn, is that you are only interested in art and I am only interested in money.
GEORGE BERNARD SHAW

Nothing in the world is worse than money. Money lays waste cities; it sets men to roaming from home; it seduces and corrupts honest men and turns virtue to baseness; it teaches villainy and impiety.
SOPHOCLES (?496–406 BC), Greek dramatist: *Antigone*

No man will take counsel, but every man will take money: therefore money is better than counsel.
JONATHAN SWIFT (1667–1745), Anglo-Irish satirist and churchman: *Thoughts on Various Subjects*

No one would remember the Good Samaritan if he'd only had good intentions. He had money as well.
MARGARET (HILDA) THATCHER (1925–), English politician and prime minister, quoted in *Observer, 'Sayings of 1980', 28 December 1980*

Make all you can, save all you can, give all you can.
JOHN WESLEY (1703–91), English preacher who founded Methodism

I don't want money. It is only people who pay their bills who want that, and I never pay mine.
OSCAR WILDE (1856–1900), Irish poet, dramatist, and wit: *The Picture of Dorian Gray*

PROPERTY

It will, generally, be found, that all great political questions end in the tenure of Land. What is the nature of that tenure is the first question a Statesman should ask himself, when forming an opinion on public events.
BENJAMIN DISRAELI, 1st Earl of Beaconsfield (1804–81), English statesman, prime minister, and novelist: *Fragment of reminiscence, 1860*

Property has its duties as well as its rights.
THOMAS DRUMMOND (1797–1840), Scottish engineer and statesman: *Letter to the Earl of Donoughmore, 22 May 1838*

If a man own land, the land owns him. Now let him leave home, if he dare.
RALPH WALDO EMERSON (1803–82), American poet, essayist, and philosopher: *The Conduct of Life, 'Wealth'*

When it comes to divide an estate, the politest men quarrel.
RALPH WALDO EMERSON, *Journals*

The earth is the first condition of our existence. To make it an object of trade was the last step towards making human beings an object of trade. To buy and sell land is an immorality surpassed only by the immorality of selling oneself into slavery.
FRIEDRICH ENGELS (1820–95), German socialist leader and political philosopher: *Outlines of a Critique of Political Economy*

By socialism we mean above all an Islamic socialism. We are a Muslim nation. We shall therefore respect, as bidden in the Quran, the principle of private property, even of hereditary property.
MOAMAR AL GADDAFI (1942–), Libyan army officer and statesman: *First Proclamation of the Revolutionary Command Council, 1 September 1969*

Private ownership of land is the nether millstone. Material progress is the upper millstone. Between them, with increasing pressure, the working classes are being ground.
HENRY GEORGE (1839–97), American economist: *Progress and poverty*

The meek shall inherit the earth, but not the mineral rights.
J(EAN) PAUL GETTY (1892–1976), American financier (Attributed)

Property is necessary, but it is not necessary that it should remain forever in the same hands.
RÉMY DE GOURMONT (1858–1915), French literary critic and novelist

We stand for the maintenance of private property.
ADOLF HITLER (1889–1945), Austrian-born German Nazi dictator

Private property in land is an obstacle to the investment of capital on land . . . The possibilities of free investment of capital in land, free competition in agriculture, are much greater under the system of free renting than under the system of private property in land . . . landlordism without the landlord.
NIKOLAI LENIN (Vladimir Ilyich Ulyanov) (1870–1924), Russian statesman and Marxist theoretician: *Selected Works*

We abuse land because we regard it as a commodity belonging to us. When we see land as a community to which we belong, we may begin to use it with love and respect.
ALDO LEOPOLD (1886–1948), American forester and conservationist, quoted in Stewart L. Udall, *The Quiet Crisis*

A son can bear with equanimity the loss of his father, but the loss of his inheritance may drive him to despair.
NICCOLÒ MACHIAVELLI (1469–1527), Italian statesman and political philosopher: *The Prince*

Landlords, like all other men, love to reap where they never sowed.
KARL MARX (1818–83), German founder of modern communism: *Early Writings*

The theory of Communism may be summed up in one sentence: Abolish all private property.
KARL MARX and FRIEDRICH ENGELS (1820–95), German socialist leader: *The Communist Manifesto*

That which is built upon the land goes with the land.
Maxim

The land of every country belongs to the people of that country. The individuals called landowners have no right in morality and justice to anything but the rent, or compensation for its salable value.
JOHN STUART MILL (1806–73), English philosopher and economist: *Principles of Political Economy, book 1*

No man made the land. It is the original inheritance of the whole species. Its appropriation is wholly a question of general expediency. When private property in land is not expedient, it is unjust. It is no hardship to any one to be excluded from what others have produced: they were not bound to produce it for his use, and he loses nothing by not sharing in what otherwise would not have existed at all. But it is some hardship to be born into the world and to find all nature's gifts previously engrossed, and no place left for the new-comer.
JOHN STUART MILL, *as above, book 2*

Riches do not consist in the possession of treasures, but in the use made of them.
NAPOLEON I (Napoleon Bonaparte)

(1769–1821), French emperor and general: *Maxims*

Property is theft.
PIERRE JOSEPH PROUDHON (1809–65), French political theorist: *Qu'est-ce que la propriété?, chapter 1*

A bird in the hand is worth two in the bush.
Proverb

Finders keepers, losers seekers.
Proverb

He that has lands, has quarrels.
Proverb

We ask not what he is but what he has.
Proverb

Whoever owns the river bank owns the fish.
Russian proverb

You cannot divorce property from power. You can only make them change hands.
JOHN RANDOLPH, Randolph of Roanoke (1773–1833), U.S. politician: *Speech to the Senate, 1826*

It should be remembered that the foundation of the social contract is property; and its first condition, that every one should be maintained in the peaceful possession of what belongs to him.
JEAN-JACQUES ROUSSEAU (1712–78), Swiss-born French philosopher and writer: *A Discourse on Political Economy*

It is preoccupation with possession, more than anything else, that prevents men from living freely and nobly.
BERTRAND (ARTHUR WILLIAM) RUSSELL, 3rd Earl Russell (1872–1970), English philosopher and mathematician

One who knows how to show and to accept kindness
Will be a friend better than any possession.
SOPHOCLES (?496–406 BC), Greek dramatist: *Philoctetes*

Next to the right of liberty, the right of property is the most important individual right guaranteed by the Constitution and the one which, united with that of personal liberty, has contributed more to the growth of civilization than any other institution established by the human race . . . Socialism proposes no adequate substitute for the motive of enlightened selfishness that today is at the basis of all human labour and effort, enterprise and new activity.
WILLIAM HOWARD TAFT (1857–1930), American statesman and U.S. president: *Popular Government, chapter 3*

The want of a thing is perplexing enough, but the possession of it is intolerable.
SIR JOHN VANBRUGH (1664–1726), English dramatist and baroque architect: *The Confederacy*

The spirit of property doubles a man's strength.
VOLTAIRE (François Marie Arouet) (1694–1778), French writer, philosopher, and historian: *Philosophical Dictionary*

It is immoral to use private property in order to alleviate the horrible evils that result from the institution of private property. It is both immoral and unfair.
OSCAR WILDE (1856–1900), Irish poet, dramatist, and wit: *Fortnightly Review, February 1891*

If property had simply pleasures, we could stand it, but its duties make it unbearable. In the interest of the rich we must get rid of it.
OSCAR WILDE, *The Soul of Man Under Socialism*

PROSPERITY

In a day of prosperity, adversity is forgotten and in a day of adversity, prosperity is not remembered.
The Apocrypha, Ecclesiasticus 11:25

There are those who believe that, if you will only legislate to make the well-to-do prosperous, their prosperity will leak through to those below. The Democratic idea, however, has been that if you legislate to make the masses prosperous, their prosperity will

find its way up through every class which rests upon them.
WILLIAM JENNINGS BRYAN (1860–1925), American political leader and orator: *Speech at the Democratic National Convention, Chicago, 8 July 1896*

Adversity is sometimes hard upon a man; but for one man who can stand prosperity, there are a hundred that will stand adversity.
THOMAS CARLYLE (1795–1881), Scottish essayist and historian: *Heroes and Hero Worship*

The rich are the scum of the earth in every country.
G(ILBERT) K(EITH) CHESTERTON (1874–1936), English essayist, novelist, poet, and critic: *The Flying Inn*

The misfortune of the wise is better than the prosperity of the fool.
EPICURUS (341–270 BC), Greek philosopher, quoted in Diogenes Laertius, *Lives and Opinions of Eminent Philosophers*

Some men never find prosperity, For all their voyaging, While others find it with no voyaging.
EURIPIDES (?480–406 BC), Greek tragic dramatist: *Iphigenia in Tauris*

The human race has had long experience and a fine tradition in surviving adversity. But we now face a task for which we have little experience, the task of surviving prosperity.
ALAN GREGG (1890–1957), American physician and foundation official: *The New York Times, 4 November 1956*

Prosperity is a great teacher; adversity is a greater.
WILLIAM HAZLITT (1778–1830), English essayist: *Sketches and Essays, 'On the Conversation of Lords'*

If you don't want prosperity to falter, then Buy, Buy, Buy – on credit, of course. In other words, the surest way of bringing on a rainy day is to prepare for it.
JOSEPH WOOD KRUTCH (1893–1970), American critic, essayist, and teacher: *Human Nature and the Human Condition*

He who wishes to be rich in a day will be hanged in a year.
LEONARDO DA VINCI (1452–1519), Italian artist, architect, and engineer: *Notebooks*

Most of our people have never had it so good.
SIR (MAURICE) HAROLD MACMILLAN, Earl of Stockton (1894–1986), English statesman and prime minister: *Speech, Bedford football ground, 20 July 1957*

In prosperity be cautious; in adversity, patient.
Proverb

The prosperity of this world is like writing on water.
Hindu proverb

Prosperity makes friends, adversity tries them.
PUBLILIUS SYRUS (1st c. BC), Latin writer of mimes: *Moral Sayings*

Nothing contributes so much to the prosperity and happiness of a

country as high profits.
DAVID RICARDO (1772–1823), English
economist: *On Protection to Agriculture*

If a nation could not prosper
without the enjoyment of perfect
liberty and perfect justice, there is
not in the world a nation which
could ever have prospered.
ADAM SMITH (1723–90), Scottish
economist and philosopher: *Wealth of
Nations, volume 2, book 4*

Prosperity is the best protector of
principle.
MARK TWAIN (Samuel Langhorne
Clemens) (1835–1910), American
novelist and humorist: *Pudd'nhead
Wilson's New Calendar*

Few of us can stand prosperity.
Another man's, I mean.
MARK TWAIN, *as above*

Prosperity is necessarily the first
theme of a political campaign.
(THOMAS) WOODROW WILSON
(1856–1924), American statesman and
U.S. president: *Address, 4 September
1912*

SUCCESS

Don't count your chickens before
they are hatched.
AESOP (ca. 620–564 BC), Greek fabulist:
Fables, 'The Milkmaid and her Pail'

Behind every successful man there
stands an amazed woman.
Anon

One's religion is whatever he is
most interested in, and yours is
Success.
SIR JAMES MATTHEW BARRIE
(1860–1937), Scottish novelist and
dramatist: *The Twelve-Pound Look*

The toughest thing about success is
that you've got to keep on being a
success.
IRVING BERLIN (Israel Baline) (1888–),
Russian-born American composer:
Theatre Arts, February 1958

To be successful you have to be
lucky, or a little mad, or very
talented, or to find yourself in a
rapid-growth field.
EDWARD DE BONO (1933–), Maltese-
born British physician and writer: *Tactics:
the art and science of success*

Success is counted sweetest
By those who ne'er succeed.
EMILY DICKINSON (1830–86),
American poet: *Poems*

The secret of success is constancy
to purpose.
BENJAMIN DISRAELI, 1st Earl of
Beaconsfield (1804–81), English
statesman, prime minister, and novelist:
*Speech, House of Commons, 24 June
1870*

She knows there's no success like
failure
And that failure's no success at all.
BOB DYLAN (Robert Allen Zimmerman)
(1941–), American folk singer and
songwriter: *Love Minus Zero/No Limit,
song*

Success, as I see it, is a result, not a goal.
GUSTAVE FLAUBERT (1821–80), French novelist: *Letter to Maxime du Camp, 26 June 1852*

Nothing is more humiliating than to see idiots succeed in enterprises we have failed in.
GUSTAVE FLAUBERT, *L'Éducation sentimentale*

Success has ruin'd many a man.
BENJAMIN FRANKLIN (1706–90), American statesman, scientist, and author: *Poor Richard's Almanac*

Early to bed and early to rise, makes a man healthy, wealthy, and wise.
BENJAMIN FRANKLIN, *as above*

He was a self-made man who owed his lack of success to nobody.
JOSEPH HELLER (1923–), American novelist: *Catch-22*

Success and failure are both difficult to endure. Along with success come drugs, divorce, fornication, bullying, travel, meditation, medication, depression, neurosis and suicide. With failure comes failure.
JOSEPH HELLER

If at first you don't succeed, Try, try again.
WILLIAM EDWARD HICKSON (1803–70), Educational writer: *Try and Try again*

Succeed we must, at all cost – even if it means being a *dead* millionaire at fifty.
LOUIS KRONENBERGER (1904–),

American critic, writer, and editor: *The Cart and the Horse*

To succeed in the world, we do everything we can to appear successful.
FRANÇOIS LA ROCHEFOUCAULD, Duc de la Rochefoucauld (1613–80), French writer: *Reflections*

Success is that old ABC – ability, breaks and courage.
CHARLES LUCKMAN (1909–), American architect: *New York Mirror, 1955*

It is important for everyone to believe, whether they succeed or not, that success is linked with some kind of logic and beholden to some notion of legitimacy . . . To put it another way, it is psychologically intolerable, having risen to the heights, to be badgered by doubt that you do not really deserve it.
ALISTAIR MANT: *The Rise and Fall of the British Manager*

The greatest thing in the world is to know how to be self-sufficient.
MICHEL DE MONTAIGNE (1533–92), French essayist: *Essays*

To succeed in the world we must look foolish but be wise.
MONTESQUIEU (Charles de Secondat), Baron de la Brède et de Montesquieu (1689–1755), French philosopher, man of letters, and lawyer: *Pensées*

Gamesmanship or The Art of Winning Games Without Actually Cheating.
STEPHEN POTTER (1900–69), English writer and radio producer: *Title of book*

If you wish to be a success in the world, acquire a knowledge of Latin, a horse, and money.
Proverb

Nothing succeeds like success.
Proverb

On the day of victory no fatigue is felt.
Proverb

Success has many friends.
Proverb

Of course there is no formula for success.
ARTUR RUBINSTEIN (1886–1982),
Polish-born American concert pianist

Unless a man has been taught what to do with success after getting it, the achievement of it must inevitably leave him a prey to boredom.
BERTRAND (ARTHUR WILLIAM) RUSSELL, 3rd Earl Russell (1872–1970), English philosopher and mathematician: *The Conquest of Happiness*

ON THE DAY OF VICTORY NO FATIGUE IS FELT.

The only place where success comes before work is in a dictionary.
VIDAL SASSOON (1928–), Hair stylist

Some are born great, some achieve greatness, and some have greatness thrust upon 'em.
WILLIAM SHAKESPEARE (1564–1616), English dramatist and poet: *Twelfth Night, Act 2*

Man can climb to the highest summits, but he cannot dwell there long.
GEORGE BERNARD SHAW (1856–1950), Irish dramatist and critic: *Candida, Act 3*

There is no success without hardship.
SOPHOCLES (?496–406 BC), Greek dramatist: *Electra*

Early to bed, early to rise, makes a man healthy, wealthy and dead.
JAMES (GROVER) THURBER (1894–1961), American humorist and cartoonist: *Fables for Our Time*

All you need in this life is ignorance and confidence, and then success is sure.
MARK TWAIN (Samuel Langhorne Clemens) (1835–1910), American novelist and humorist: *Letter to Mrs Foote, 2 December 1887*

WEALTH

It is better to be miserable and rich than it is to be miserable and poor.
Anon

Wealth is not only what we have, but what we are.
Anon

A man who has a million dollars is as well off as if he were rich.
JOHN JACOB ASTOR THE THIRD (1918–), American millionaire (Attributed)

Riches are for spending.
FRANCIS BACON, 1st Baron Verulam, Viscount St Albans (1561–1626), English writer, philosopher, and statesman: *Essays, 'Of Expense'*

The control of the production of wealth is the control of human life itself.
(JOSEPH) HILAIRE (PIERRE) BELLOC (1870–1953), Anglo-French author

The poor is hated even of his neighbour: but the rich hath many friends.
The Bible, Authorized (King James) Version, Proverbs 14:20

It is easier for a camel to go through the eye of a needle, than for a rich man to enter the kingdom of God.
The Bible, Authorized (King James) Version, Matthew 19:24

As wealth is power, so all power will infallibly draw wealth to itself by some means or other.
EDMUND BURKE (1729–97), British statesman, orator, and writer: *Speech, House of Commons, 11 February 1780*

If you aren't rich, you should always look useful.
LOUIS-FERDINAND CÉLINE (Louis-Ferdinand Destouches) (1894–1961), French novelist: *Journey to the End of the Night*

The first wealth is health.
RALPH WALDO EMERSON (1803–82), American poet, essayist, and philosopher: *The Conduct of Life*

Wealth stays with us a little moment if at all;
Only our characters are steadfast, not our gold.
EURIPIDES (?480–406 BC), Greek tragic dramatist: *Electra*

There seem to be but three ways for a nation to acquire wealth. The first is by war, as the Romans did, in plundering their conquered neighbors. This is robbery. The second by commerce, which is generally cheating. The third by agriculture, the only honest way, wherein man receives a real increase of the seed thrown into the ground, in a kind of continual miracle, wrought by the hand of God in his favor, as a reward for his innocent life and his virtuous industry.
BENJAMIN FRANKLIN (1706–90), American statesman, scientist, and author: *Positions to be Examined Concerning National Wealth*

Riches have made more covetous men than covetousness hath made rich men.
THOMAS FULLER (1654–1734), English physician, writer, and compiler: *Gnomologia*

Wealth is not without its advantages, and the case to the contrary, although it has often been made, has never proved widely persuasive.
JOHN KENNETH GALBRAITH (1908–), Canadian-born American economist, diplomat, and writer: *The Affluent Society, chapter 1*

Wealth has never been a sufficient source of honour in itself. It must be advertised, and the normal medium is obtrusively expensive goods.
JOHN KENNETH GALBRAITH, *as above, chapter 7*

F. Scott Fitzgerald
You know, Ernest, the rich are different from us.
Ernest Hemingway
Yes I know. They have more money than we do.
ERNEST HEMINGWAY (1899–1961), American novelist and short-story writer

The increase of riches and commerce in any one nation, instead of hurting, commonly promotes the riches and commerce of all its neighbours.
DAVID HUME (1711–76), Scottish philosopher and historian: *Essays, 'Of the Jealousy of Trade'*

15

It is better to *live* rich than to *die* rich.
SAMUEL JOHNSON (1709–84), English lexicographer, essayist, and poet: Boswell, *Life of Johnson*

It is Enterprise which builds and improves the world's possessions ... If Enterprise is afoot, wealth accumulates whatever may be happening to Thrift; and if Enterprise is asleep, Wealth decays, whatever Thrift may be doing.
JOHN MAYNARD KEYNES (1883–1946), English economist: *Treatise on Money*

No just man ever became rich suddenly.
MENANDER (?342–?292 BC), Greek comic dramatist: *Adsentator*

The distribution of wealth ... depends on the laws and customs of society. The rules by which it is determined are what the opinions and feelings of the ruling portion of the community make them, and are very different in different ages and countries; and might be still more different, if mankind so chose.
JOHN STUART MILL (1806–73), English philosopher and economist: *Principles of Political Economy, book 2*

Men do not desire to be *rich*, but to be richer than other men.
JOHN STUART MILL, *Oxford and Cambridge Review, Posthumous Essay on Social Freedom, January 1907*

Give us the luxuries of life, and we will dispense with its necessities.
JOHN LOTHROP MOTLEY (1814–77), American historian and diplomat, comment, O.W. Holmes, *The Autocrat of the Breakfast Table, chapter 6*

God shows his contempt for wealth by the kind of person he selects to receive it.
AUSTIN O'MALLEY (1858–1932)

Rich men long to be richer.
Proverb

A man seldom gets rich without ill-got gain; as a horse does not fatten without feeding in the night.
Chinese proverb

Nobody ever feels rich.
ESTHER RANTZEN (1940–), TV journalist, quoted in *Observer, 'Sayings of the Year', 2 January 1983*

Man does not live by GNP alone.
PAUL ANTHONY SAMUELSON (1915–), American economist: *Economics*

Many a man has found the acquisition of wealth only a change, not an end of miseries.
MARCUS or LUCIUS ANNAEUS SENECA (The Elder) (?55 BC–?39 AD), Roman writer on oratory and history: *Letters to Lucilius*

Petruchio
Our purses shall be proud, our garments poor;
For 'tis the mind that makes the body rich;
And as the sun breaks through the darkest clouds,
So honour peereth in the meanest habit.
WILLIAM SHAKESPEARE (1564–1616), English dramatist and poet: *The Taming of the Shrew*, Act 4

I am a Millionaire. That is my religion.
GEORGE BERNARD SHAW (1858–1950), Irish dramatist and critic: *Major Barbara*, Act 1

The wretchedness of being rich is that you live with rich people.
LOGAN PEARSALL SMITH (1865–1946), American-born English man of letters: *Afterthoughts*

Nobody who has wealth to distribute ever omits himself.
LEON TROTSKY (Lev Davidovich Bronstein) (1879–1940), Russian revolutionary and Communist theorist: *Observer, 'Sayings of the Week', 23 March 1937*

When I was young I thought money was the most important thing in life; now that I am old I know that it is.
OSCAR WILDE (1856–1900), Irish poet, dramatist, and wit

BUSINESS ACTIVITIES

What are the functions of business? What is industry actually doing? 'Business? It's quite simple. It's other people's money' according to the French writer Alexandre Dumas; 'Business has only two functions – marketing and innovation' according to the management expert Peter Drucker. The quotations in this section move from decision-making and meetings ('A conference is a gathering of important people who singly can do nothing, but together can decide that nothing can be done' – Fred Allen) to the sheer hard graft of work. We also look at the industrial process from ideas and planning ('You can't really separate the inventor and the businessman' – Sir Clive Sinclair) through to production . . . and problems.

ACCOUNTANTS

An accountant is a man hired to explain that you didn't make the money you did.
Anon

In your report here, it says that you are an extremely dull person. Our experts describe you as an appallingly dull fellow, unimaginative, timid, spineless, easily dominated, no sense of humour, tedious company and irrepressibly drab and awful. And whereas in most professions these would be considered drawbacks, in accountancy they are a positive boon.
JOHN CLEESE, GRAHAM CHAPMAN, TERRY JONES, MICHAEL PALIN, and ERIC IDLE: *And Now for Something Completely Different, screenplay*

He that gains well and spends well needs no account book.
GEORGE HERBERT (1593–1633), English metaphysical poet: *Outlandish Proverbs*

ADMINISTRATION

It is common for professional economists, when they first come in contact with administrators, to feel that the administrator is grossly ignorant of elementary economics. Sometimes this is

justified; but it is equally true that the professional economist may be grossly ignorant of administration.
SIR ALEC CAIRNCROSS (1911–), Scottish economist: *Essays in Economic Management*

An administration, like a machine, does not create. It carries on.
ANTOINE DE SAINT-EXUPÉRY (1900–44), French novelist and aviator: *Flight to Arras*

Bad administration, to be sure, can destroy good policy; but good administration can never save bad policy.
ADLAI (EWING) STEVENSON (1900–68), American statesman: *Speech, Los Angeles, 11 September 1952*

ADVERTISING

Advertising agency: eighty-five per cent confusion and fifteen per cent commission.
FRED ALLEN (John F. Sullivan) (1894–1956), American comedian

When business is good it pays to advertise; when business is bad you've got to advertise.
Anon

When the client moans and sighs
Make his logo twice the size.
If he still should prove refractory,
Show a picture of his factory.
Only in the gravest cases
Should you show the clients' faces.
Anon

Advertising is the very essence of democracy.
BRUCE BARTON (1935–), American advertising man: *Reader's Digest, 1955*

The advertisements in a newspaper are more full of knowledge in respect to what is going on in a state or community than the editorial columns are.
HENRY WARD BEECHER (1813–87), American clergyman, editor, and writer: *Proverbs from Plymouth Pulpit*

The philosophy behind much advertising is based on the old observation that every man is really two men – the man he is and the man he wants to be.
WILLIAM FEATHER (1889–), American businessman: *The Business of Life*

It is not necessary to advertise food to hungry people, fuel to cold people, or houses to the homeless.
JOHN KENNETH GALBRAITH (1908–), Canadian-born American economist, diplomat, and writer: *American Capitalism, chapter 8*

Few people at the beginning of the nineteenth century needed an adman to tell them what they wanted.
JOHN KENNETH GALBRAITH

Give them quality. That's the best kind of advertising.
MILTON SNAVELY HERSHEY (1857–1945), American industrialist

Doing business without advertising is like winking at a girl in the dark:

you know what you are doing, but nobody else does.
EDGAR WATSON HOWE (1853–1937), American journalist, novelist, and essayist

Advertisements contain the only truths to be relied on in a newspaper.
THOMAS JEFFERSON (1743–1826), American statesman and U.S. president: *Letter to Nathaniel Macon, 1819*

Advertisements are now so numerous that they are very negligently perused, and it is therefore become necessary to gain attention by magnificence of promises, and by eloquences sometimes sublime and sometimes pathetic.
SAMUEL JOHNSON (1709–84), English lexicographer, essayist, and poet: *The Idler*

Promise, large promise, is the soul of an advertisement.
SAMUEL JOHNSON, *as above*

You can fool all the people all of the time if the advertising is right and the budget is big enough.
JOSEPH E. LEVINE (1905–), American film producer: *Joseph E. Levine Presents*

When producers want to know what the public wants, they graph it in curves. When they want to tell the public what to get, they say it in curves.
(HERBERT) MARSHALL McLUHAN (1911–80), Canadian educator, author, and media expert: *The Mechanical Bride*

Ads push the principle of noise all the way to the plateau of persuasion. They are quite in accord with the procedures of brain-washing.
(HERBERT) MARSHALL McLUHAN, *Understanding Media*

Advertising is the greatest art form of the twentieth century.
(HERBERT) MARSHALL McLUHAN, *Advertising Age*

Most of the people who are writing advertising today have never had to sell anything to anybody. They've never seen a consumer.
DAVID OGILVY (1911–), British advertising executive

The Hidden Persuaders.
VANCE (OAKLEY) PACKARD (1914–), American writer and social critic: *Title of book*

Any publicity is good publicity.
Proverb

It pays to advertise.
Proverb

One Ad is worth more to a paper than forty Editorials.
WILL(IAM PENN ADAIR) ROGERS (1879–1935), American actor and humorist: *The Illiterate Digest*

ADVICE

There is nothing which we receive with so much reluctance as advice.
JOSEPH ADDISON (1672–1719), English essayist and dramatist: *The Spectator, 1711*

Never trust the advice of a man in difficulties.
AESOP (ca. 620–564 BC), Greek fabulist: *Fables, 'The Fox and the Goat'*

In the multitude of counsellors there is safety.
The Bible, Authorized (King James) Version, Proverbs 11:14

Consult
To seek another's approval of a course already decided on.
AMBROSE (GWINETT) BIERCE (1842–?1914), American journalist and humorist: *The Devil's Dictionary*

Advice is seldom welcome; and those who want it the most always like it the least.
LORD CHESTERFIELD, Philip Dormer Stanhope, 4th Earl of (1694–1773), English statesman and writer: *Letter to his son, 29 January 1748*

When we feel a strong desire to thrust our advice upon others, it is usually because we suspect their weakness; but we ought rather to suspect our own.
CHARLES CALEB COLTON (?1780–1832), English clergyman and writer: *Lacon*

Whatever your advice, make it brief.
HORACE (Quintus Horatius Flaccus) (65–8 BC), Roman poet and satirist: *De arte poetica*

You will always find some Eskimos ready to instruct the Congolese on how to cope with heat waves.
STANISLAW (JERZY) LEC (1909–), Polish poet and aphorist: *Unkempt Thoughts*

Advice after injury is like medicine after death.
Proverb

Ask advice only of your equals.
Proverb

Many receive advice, few profit by it.
PUBLILIUS SYRUS (1st c. BC), Latin writer of mimes: *Moral Sayings*

No man will take counsel, but every man will take money: therefore money is better than counsel.
JONATHAN SWIFT (1667–1745), Anglo-Irish satirist and churchman: *Thoughts on Various Subjects*

I always pass on good advice. It is the only thing to do with it. It is never any use to oneself.
OSCAR WILDE (1856–1900), Irish poet, dramatist, and wit: *An Ideal Husband*

AGREEMENT & CONTRACTS

'My idea of an agreeable person,' said Hugo Bohun, 'is a person who agrees with me.'
BENJAMIN DISRAELI, lst Earl of Beaconsfield (1804–81), English statesman, prime minister, and novelist: *Lothair, chapter 35*

A verbal contract isn't worth the paper it's written on.
SAMUEL GOLDWYN (1882–1974), American film producer (Attributed)

If two people agree all the time, one of them is unnecessary.
DAVID MAHONEY (1923–), American businessman, quoted in M. Korda, *Power in the Office*

Some people mistake weakness for tact. If they are silent when they ought to speak and so feign an agreement they do not feel, they call it being tactful. Cowardice would be a much better name.
SIR FRANK MEDLICOTT (1903–), English solicitor: *Reader's Digest, July 1958*

Every law is a contract between the king and the people and therefore to be kept.
JOHN SELDEN (1584–1654), English historian and antiquary: *Table Talk*

There is nothing more likely to start disagreement among people or countries than an agreement.
E(LWYN) B(ROOKS) WHITE (1899–), American humorist and essayist: *One Man's Meat*

Ah! don't say you agree with me. When people agree with me I always feel that I must be wrong.
OSCAR WILDE (1856–1900), Irish poet, dramatist, and wit: *The Critic as Artist, Part 2*

If two men on the same job agree all the time, then one is useless. If they disagree all the time, then both are useless.
DARRYL F(RANCIS) ZANUCK (1902–79), Film executive, quoted in *Observer, 23 October 1949*

One of my favourite philosophical tenets is that people will agree with you only if they already agree with you. You do not change people's minds.
FRANK ZAPPA (1940–), American rock musician and producer

ARGUMENTS

When quarrels and complaints arise, it is when people who are equal have not got equal shares, or vice versa.
ARISTOTLE (384–322 BC), Greek philosopher and scientist: *Nicomachean Ethics, book 5*

When an argument is over, how many weighty reasons does a man recollect which his heat and violence made him utterly forget?
EUSTACE BUDGELL (1686–1737), English essayist and man of letters: *The Spectator, 1711*

The only way to get the best of an argument is to avoid it.
DALE CARNEGIE (1888–1955), American writer

The best way I know of to win an argument is to start by being in the right.
LORD HAILSHAM (Quintin McGarel Hogg) (1907–), British lawyer and government official: *The New York Times, 16 October 1960*

The test of a man or woman's breeding is how they behave in a quarrel.
GEORGE BERNARD SHAW (1856–1950), Irish dramatist and critic: *The Philanderer*

I am not arguing with you – I am telling you.
JAMES ABBOTT McNEILL WHISTLER (1834–1903), American painter: *Gentle Art of Making Enemies*

Arguments are to be avoided; they are always vulgar and often convincing.
OSCAR WILDE (1856–1900), Irish poet, dramatist, and wit: *The Importance of Being Earnest*

AUTOMATION & COMPUTERS

Don't worry about our future if we automate. Worry about our future if we don't automate.
Anon

GIGO: Garbage in, garbage out.
Anon

To err is human, but to really foul things up requires a computer.
Anon

One cannot walk through a mass-production factory and not feel that one is in Hell.
W(YSTAN) H(UGH) AUDEN (1907–73), English poet, dramatist, critic, and librettist

Automation is not gadgeteering, it is not even engineering; it is a concept of the structure and order of economic life, the design of its basic patterns integrated into a harmonious, balanced, organic whole.
PETER F. DRUCKER (1909–), American management expert: *America's Next Twenty Years*

The automatic factory is the end product rather than the beginning of automation. Automation properly does not start with production at all, but with an analysis of the business and its redesign on automation principles. The form that automatic production takes in the plant is determined by that analysis and redesign; and mechanization, the replacement of human labor by machines, is a detail of automation and not always the essential one. The reason for this, the reason why automation has to be business-focused rather than production-focused, is that it radically shifts the area of *business risk*.
PETER F. DRUCKER, *as above*

The danger of the past was that men became slaves. The danger of the future is that men may become robots.
ERICH FROMM (1900–80), German-born American psychoanalyst and philosopher: *The Sane Society*

One machine can do the work of fifty ordinary men. No machine can do the work of one extraordinary man.
ELBERT (GREEN) HUBBARD (1856–1915), American businessman, writer, and printer: *Roycroft Dictionary and Book of Epigrams*

We believe that if men have the talent to invent new machines that put men out of work, they have the talent to put those men back to work.
JOHN FITZGERALD KENNEDY (1917–63), U.S. statesman and president: *Address, Wheeling, West Virginia, 27 September 1962*

TO ERR IS HUMAN, BUT TO REALLY FOUL THINGS UP REQUIRES A COMPUTER.

Man is still the most extraordinary computer of all.
JOHN FITZGERALD KENNEDY, *Address,*
21 May 1963

It is critical vision alone which can mitigate the unimpeded operation of the automatic.
(HERBERT) MARSHALL McLUHAN (1911–80), Canadian educator, author, and media expert: *The Mechanical Bride*

The world is dying of machinery; that is the great disease, that is the plague that will sweep away and destroy civilization; man will have to rise against it sooner or later.
GEORGE MOORE (1852–1933), Irish novelist, poet, and critic: *Confessions of a Young Man*

The evil that machinery is doing is not merely in the consequences of its work but in the fact that it makes men themselves machines also.
OSCAR WILDE (1856–1900), Irish poet, dramatist and wit: *(Omaha) Weekly Herald, 22 March 1882*

BUSINESS

John Knightley
Business, you know, may bring money, but friendship hardly ever does.
JANE AUSTEN (1775–1817), English novelist: *Emma, chapter 34*

The 'theory of business' leads a life of obstruction, because theorists do not see the business, and the men of business will not reason out the theories.
WALTER BAGEHOT (1826–77), English economist and journalist: *Economic Studies*

They that go down to the sea in ships, that do business in great waters.
The Bible, Authorized (King James) Version, Psalm 107:23

A business must have a conscience as well as a counting house.
SIR MONTAGUE BURTON, British tailor

Few people do business well who do nothing else.
LORD CHESTERFIELD, Philip Dormer Stanhope, 4th Earl of (1694–1773), English statesman and writer: *Letter to his son, 7 August 1749*

The maxim of the British people is 'Business as usual.'
SIR WINSTON LEONARD SPENCER CHURCHILL (1874–1965), English statesman, writer, and prime minister: *Speech, Guildhall, 9 November 1914*

The fact that a business is large, efficient and profitable does not mean it takes advantage of the public.
CHARLES CLORE (1904–79), British businessman

The business of America is business.
(JOHN) CALVIN COOLIDGE (1872–1933), U.S. president: *Address before the Society of American Newspaper Editors, Washington, 17 January 1925*

Business has only two functions – marketing and innovation.
PETER F. DRUCKER (1909–),
American management expert

Business? It's quite simple. It's other people's money.
ALEXANDRE DUMAS, known as Dumas Fils (1824–95), French novelist and dramatist: *La Question d'Argent*

Business is the salt of life.
THOMAS FULLER (1654–1734), English physician, writer, and compiler: *Gnomologia*

Everything which is properly *business* we must keep carefully separate from *life*. Business requires earnestness and method; life must have a freer handling.
JOHANN WOLFGANG VON GOETHE (1749–1832), German poet, scientist, and writer: *Elective Affinities*

Business is a competition, and any high-level, sophisticated competition is almost exclusively a head game. The Inner Game of Business, as this could be called, is understanding the Business Paradox: the better you think you are doing, the greater should be your cause for concern; the more self-satisfied you are with your accomplishments, your past achievements, your 'right moves', the less you should be.
MARK H. McCORMACK (1930–), Founder, International Management Group: *What They Don't Teach You at Harvard Business School*

I believe strongly in the social function of business . . . It is industry which creates our social patterns, it determines the whole form of our society, whether it is education or the design of cities. And I am concerned with the splits that I see in industry as they run right out into the fabric of our society.
SIR PETER PARKER (1924–), Former chairman of British Rail, quoted in Cary L. Cooper and Peter Hingley, *The Change Makers*

Business before pleasure.
Proverb

Let business wait till tomorrow.
Proverb

Mind your own business.
Proverb

Live together like brothers and do business like strangers.
Arabic proverb

We demand that big business give people a square deal; in return we must insist that when anyone engaged in big business honestly endeavors to do right, he shall himself be given a square deal.
THEODORE ROOSEVELT (1858–1919), U.S. statesman and president

That which is everybody's business is nobody's business.
IZAAK WALTON (1593–1683), English writer: *The Compleat Angler*

My own business always bores me to death; I prefer other people's.
OSCAR WILDE (1856–1900), Irish poet, dramatist, and wit: *Lady Windermere's Fan*

I thought what was good for the country was good for General Motors and vice versa.
CHARLES ERWIN WILSON (1890–1961), American engineer and industrialist: *Statement to U.S. Congressional Committee, 23 January 1953*

Big business is not dangerous because it is big, but because its bigness is an unwholesome inflation created by privileges and exemptions which it ought not to enjoy.
(THOMAS) WOODROW WILSON (1856–1924), U.S. statesman and president: *Acceptance speech, Democratic National Convention, 7 July 1912*

Business underlies everything in our national life, including our spiritual life. Witness the fact that in the Lord's Prayer the first petition is for daily bread. No one can worship God or love his neighbor on an empty stomach.
(THOMAS) WOODROW WILSON, *Speech, New York, 1912*

COMMITTEES & MEETINGS

A conference is a gathering of important people who singly can do nothing, but together can decide that nothing can be done.
FRED ALLEN (John F. Sullivan) (1894–1956), American comedian

A camel looks like a horse that was planned by a committee.
Anon

Committee
A group of men who keep minutes and waste hours.
Anon

Meetings . . . are rather like cocktail parties. You don't want to go, but you're cross not to be asked.
JILLY COOPER (1937–), British writer: *How to Survive from Nine to Five*

To get something done a committee should consist of no more than three men, two of whom are absent.
ROBERT COPELAND, quoted in *Penguin Dictionary of Modern Humorous Quotations*

Meetings are indispensable when you don't want to do anything.
JOHN KENNETH GALBRAITH (1908–), Canadian-born American economist, diplomat, and writer: *Ambassador's Journal, 1969*

What is a committee? A group of the unwilling, picked from the unfit, to do the unnecessary.
RICHARD (LONG) HARKNESS (1907–), American radio and television commentator and journalist: *New York Herald Tribune, 1960*

Civil Servant
What I mean is that I'm fully seized of your aims and, of course, I will do

my utmost to see that they're put into practice. To that end, I recommend that we set up an inter-departmental committee with fairly broad terms of reference so that at the end of the day we'll be in a position to think through the various implications and arrive at a decision based on long-term considerations rather than rush prematurely into precipitate and possibly ill-conceived action which might well have unforeseen repercussions.
Minister
You mean, no?
ANTHONY JAY and JONATHAN LYNN, Scriptwriters: *Yes, Minister, BBC television, 1981*

A committee is an animal with four back legs.
JOHN LE CARRÉ (David John Cornwall) (1931–), English novelist: *Tinker Tailor Soldier Spy, Part 3*

The Law of Triviality . . . means that the time spent on any item on the agenda will be in inverse proportion to the sum involved.
C(YRIL) NORTHCOTE PARKINSON (1909–), English historian and journalist: *Parkinson's Law*

We to a committee of the Council to discourse concerning pressing of men; but Lord how they meet; never sit down – one comes, now another goes, then comes another – one complaining that nothing is done, another swearing that he hath been there these two hours and nobody came. At last it came to this: my Lord Annesly, says he, 'I think we must be forced to get the King to come to every committee, for I do not see that we do anything, at any time but when he is here.'
SAMUEL PEPYS (1633–1703), English diarist and naval administrator: *Diary, 27 February 1665*

The length of a meeting rises with the square of the number of people present.
EILEEN SHANAHAN, American news-paperwoman, quoted by Harold Faber in *The New York Times Magazine, 17 March 1968*

COMPROMISE

All life is essentially the contributions that come from compromise.
SPIRO T. AGNEW (1918–), U.S. vice-president

Compromise
Such an adjustment of conflicting interests as gives each adversary the satisfaction of thinking he has got what he ought not to have, and is deprived of nothing except what was justly his due.
AMBROSE (GWINETT) BIERCE (1862–?1914), American journalist and humorist: *The Devil's Dictionary*

Compromise never pays. One must be intransigent. If you do something out of conviction, and you are wrong, you are wrong in an interesting way. But if you are wrong because you have compromised, all

you have is a sense of failure and discouragement.
PIERRE BOULEZ (1925–), French composer: *Esquire, 1969*

All government – indeed, every human benefit and enjoyment, every virtue and every prudent act – is founded on compromise and barter.
EDMUND BURKE (1729–97), British statesman, orator, and writer: *Speech on Conciliation with America, 22 March 1775*

Compromise used to mean that half a loaf was better than no bread. Among modern statesmen it really seems to mean that half a loaf is better than a whole loaf.
G(ILBERT) K(EITH) CHESTERTON (1874–1936), English essayist, novelist, poet, and critic: *What's Wrong with the World*

It is better to lose the saddle than the horse.
Proverb

DECISION-MAKING & INDECISION

We know what happens to people who stay in the middle of the road. They get run over.
ANEURIN BEVAN (1897–1960), British statesman: *Observer, 'Sayings of the Week', 9 December 1953*

What is a rebel? A man who says no.
ALBERT CAMUS (1913–60), French philosopher and writer: *The Rebel*

Resolve to perform what you ought. Perform without fail what you resolve.
BENJAMIN FRANKLIN (1706–90), American statesman, scientist, and author: *Autobiography*

I'll give you a definite maybe.
SAMUEL GOLDWYN (1882–1974), American film producer (Attributed)

The minority is always right.
HENRIK IBSEN (1828–1906), Norwegian dramatist and poet: *An Enemy of the People, Act 4*

Like all weak men he laid an exaggerated stress on not changing one's mind.
W(ILLIAM) SOMERSET MAUGHAM (1874–1965), English writer: *Of Human Bondage, chapter 37*

Nothing is more difficult, and therefore more precious, than to be able to decide.
NAPOLEON I (Napoleon Bonaparte) (1769–1821), French emperor and general: *Maxims*

The man who is denied the opportunity of taking decisions of importance begins to regard as important the decisions he is allowed to take. He becomes fussy about filing, keen on seeing that pencils are sharpened, eager to ensure that the windows are open (or shut) and apt to use two or three different-colored inks.
C(YRIL) NORTHCOTE PARKINSON (1909–), English historian and journalist: *Parkinson's Law*

Between two stools one sits on the ground.
Proverb

A decision is the action an executive must take when he has information so incomplete that the answer does not suggest itself.
ARTHUR WILLIAM RADFORD (1896–),
American admiral and business consultant: *Time, 25 February 1957*

He who hesitates is lost.
Saying

Don't vacillate. A poor plan persevered in is better than a good one shifted while being performed.
ERWIN H. SCHELL (1889–1965):
The Technique of Executive Control

BETWEEN TWO STOOLS ONE SITS ON THE GROUND.

Procrastination is the thief of time.
EDWARD YOUNG (1683–1765), English
poet and dramatist: *Night Thoughts*

EATING & DRINKING

There is no such thing as a free
lunch.
Anon

Tell me what you eat, and I will tell
you what you are.
ANTHELME BRILLAT-SAVARIN (1755–
1826), French politician and gourmet:
Physiologie du goût

Quick at meals, quick at work, is a
saying as old as the hills.
WILLIAM COBBETT (1762–1835),
English farmer, social reformer, and
writer: *Advice to Young Men*

Never drink black coffee at lunch;
it will keep you awake in the
afternoon.
JILLY COOPER (1937–), British writer:
How to Survive from Nine to Five

More die in the United States of too
much food than of too little.
JOHN KENNETH GALBRAITH (1908–),
Canadian-born American economist,
diplomat, and writer: *The Affluent Society*

Conversation is the enemy of good
wine and food.
SIR ALFRED (JOSEPH) HITCHCOCK
(1889–1980), English film director

The morning cup of coffee has an
exhilaration about it which the

cheering influence of the afternoon
or evening cup of tea cannot be
expected to reproduce.
OLIVER WENDELL HOLMES, SR
(1809–94), American physician,
professor, and author: *Over the Teacups*

Melancholy, indeed, should
be diverted by every means but
drinking.
SAMUEL JOHNSON (1709–84), English
lexicographer, essayist, and poet:
Boswell, *Life of Johnson*

At a dinner party one should eat
wisely but not too well, and talk
well, but not too wisely.
W(ILLIAM) SOMERSET MAUGHAM
(1874–1965), English writer: *A Writer's
Notebook*

I've made it a rule never to drink by
daylight and never to refuse a drink
after dark.
HENRY LOUIS MENCKEN (1880–1956),
American philologist, editor, and satirist:
New York Post, 18 September 1945

On the Continent people have good
food; in England people have good
table manners.
GEORGE MIKES (1912–), Hungarian-
English writer: *How to be an Alien*

One should eat to live,
not live to eat.
MOLIÈRE, (Jean Baptiste Poquelin)
(1622–73), French dramatist: *L'Avare,
Act 3*

Mr Portpipe
There are two reasons for drinking;
one is, when you are thirsty, to cure
it; the other, when you are not

thirsty, to prevent it . . . Prevention is better than cure.
THOMAS LOVE PEACOCK (1785–1866), English novelist: *Melincourt, chapter 16*

Strange to see how a good dinner and feasting reconciles everybody.
SAMUEL PEPYS (1633–1703), English diarist and naval administrator: *Diary, 9 November 1665*

Appetite comes with eating.
FRANÇOIS RABELAIS (?1494–1553), French writer: *Gargantua I:5*

A dinner lubricates business.
WILLIAM SCOTT, 1st Baron Stowell (1745–1836), English judge: Boswell, *Life of Johnson*

Bad men live that they may eat and drink, whereas good men eat and drink that they may live.
SOCRATES (?470–399 BC), Athenian philosopher: *How a Young Man Ought to Hear Poems (Plutarch)*

But I'm not so think as you drunk I am.
SIR JOHN COLLINGS SQUIRE (1884–1958), English writer: *Ballade of Soporific Absorption*

EDUCATION & TRAINING

Education is an ornament in prosperity and a refuge in adversity.
ARISTOTLE (384–322 BC), Greek philosopher and scientist, quoted in *Lives and Opinions of Eminent Philosophers*

I had a good education but it never went to my head, somehow. It should be a journey ending up with you at a different place. It didn't take with me. My degree was a kind of inoculation. I got just enough education to make me immune from it for the rest of my life.
ALAN BENNETT (1934–), English dramatist and actor: *Getting On, Act 1*

The dons are too busy educating the young men to be able to teach them anything.
SAMUEL BUTLER (1835–1902), English author, painter, and musician: *Notebooks*

Life at a university, with its intellectual and inconclusive discussions at a postgraduate level is on the whole a bad training for the real world. Only men of very strong character surmount this handicap.
PAUL CHAMBERS (1904–81), British chairman of ICI, quoted in *Observer, 1964*

Education is a sieve as well as a lift.
SID CHAPLIN: *The Day of the Sardine, chapter 2*

Headmasters have powers at their disposal with which Prime Ministers have never yet been invested.
SIR WINSTON LEONARD SPENCER CHURCHILL (1874–1965), English statesman, writer, and prime minister: *My Early Life, chapter 2*

Examinations are formidable even to the best prepared, for the greatest fool may ask more than the wisest man can answer.
CHARLES CALEB COLTON (?1780–1832), English clergyman and writer: *Lacon, II*

Learning without thought is labour lost; thought without learning is perilous.
CONFUCIUS (Kong Zi) (551–479 BC), Chinese philosopher: *Analects*

I've over-educated myself in all the things I shouldn't have known at all.
SIR NOËL (PIERCE) COWARD (1899–1973), English actor and dramatist: *Wild Oats*

The one real object of education is to leave a man in the condition of continually asking questions.
BISHOP MANDELL CREIGHTON (1843–1901), English prelate and historian, quoted in C.A. Alington, *Things Ancient and Modern*

Higher education and business are basically interdependent. The one needs money to produce educated people. The other needs educated people to produce money.
MILTON EISENHOWER, quoted in *The Times Higher Education Supplement, 22 January 1982*

I pay the schoolmaster, but 'tis the schoolboys that educate my son.
RALPH WALDO EMERSON (1803–82), American poet, essayist, and philosopher: *Journals, 1849*

It is not that the Englishman can't feel – it is that he is afraid to feel. He has been taught at his public school that feeling is bad form. He must not express great joy or sorrow, or even open his mouth too wide when he talks – his pipe might fall out if he did.
EDWARD MORGAN FORSTER (1879–1970), English novelist: *Abinger Harvest, 'Notes on the English character'*

Spoon feeding in the long run teaches us nothing but the shape of the spoon.
EDWARD MORGAN FORSTER, *Observer, 'Sayings of the Week', 7 October 1951*

The world's great men have not commonly been great scholars, nor great scholars great men.
OLIVER WENDELL HOLMES, SR (1809–94), American physician, professor, and author: *The Autocrat of the Breakfast Table, chapter 6*

Perhaps the most valuable result of all education is the ability to make yourself do the thing you have to do, when it ought to be done, whether you like it or not; it is the first lesson that ought to be learned; and however early a man's training begins, it is probably the last lesson that he learns thoroughly.
THOMAS HENRY HUXLEY (1825–95), English biologist, teacher, and writer: *Technical Education*

State a moral case to a ploughman and a professor. The former will decide it as well, and often better than the latter, because he has not been led astray by artificial rules.
THOMAS JEFFERSON (1743–1826), U.S. statesman and president: *Letter to Peter Carr, 10 August 1787*

The goal of education is the advancement of knowledge and the dissemination of truth.
JOHN FITZGERALD KENNEDY (1917–63), U.S. statesman and president: *Address, Harvard University, Cambridge, Massachusetts, 1956*

A man who knows a subject thoroughly, a man so soaked in it that he eats it, sleeps it and dreams it – this man can always teach it with success, no matter how little he knows of technical pedagogy.
HENRY LOUIS MENCKEN (1880–1956), American philologist, editor, and satirist: *Prejudices: Third Series*

***All* education is, in a sense, vocational, vocational for living.**
SIR JOHN NEWSOM (1910–71), Chairman of Central Advisory Council for Education (England): *Observer, 6 September 1964, 'The Education Women Need'*

A little learning is a dangerous thing.
ALEXANDER POPE (1688–1744), English poet and satirist: *An Essay on Criticism*

Experience is the best teacher.
Proverb

Live and learn.
Proverb

Once bitten, twice shy.
Proverb

Those who can, do; those who can't, teach.
Proverb

Give a man a fish and you feed him for one day. Teach a man to fish and you feed him for a lifetime.
Chinese proverb

The schools of the country are its future in miniature.
Chinese proverb

Education is the leading human souls to what is best ... the training which makes men happiest in themselves also makes them most serviceable to others.
JOHN RUSKIN (1819–1900), English art critic and social reformer: *The Stones of Venice*

He who can, does. He who cannot, teaches.
GEORGE BERNARD SHAW (1856–1950), Irish dramatist and critic: *Man and Superman, Maxims for Revolutionists*

Education has for its object the formation of character.
HERBERT SPENCER (1820–1903), English philosopher: *Social Statics*

Education is an admirable thing, but it is well to remember from time to time that nothing that is worth knowing can be taught.
OSCAR WILDE (1856–1900), Irish poet, dramatist, and wit: *Intentions, 'The Critic As Artist'*

FACTS

On Harold Wilson
All facts – no bloody ideas.
ANEURIN BEVAN (1897–1960), British
statesman

The trouble with facts is that there are so many of them.
SAMUEL McCHORD CROTHERS, *The Gentle Reader*

Gradgrind
Now, what I want is Facts . . . Facts alone are wanted in life.
CHARLES (JOHN HUFFAM) DICKENS (1812–70), English novelist: *Hard Times*

It is a capital mistake to theorise before one has data. Insensibly one begins to twist facts to suit theories, instead of theories to suit facts.
SIR ARTHUR CONAN DOYLE (1859–1930), English writer: *The Adventures of Sherlock Holmes, 'Scandal in Bohemia'*

I think there is one smashing rule – never face the facts.
RUTH GORDON (1896–), American actress: *New York Post, 1971*

All fact-collectors, who have no aim beyond their facts, are one-story men. Two-story men compare, reason, generalize, using the labors of the fact-collectors as well as their own. Three-story men idealize, imagine, predict; their best illumi-nation comes from above, through the skylight.
OLIVER WENDELL HOLMES, SR (1809–94), American physician, professor, and author: *The Poet at the Breakfast Table*

A wise man recognizes the conveni-ence of a general statement, but he bows to the authority of a particular fact.
OLIVER WENDELL HOLMES, SR, *as above*

Facts do not cease to exist because they are ignored.
ALDOUS (LEONARD) HUXLEY (1894–1963), English novelist and essayist: *Proper Studies*

Facts by themselves are silent.
ALFRED MARSHALL (1842–1924), English classical economist: *The Present Position of Economics*

Why, a four-year-old child could understand this report. Run out and find me a four-year-old child. I can't make head or tail out of it.
GROUCHO MARX (1895–1977), American film comedian: *Duck Soup, film*

The facts are to blame, my friend. We are all imprisoned by facts: I was born, I exist.
LUIGI PIRANDELLO (1867–1936), Italian playwright and novelist: *The Rules of the Game*

When you have duly arrayed your 'facts' in logical order, lo, it is like an oil-lamp that you have made, filled

and trimmed, but which sheds no light unless first you light it.
ANTOINE DE SAINT-EXUPÉRY (1900–44), French novelist and aviator: *The Wisdom of the Sands*

Comment is free but facts are sacred.
C(HARLES) P(RESTWICK) SCOTT (1846–1932), Editor, Manchester Guardian

Get your facts first, and then you can distort them as much as you please.
MARK TWAIN (Samuel Langhorne Clemens) (1835–1910), American novelist and humorist

GIFTS

What you get free costs too much.
JEAN ANOUILH (1910–), French dramatist: *The Lark*

Bath salts and inexpensive scent And hideous tie so kindly meant.
SIR JOHN BETJEMAN (1906–84), English poet: *Christmas*

The only gift is a portion of thyself.
RALPH WALDO EMERSON (1803–82), American poet, essayist, and philosopher: *Essays: Second Series, 'Gifts'*

It is not good to refuse a gift.
HOMER (ca. 800 BC), Greek poet: *Odyssey*

The charity that is a trifle to us can be precious to others.
HOMER, *as above*

You never want to give a man a present when he's feeling good. You want to do it when he's down.
LYNDON B(AINES) JOHNSON (1908–), U.S. statesman and president (Attributed)

People seldom read a book which is given to them; and few are given. The way to spread a work is to sell it at a low price. No man will send to buy a thing that costs even sixpence, without an intention to read it.
SAMUEL JOHNSON (1709–84), English lexicographer, essayist, and poet: Boswell, *Life of Johnson*

The selection of presents for children is never easy, because in order to extract real pleasure from the purchase, it is necessary to find something that excites the donor as much as it is likely to excite the recipient.
SIR COMPTON MACKENZIE (1883–1972), British author: *Poor Relations*

He who cannot give anything away cannot feel anything either.
FRIEDRICH WILHELM NIETZSCHE (1844–1900), German philosopher, poet, and critic: *The Will to Power*

Say it with flowers.
PATRICK O'KEEFE (1874–1934), American advertising agent: *Slogan for Society of American Florists*

Fear the Greeks bearing gifts.
Proverb

Small gifts make friends, great ones make enemies.
Proverb

It's the thought that counts.
Saying

The spirit in which a thing is given determines that in which the debt is acknowledged; it's the intention, not the face-value of the gift, that's weighed.
MARCUS or LUCIUS ANNAEUS SENECA (The Elder) (?55 BC–?39 AD), Roman writer on oratory and history: *Letters to Lucilius*

HOTELS

I have always had a hidden wish, a frustrated desire, to run a hotel.
EDWARD (RICHARD GEORGE) HEATH (1916–), British statesman and prime minister: *Observer, 'Sayings of the Year', 18 December 1966*

I want to register a complaint. Do you know who sneaked into my room at three o'clock this morning? —Who?
Nobody, and that's my complaint.
GROUCHO MARX (1895–1977), American film comedian: *Monkey Business, film*

Send two dozen red roses to Room 424 and put 'Emily, I love you' on the back of the bill.
GROUCHO MARX, *A Night in Casablanca, film*

The great advantage of a hotel is that it's a refuge from home life.
GEORGE BERNARD SHAW (1856–1950), Irish dramatist and critic: *You Never Can Tell*

It used to be a good hotel, but that proves nothing – I used to be a good boy.
MARK TWAIN (Samuel Langhorne Clemens) (1835–1910), American novelist and humorist: *Letter from New York to the Alta Californian (San Francisco), 19 April 1867*

I prefer temperance hotels – although they sell worse kinds of liquor than any other kind of hotels.
ARTEMUS WARD (Charles Farrar Browne) (1834–67), American humorist, editor, and lecturer: *Artemus Ward's Lecture*

IDEAS & INVENTIONS

As the births of living creatures at first are ill-shapen, so are all innovations, which are the births of time.
FRANCIS BACON, 1st Baron Verulam, Viscount St Albans (1561–1626), English writer, philosopher, and statesman: *Essays*

There is no new thing under the sun.
The Bible, Authorized (King James) Version, Ecclesiastes 1:9

I never actually set out to see how I could make the most cash. I've always merely tried to make the figures fit the ideas I've had rather than the other way around. I guess that's doing it backwards.
RICHARD BRANSON, Head of Virgin Group, quoted in Jeffrey Robinson, *The Risk Takers, chapter 4*

Let's remind ourselves that last year's fresh idea is today's cliché.
AUSTEN BRIGGS (1931–), American commercial artist

A new idea is delicate. It can be killed by a sneer or a yawn; it can be stabbed to death by a quip and worried to death by a frown on the right man's brow.
CHARLES (HENDRICKSON) BROWER (1901–), American advertising executive: *Advertising Age, 10 August 1959*

Inventors and men of genius have almost always been regarded as fools at the beginning (and very often at the end) of their careers.
FYODOR MIKHAILOVICH DOSTOEVSKY (1821–81), Russian novelist: *The Idiot*

Innovation is the new conservatism.
PETER F. DRUCKER (1909–), American management expert, quoted in Jeremy Tunstall, *The Advertising Man*

Invention breeds invention.
RALPH WALDO EMERSON (1803–82), American poet, essayist, and philosopher: *Society and Solitude*

No grand idea was ever born in a conference, but a lot of foolish ideas have died there.
FRANCIS SCOTT (KEY) FITZGERALD (1896–1940), American novelist: *The Crack-Up*

It is easy to overlook the absence of appreciable advance in an industry. Inventions that are not made, like babies that are not born, are rarely missed.
JOHN KENNETH GALBRAITH (1908–), Canadian-born American economist, diplomat, and writer: *The Affluent Society, chapter 9*

One doesn't discover new lands without consenting to lose sight of the shore for a very long time.
ANDRÉ GIDE (1869–1951), French novelist, dramatist, critic, diarist, and translator: *The Counterfeiters*

As soon as an idea is accepted it is time to reject it.
HOLBROOK JACKSON (1874–1948), English literary scholar and editor

If you are possessed by an idea, you find it expressed everywhere, you even *smell* it.
THOMAS MANN (1875–1955), German novelist and essayist: *Death in Venice*

An idea isn't responsible for the people who believe in it.
DON(ALD ROBERT PERRY) MARQUIS (1878–1937), American humorist: *New York Sun, 'Sun Dial'*

The full importance of an epoch-making idea is often not perceived in the generation in which it is made ... The mechanical inventions of every age are apt to be underrated relatively to those of earlier times. For a new discovery is seldom fully effective for practical purposes till many minor improvements and subsidiary discoveries have gathered themselves around it.
ALFRED MARSHALL (1842–1924), English classical economist: *Principles of Economics, book 4*

By his very success in inventing labor-saving devices, modern man has manufactured an abyss of boredom that only the privileged classes in earlier civilizations have ever fathomed.
LEWIS MUMFORD (1895–), American sociologist, historian, and critic: *The Conduct of Life*

As soon as we are shown the existence of something old in a new thing, we are pacified.
FRIEDRICH WILHELM NIETZSCHE (1844–1900), German philosopher, poet, and critic: *The Will to Power*

Thinking is the endeavor to capture reality by means of ideas.
JOSÉ ORTEGA Y GASSET (1883–1955), Spanish philosopher and statesman: *The Dehumanization of Art*

Innovations are dangerous.
Proverb

Necessity is the mother of invention.
Proverb

The great difficulty in education is to get experience out of ideas.
GEORGE SANTAYANA (1863–1952), American philosopher and poet: *The Life of Reason: Reason in Common Sense*

You can't really separate the inventor and the businessman. The idea of the lone inventor sitting in an attic somewhere is pretty impractical. By its very nature, invention itself is improbable. If you rush around with all your ideas in a brown paper bag, knocking on doors of big companies, those big companies are going to say, no. The way society arranges things makes it very difficult for all inventors. So the way you get around that problem, the way you turn your invention into something, is by being a sort of businessman. You go out there and you start a company and you get your own invention off the ground.
SIR CLIVE (MARLES) SINCLAIR (1940–), English computer entrepreneur, quoted in Jeffrey Robinson, *The Risk Takers*

Name the greatest of all the inventors. Accident.
MARK TWAIN (Samuel Langhorne Clemens) (1835–1910), American novelist and humorist: *Notebook*

The radical invents the views. When he has worn them out the conservative adopts them.
MARK TWAIN, *as above*

Wit is the sudden marriage of ideas which before their union were not perceived to have any relation.
MARK TWAIN, *as above*

Everyone likes innovation until it affects himself, and then it's bad.
WALTER WRISTON, Chairman, First National City Bank, New York: *Observer*, 'Sayings of the Year', 29 December 1974

INSURANCE

I don't want to tell you how much insurance I carry with the Prudential, but all I can say is: when I go, *they* go.
JACK BENNY (1894–1974), American comedian (Attributed)

Insurance
An ingenious modern game of chance in which the player is permitted to enjoy the comfortable conviction that he is beating the man who keeps the table.
AMBROSE (GWINETT) BIERCE (1842–?1914), American journalist and humorist: *The Devil's Dictionary*

When the praying does no good, insurance does help.
BERTOLT BRECHT (1898–1956), German dramatist: *The Mother*

The Act of God designation on all insurance policies . . . means

roughly that you cannot be insured for the accidents that are most likely to happen to you. If your ox kicks a hole in your neighbour's Maserati, however, indemnity is instantaneous.
ALAN COREN (1938–), British humorist: *The Lady from Stalingrad Mansions*

I detest life-insurance agents; they always argue that I shall some day die, which is not so.
STEPHEN BUTLER LEACOCK (1869–1944), Canadian economist and humorist: *Literary Lapses, 'Insurance. Up to Date'*

will find that nearly all of them have answered themselves.
ARTHUR BINSTEAD: *Pitcher's Proverbs*

Of the Persian post-riders
Neither snow nor rain nor heat nor gloom of night stays these couriers from the swift accomplishment of their appointed routes.
HERODOTUS (?485–?425 BC), Greek historian: *Histories*

No, I don't know his telephone number. But it was up in the high numbers.
JOHN MAYNARD KEYNES (1883–1946), English economist (Attributed)

LETTERS & THE TELEPHONE

Letters of thanks, letters from banks,
Letters of joy from girl and boy.
W(YSTAN) H(UGH) AUDEN (1907–73), English poet, dramatist, critic, and librettist: *Night Mail*

Telephone
An invention of the devil which abrogates some of the advantages of making a disagreeable person keep his distance.
AMBROSE (GWINETT) BIERCE (1842–?1914), American journalist and humorist: *The Devil's Dictionary*

The great secret in life ... not to open your letters for a fortnight. At the expiration of that period you

MACHINERY

Faith in machinery is our besetting danger; often in machinery most absurdly disproportioned to the end which this machinery, if it is to do any good at all, is to serve; but always in machinery, as if it had a value in and for itself.
MATTHEW ARNOLD (1822–88), English poet, essayist, and literary critic: *Culture and Anarchy*

If it works, it's out of date.
STAFFORD BEER (1926–), British writer and scientist: *Brain of the Firm*

Man is a tool-using animal.
THOMAS CARLYLE (1795–1881), Scottish essayist and historian: *Sartor Resartus*

One machine can do the work of fifty ordinary men. No machine can do the work of one extraordinary man.
ELBERT (GREEN) HUBBARD (1856–1915), American businessman, writer, and printer

It is only when they go wrong that machines remind you how powerful they are.
CLIVE JAMES (1939–), Australian critic: *Observer, 1976*

We believe that if men have the talent to invent new machines that

ONE MACHINE CAN DO THE WORK OF FIFTY ORDINARY MEN. NO MACHINE CAN DO THE WORK OF ONE EXTRAORDINARY MAN.

put men out of work, they have the talent to put those men back to work.
JOHN FITZGERALD KENNEDY (1917–63), U.S. statesman and president: *Address, Wheeling, West Virginia, 27 September 1962*

Without doubt, machinery has greatly increased the number of well-to-do idlers.
KARL MARX (1818–83), German founder of modern communism: *Capital, volume 1*

Since the introduction of inanimate mechanism into British manufactories, man, with few exceptions, has been treated as a secondary and inferior machine; and far more attention has been given to perfect the raw materials of wood and metals than those of body and mind. Give but due reflection to the subject, and you will find that man, even as an instrument for the creation of wealth, may be still greatly improved.
ROBERT OWEN (1771–1858), Welsh industrialist and social reformer: *A New View of Society or Essays on the Principle of the Formation of the Human Character and the Application of the Principle of Practice*

The great mechanical impulses of the age, of which most of us are so proud, are a mere passing fever, half-speculative, half-childish.
JOHN RUSKIN (1819–1900), English art critic and social reformer: *Modern Painters*

NEGOTIATION & PERSUASION

The advantage of doing one's praising for oneself is that one can lay it on so thick and exactly in the right places.
SAMUEL BUTLER (1835–1902), English author, painter, and musician: *The Way of All Flesh, chapter 34*

How to Win Friends and Influence People.
DALE CARNEGIE (1888–1955), American writer: *Title of Book*

Most people have ears, but few have judgment; tickle those ears, and, depend upon it, you will catch their judgments, such as they are.
LORD CHESTERFIELD, Philip Dormer Stanhope, 4th Earl of (1694–1773), English statesman and writer: *Letter to his son, 9 December 1749*

Money is the best bait to fish for man with.
THOMAS FULLER (1654–1734), English physician, writer, and compiler: *Gnomologia*

When a man tells me he's going to put all his cards on the table, I always look up his sleeve.
LORD (ISAAC) LESLIE HORE-BELISHA (1893–1957), British politician

Whenever you're sitting across from some important person, always picture him sitting there in a suit of long red underwear. That's

the way I always operated in business.
JOSEPH PATRICK KENNEDY (1888–1969), American businessman and diplomat

By winning words to conquer willing hearts,
And make persuasion do the work of fear.
JOHN MILTON (1608–74), English poet: *Paradise Regained*

We are more easily persuaded, in general, by the reasons we ourselves discover than by those which are given to us by others.
BLAISE PASCAL (1623–62), French philosopher, mathematician, and physicist: *Pensées*

There are two fools in every market: one asks too little, one asks too much.
Proverb

Never take no for an answer.
Saying

There is a danger in being persuaded before one understands.
(THOMAS) WOODROW WILSON (1856–1924), American statesman and U.S. president: *Maxims of Piety and of Christianity*

(HERBERT) MARSHALL McLUHAN (1911–80), Canadian educator, author, and media expert, quoted in *Guardian Weekly, 12 June 1977*

Papyromania
Compulsive accumulation of papers.
Papyrophobia
Abnormal desire for 'a clean desk'.
DR LAURENCE J. PETER (1919–), Canadian educator and RAYMOND HULL (1919–), *The Peter Principle, Glossary*

A man who has no office to go to – I don't care who he is – is a trial of which you can have no conception.
GEORGE BERNARD SHAW (1856–1950), Irish dramatist and critic: *The Irrational Knot*

I yield to no one in my admiration for the office as a social centre, but it's no place actually to get any work done.
KATHERINE WHITEHORN, British journalist: *Sunday Best, Introduction*

Filing is concerned with the past; anything you actually need to see again has to do with the future.
KATHERINE WHITEHORN, *as above*, 'Sorting Out'

PROBLEMS

There's no problem so big or complicated that it can't be run away from.
Anon

OFFICES

Gutenberg made everybody a reader. Xerox makes everybody a publisher.

If you can't tell me what you'd like to be happening ... you don't have a problem yet. You're just complaining. A problem exists only if there is a difference between what is *actually* happening and what you *desire* to be happening.
KENNETH BLANCHARD, American management consultant and SPENCER JOHNSON, American doctor, psychologist, and author: *The One Minute Manager*

When I look back on all these worries I remember the story of the old man who said on his deathbed that he had had a lot of trouble in his life, most of which had never happened.
SIR WINSTON LEONARD SPENCER CHURCHILL (1874–1965), English statesman, writer, and prime minister: *Their Finest Hour*

You're either part of the solution or part of the problem.
ELDRIDGE CLEAVER (1935–), American writer and radical: *Slogan, 1968*

The government solution to a problem is usually as bad as the problem.
MILTON FRIEDMAN (1912–), American economist (Attributed)

It is not always by plugging away at a difficulty and sticking at it that one overcomes it; but, rather, often by working on the one next to it.

Certain people and certain things require to be approached on an angle.
ANDRÉ GIDE (1869–1951), French novelist, dramatist, critic, diarist, and translator: *Journals, 26 October 1924*

There are two problems in my life. The political ones are insoluble and the economic ones are incomprehensible.
SIR ALEC DOUGLAS-HOME, Lord Home of Hirsel (1903–), British statesman and prime minister

Nothing will ever be attempted, if all possible objections must be first overcome.
SAMUEL JOHNSON (1709–84), English lexicographer, essayist, and poet: *Rasselas*

Problems are only opportunities in work clothes.
HENRY J. KAISER (1882–1967), American industrialist

There cannot be a crisis next week. My schedule is already full.
HENRY KISSINGER (1923–), German-born American academic and diplomat: *New York Times Magazine, 1969*

PRODUCTION

Man produces in order to consume.
FRÉDÉRIC BASTIAT (1801–50): *Sophismes Économiques, chapter 1*

Every production must resemble its author.
MIGUEL DE CERVANTES (SAAVEDRA) (1547–1616), Spanish writer: *Don Quixote, Preface*

Production only fills a void that it has itself created.
JOHN KENNETH GALBRAITH (1908–), Canadian-born American economist, diplomat, and writer: *The Affluent Society, chapter 11*

An object of art creates a public capable of finding pleasure in its beauty. Production, therefore, not only produces an object for the subject, but also a subject for the object.
KARL MARX (1818–83), German founder of modern communism: *A Critique of Political Economy*

Production goes up and up because high pressure advertising and salesmanship constantly create new needs that must be satisfied: this is *Admass* – a consumer's race with donkeys chasing an electric carrot.
J(OHN) B(OYNTON) PRIESTLEY (1894–1984), English author: *Thoughts in the Wilderness*

It is production which opens a demand for production . . . a product is no sooner created, than it, from that instant, affords a market for other products to the full extent of its own value . . . the only way of getting rid of money is in the purchase of some product or other.
JEAN-BAPTISTE SAY (1767–1832), French economist: *A Treatise on Political Economy, volume 1*

Industry does nothing but produce scarce things.
(MARIE-ESPRIT) LÉON WALRAS (1834–1910), French economist and reformer: *Elements of Pure Economics, Part 1*

PROGRESS

In the youth of a state arms do flourish; in the middle age of a state, learning; and then both of them together for a time; in the declining age of a state, mechanical arts and merchandise.
FRANCIS BACON, 1st Baron Verulam, Viscount St Albans (1561–1626), English writer, philosopher, and statesman: *Essays, 'Of Vicissitude of Things'*

All progress is based upon a universal innate desire of every organism to live beyond its income.
SAMUEL BUTLER (1835–1902), English author, painter, and musician: *Note Books*

As enunciated today, 'progress' is simply a comparative of which we have not settled the superlative.
G(ILBERT) K(EITH) CHESTERTON (1874–1936), English essayist, novelist, poet, and critic: *Heretics, chapter 2*

All conservatism is based upon the idea that if you leave things alone you leave them as they are. But you do not. If you leave a thing alone you leave it to a torrent of change.
G(ILBERT) K(EITH) CHESTERTON, *Orthodoxy, chapter 7*

Economic advance is not the same
thing as human progress.
SIR JOHN CLAPHAM (1873–1946),
British economic historian: *A Concise
Economic History of Britain*

Change comes about because of
two factors broadly, I think. One is
the interaction of other nations on
us, who are exploiting our lack of
competitiveness ... And then you've
got people like me who bring about
change with a view to trying to
recoup the situation and to make us
more competitive; and it is thought
that the only way you do that is now
by rushing out and employing a lot
of people. You do it, in fact, by
scaling down organizations to be
lean, hungry and competitive, and
to take on the Japanese and the
Americans and the Germans.
SIR MICHAEL EDWARDES, (1930–),
British industrialist, quoted in Cary L.
Cooper and Peter Hingley, *The Change
Makers*

The strongest principle of growth
lies in human choice.
GEORGE ELIOT (Mary Ann Evans)
(1819–90), English novelist: *Daniel
Deronda, book 6*

There is always a certain meanness
in the argument of conservatism,
joined with a certain superiority in
its fact.
RALPH WALDO EMERSON (1803–82),
American poet, essayist, and philosopher:
The Conservative

All is change; all yields its place
and goes.
EURIPIDES (?480–406 BC), Greek
tragic dramatist: *Heracles*

The modern conservative is engaged
in one of man's oldest exercises in
moral philosophy, that is the search
for a superior moral justification for
selfishness.
JOHN KENNETH GALBRAITH (1908–),
Canadian-born American economist,
diplomat, and writer

All that is human must retrograde if
it do not advance.
EDWARD GIBBON (1737–94), English
historian: *Decline and Fall of the Roman
Empire*

There is no way to make people like
change. You can only make them
feel less threatened by it.
FREDERICK HAYES, American bureaucrat: *Fortune, 1969*

The reason men oppose progress is
not that they hate progress, but
that they love inertia.
ELBERT (GREEN) HUBBARD (1856–
1915), American businessman, writer,
and printer: *The Note Book*

What is conservatism? Is it not
adherence to the old and tried,
against the new and untried?
ABRAHAM LINCOLN (1809–65), U.S.
statesman and president: *Speech, New
York, 27 February 1860*

If we have had a formula for growth
it has been: start with the best;
learn from the best, expand slowly
and solidify our position; then
horizontally diversify our expertise.
MARK H. McCORMACK (1930–),
Founder, International Management
Group: *What They Don't Teach You At
Harvard Business School*

**Progress – progress is the dirtiest word in the language – who ever told us –
And made us believe it – that to take a step forward was necessarily, was always
A good idea?**
EDNA ST VINCENT MILLAY (1892–1950), American poet: *Make Bright the Arrows*

No progress is going back.
Proverb

If you are planning for one year plant rice. If you are planning for ten years plant trees. If you are planning for 100 years plant people.
Indian proverb

You can't stand still.
Saying

Small Is Beautiful: Economics As If People Mattered.
ERNST FRIEDRICH SCHUMACHER (1911–77), German-born economist and conservationist: *Title of book*

Economic progress, in capitalist society, means turmoil.
JOSEPH ALOIS SCHUMPETER (1883–1950), Austrian-born American economist: *Capitalism, Socialism and Democracy*

The reasonable man adapts himself to the world: the unreasonable one persists in trying to adapt the world to himself. Therefore all progress depends on the unreasonable man.
GEORGE BERNARD SHAW (1856–1950), Irish dramatist and critic: *Man and Superman, Maxims for Revolutionists*

All progress means war with Society.
GEORGE BERNARD SHAW, *Getting Married*

Economic growth is not only unnecessary, but ruinous.
ALEXANDER ISAYEVICH SOLZHENITSYN (1918–), Exiled Russian novelist

Things do not change; we change.
HENRY DAVID THOREAU (1817–62), American essayist and poet: *Walden, 'Economy'*

Progress was all right. Only it went on too long.
JAMES (GROVER) THURBER (1894–1961), American humorist and cartoonist (Attributed)

Civilization advances by extending the number of important operations which we can perform without thinking about them.
ALFRED NORTH WHITEHEAD (1861–1947), English mathematician and philosopher

Conservatism is the policy of 'make no change and consult your grandmother when in doubt.'
(THOMAS) WOODROW WILSON (1856-1924), U.S. statesman and president

PUBLIC SPEAKING

An after-dinner speech should be like a lady's dress: long enough to cover the subject and short enough to be interesting.
Anon

KISS: Keep it short, stupid.
Anon

I do not object to people looking at their watches when I am speaking – but I strongly object when they start shaking them to make certain they are still going.
LORD BIRKETT, quoted in A. Andrews, *Quotations for Speakers and Writers*

First learn the meaning of what you say, and then speak.
EPICTETUS (?50–?120 AD), Greek philosopher: *Discourses*

There may be other reasons for a man's not speaking in publick than want of resolution: he may have nothing to say.
SAMUEL JOHNSON (1709–84), English lexicographer, essayist, and poet: Boswell, *Life of Johnson*

Beware of the conversationalist who adds 'In other words'. He is merely starting afresh.
ROBERT MORLEY (1908–), British actor and wit: *Observer, 1964*

Polonius
Brevity is the soul of wit.
WILLIAM SHAKESPEARE (1564–1616), English dramatist and poet: *Hamlet, Act 2*

Men of few words are the best men.
WILLIAM SHAKESPEARE, *King Henry the Fifth, Act 3*

I am the most spontaneous speaker in the world because every word, every gesture, and every retort has been carefully rehearsed.
GEORGE BERNARD SHAW (1856–1950), Irish dramatist and critic

It is terrible to speak well and be wrong.
SOPHOCLES (?496–406 BC), Greek dramatist: *Electra*

It usually takes me more than three weeks to prepare a good impromptu speech.
MARK TWAIN (Samuel Langhorne Clemens) (1835–1910), American novelist and humorist

TECHNOLOGY

Technology . . . the knack of so arranging the world that we don't have to experience it.
MAX FRISCH (1911–), Swiss dramatist and novelist: *Homo Faber*

Every technical improvement creates a new complication to the economic apparatus, causes the appearance of new factors and combinations, which the masses cannot penetrate for a time. Every jump of technical progress leaves the relative intellectual development of the masses a step behind, and thus causes a fall in the political-maturity thermometer. It takes sometimes tens of years, sometimes generations, for a people's level of understanding gradually to adapt itself to the changed state of affairs, until it has recovered the same capacity for self-government, as it had already

possessed at a lower stage of civilization.
ARTHUR KOESTLER (1905–83), Hungarian-born English author: *Darkness at Noon, book 3*

For tribal man space was the uncontrollable mystery. For technological man it is time that occupies the same role.
(HERBERT) MARSHALL McLUHAN (1911–80), Canadian educator, author, and media expert: *The Mechanical Bride, 'Magic that Changes Mood'*

THOUGHT

Analysis kills spontaneity. The grain once ground into flour springs and germinates no more.
HENRI FRÉDÉRIC AMIEL (1821–81), Swiss philosopher and poet: *Journal, 7 November 1878*

Reflection
An action of the mind whereby we obtain a clearer view of our relation to the things of yesterday and are able to avoid the perils that we shall not again encounter.
AMBROSE (GWINETT) BIERCE (1842–?1914), American journalist and humorist: *The Devil's Dictionary*

Cogito, ergo sum.
I think; therefore I am.
RENÉ DESCARTES (1596–1650), French philosopher and mathematician: *Discourse on Method*

If a man sits down to think, he is immediately asked if he has the headache.
RALPH WALDO EMERSON (1803–82), American poet, essayist, and philosopher: *Journals*

What is the hardest task in the world? To think.
RALPH WALDO EMERSON, *Intellect*

Second thoughts are ever wiser.
EURIPIDES (?480–406 BC), Greek tragic dramatist: *Hippolytus*

Thinking is more interesting than knowing, but less interesting than looking.
JOHANN WOLFGANG VON GOETHE (1749–1832), German poet, scientist, and writer

When half the people believe one thing, and the other half another, it is usually safe to accept either opinion.
EDGAR WATSON HOWE (1853–1937), American journalist, novelist, and essayist: *Ventures in Common Sense*

Most of one's life . . . is one prolonged effort to prevent oneself thinking.
ALDOUS (LEONARD) HUXLEY (1894–1963), English novelist and essayist: *Mortal Coils, 'Green Tunnels'*

As the development of the mind proceeds, symbols, instead of being employed to convey images, are substituted for them. Civilized men think as they trade, not in kind, but

by means of a circulating medium.
THOMAS BABINGTON MACAULAY
(1800–59), English historian, essayist,
and statesman: *Edinburgh Review,
January 1828, 'John Dryden'*

Think.
Motto of IBM

**Profundity of thought belongs to
youth, clarity of thought to old age.**
FRIEDRICH WILHELM NIETZSCHE
(1844–1900), German philosopher,
poet, and critic: *Miscellaneous Maxims
and Opinions*

**We do not live to think, but, on the
contrary, we think in order that we
may succeed in surviving.**
JOSÉ ORTEGA Y GASSET (1883–1955),
Spanish philosopher and statesman:
Partisan Review, December 1949

**There are two distinct classes of
what are called thoughts: those
that we produce in ourselves by
reflection and the act of thinking,
and those that bolt into the mind of
their own accord.**
THOMAS PAINE (1737–1809), English
philosopher and writer: *The Age of
Reason*

**After you've done a thing the same
way for two years look it over
carefully. After five years look at it
with suspicion and after ten years
throw it away and start all over
again.**
ALFRED EDWARD PERLMAN (1902–),
American railway executive: *New York
Times, 1958*

A penny for your thoughts.
Proverb

**While we stop to think, we often
miss our opportunity.**
PUBLILIUS SYRUS (1st c. BC), Latin
writer of mimes: *Sententiae*

**You can't think rationally on an
empty stomach, and a whole lot of
people can't do it on a full one
either.**
LORD REITH, John (Charles Walsham),
1st Baron (1889–1971), British
broadcasting executive (Attributed)

**The real problem is not whether
machines think but whether men
do.**
B(URRHUS) F(REDERIC) SKINNER
(1904–), American behaviourist:
Contingencies of Reinforcement

**Thoughts may be bandits. Thoughts
may be raiders. Thoughts may be
invaders. Thoughts may be disturb-
ers of the international peace.**
(THOMAS) WOODROW WILSON
(1856–1924), U.S. statesman and
president: *Speech, 16 May 1916*

TRAVEL

Telegram of employee during traffic crisis
**Regret cannot come today; have not
yet got home yesterday.**
Anon

Travel teaches toleration.
BENJAMIN DISRAELI, 1st Earl of
Beaconsfield (1804–81), English
statesman, prime minister, and novelist:
Contarini Fleming

**No man should travel until he has
learned the language of the country
he visits. Otherwise he voluntarily
makes himself a great baby – so
helpless and so ridiculous.**
RALPH WALDO EMERSON (1803–82),
American poet, essayist, and philosopher:
Journals, 1833

Of railway termini
**They are our gates to the glorious
and the unknown. Through them
we pass out into adventure and
sunshine, and to them, alas! we
return.**
EDWARD MORGAN FORSTER (1879–
1970), English novelist: *Howard's End*,
chapter 2

**Travel is atavistic, the day will
come when there will be no more
traffic at all and only newlyweds will
travel.**
MAX FRISCH (1911–), Swiss dramatist
and novelist, quoted in D.J. Boorstin, *The
Image*

**A gentleman ought to travel abroad
but dwell at home.**
THOMAS FULLER (1654–1734), English
physician, writer, and compiler:
Gnomologia

He that travels much knows much.
THOMAS FULLER, *as above*

**One of the pleasantest things in the
world is going a journey; but I like
to go by myself.**
WILLIAM HAZLITT (1778–1830),
English essayist: *On Going a Journey*

**Flying? I've been to almost as many
places as my luggage!**
BOB HOPE (1904–), English-born
American comedian and comic actor

**Traveling makes men wiser, but
less happy. When men of sober age
travel, they gather knowledge
which they may apply usefully for
their country; but they are subject
ever after to recollections mixed
with regret; their affections are
weakened by being extended over
more objects; and they learn new
habits which cannot be gratified
when they return home.**
THOMAS JEFFERSON (1743–1826),
U.S. statesman and president: *Letter to
Peter Carr*

**In the space age, man will be able to
go around the world in two hours –
one hour for flying and the other to
get to the airport.**
NEIL H. McELROY (1904–), American
business executive and public official:
Look, 18 February 1958

**The car has become the carapace,
the protective and aggressive shell,
of urban and suburban man.**
(HERBERT) MARSHALL McLUHAN
(1911–80), Canadian educator, author,
and media expert: *Understanding Media*

**Nothing so necessary for travellers
as languages.**
Proverb

Travel broadens the mind.
Proverb

A pleasant companion reduces the length of the journey.
PUBLILIUS SYRUS (1st c. BC), Latin writer of mimes: *Sententiae*

He who would travel happily must travel light.
ANTOINE DE SAINT-EXUPÉRY (1900–44), French novelist and aviator

The more I see of other countries the more I love my own.
MADAME DE STAËL, Baronne Anne Louise Germaine de Staël-Holstein (1766–1817), Swiss-born French writer: *Corinne*

IN THE SPACE AGE, MAN WILL BE ABLE TO GO AROUND THE WORLD IN TWO HOURS – ONE HOUR FOR FLYING AND THE OTHER TO GET TO THE AIRPORT.

For my part, I travel not to go anywhere, but to go. I travel for travel's sake. The great affair is to move.
ROBERT LOUIS BALFOUR STEVENSON (1850–94), Scottish writer: *Travels with a Donkey*

To travel hopefully is a better thing than to arrive, and the true success is to labour.
ROBERT LOUIS BALFOUR STEVENSON, *Virginibus Puerisque*, 'El Dorado'

Everything in life is somewhere else, and you get there in a car.
E(LWYN) B(ROOKS) WHITE (1899–), American humorist and essayist: *One Man's Meat*

WORK

We continue to overlook the fact that work has become a leisure activity.
MARK ABRAMS: *Observer*, 'Sayings of the Week', 3 June 1962

Work was like cats were supposed to be; if you disliked and feared it and tried to keep out of its way, it knew at once and sought you out.
KINGSLEY AMIS (1922–), English novelist and poet: *Take a Girl Like You*

Even the best plan degenerates into work.
Anon

The difficult we do immediately. The impossible takes a little longer.
Anon

The first 90% of the project takes the first 90% of the time. The last 10% of the project takes the last 90% of the time.
Anon

Work is the price you pay for money.
Anon

How can I take an interest in my work when I don't like it?
FRANCIS BACON (1909–), Irish artist

He had insomnia so bad that he couldn't sleep when he was working.
ARTHUR BAER (1885–1969), quoted in Robert W. Kent, *Money Talks*

It is necessary to work, if not from inclination, at least from despair. Everything considered, work is less boring than amusing oneself.
CHARLES PIERRE BAUDELAIRE (1821–67), French poet: *Mon coeur mis à nu*

Overwork
A dangerous disorder affecting high public functionaries who want to go fishing.
AMBROSE (GWINETT) BIERCE (1842–?1914), American journalist and humorist: *The Devil's Dictionary*

What is the use of health, or of life, if not to do some work therewith?
THOMAS CARLYLE (1795–1881), Scottish essayist and historian: *Sartor Resartus*

Whatever is worth doing at all is worth doing well.
LORD CHESTERFIELD, Philip Dormer Stanhope, 4th Earl of (1694–1773), English statesman and writer: *Letter to his son, 10 March 1746*

Work is much more fun than fun.
SIR NOËL (PIERCE) COWARD (1899–1973), English actor and dramatist: *Observer, 'Sayings of the Week', 21 June 1963*

Whistle While You Work.
WALT(ER ELIAS) DISNEY (1901–66), U.S. film director and LARRY MOREY: *Snow White, title of song*

Genius is one percent inspiration and ninety-nine percent perspiration.
THOMAS ALVA EDISON (1847–1931), American inventor: *Life*

The idea that to make a man work you've got to hold gold in front of his eyes is a growth, not an axiom. We've done that for so long that we've forgotten there's any other way.
FRANCIS SCOTT (KEY) FITZGERALD (1896–1940), American novelist: *This Side of Paradise, book 2*

Diligence is the mother of good luck, and God gives all things to industry. Then plough deep while sluggards sleep, and you shall have corn to sell and to keep.
BENJAMIN FRANKLIN (1706–90), American statesman, scientist, and author: *Poor Richard's Almanac*

One of the best ways of avoiding necessary and even urgent tasks is to seem to be busily employed on things that are already done.
JOHN KENNETH GALBRAITH (1908–), Canadian-born American economist, diplomat, and writer: *The Affluent Society*

I like work; it fascinates me. I can sit and look at it for hours. I love to keep it by me: the idea of getting rid of it nearly breaks my heart.
JEROME K(LAPKA) JEROME (1859–1927), English humorous writer: *Three Men in a Boat, chapter 15*

It is impossible to enjoy idling thoroughly unless one has plenty of work to do.
JEROME K(LAPKA) JEROME, *Idle Thoughts of an Idle Fellow*

It's all in the day's work, as the huntsman said when the lion ate him.
CHARLES KINGSLEY (1819–75), English clergyman, novelist, and poet

Too much work and too much energy kill a man just as effectively as too much assorted vice or too much drink.
(JOSEPH) RUDYARD KIPLING (1865–1936), English novelist, poet and short story writer: *Plain Tales from the Hills, 'Thrown Away'*

My father taught me to work; he did not teach me to love it.
ABRAHAM LINCOLN (1809–65), U.S. statesman and president

Work . . . does not exist in a non-literate world . . . Where the

whole man is involved there is no work. Work begins with the division of labour.
(HERBERT) MARSHALL McLUHAN (1911–80), Canadian educator, author, and media expert: *Understanding Media*

It seems to me that a great deal of nonsense is talked about the dignity of work. Work is a drug that dull people take to avoid the pangs of unmitigated boredom.
W(ILLIAM) SOMERSET MAUGHAM (1874–1965), English writer: *The Explorer, chapter 3*

The really exhausting and the really repulsive labours, instead of being better paid than others, are almost invariably paid the worst of all . . . The hardships and the earnings, instead of being directly proportional, as in any just arrangements of society they would be, are generally in an inverse ratio to one another.
JOHN STUART MILL (1806–73), English philosopher and economist: *Principles of Political Economy, book 2*

Work seven days a week and nothing can stop you.
JOHN MOORES (1896–), British businessman

Work expands so as to fill the time available for its completion.
C(YRIL) NORTHCOTE PARKINSON (1909–), English historian and journalist: *Parkinson's Law*

Work is accomplished by those employees who have not yet reached their level of incompetence.
DR LAURENCE J. PETER (1919–), Canadian educator and RAYMOND HULL (1919–), *The Peter Principle, chapter 1*

All work and no play makes Jack a dull boy.
Proverb

Elbow-grease is the best polish.
Proverb

If a job's worth doing, it's worth doing well.
Proverb

Nothing is got without pain but dirt and long nails.
Proverb

It's all in a day's work.
Saying

The test of a vocation is the love of the drudgery it involves.
LOGAN PEARSALL SMITH (1865–1946), American-born English man of letters: *Afterthoughts*

Nothing so difficult but it may be won by industry.
TERENCE (Publius Terentius Afer) (?190–159 BC), Roman comic dramatist: *Heauton Timoroumenos*

Of work
It is about a search, too, for daily meaning as well as daily bread, for recognition as well as cash, for astonishment rather than torpor; in short, for a sort of life rather than a

Monday through Friday sort of dying.
STUDS TERKEL (1912–): *Working*

The buck stops here.
HARRY S. TRUMAN (1884–1972), U.S. statesman and president: *Notice on the presidential desk*

Work spares us from three great evils: boredom, vice and need.
VOLTAIRE (François Marie Arouet) (1694–1778), French writer, philosopher, and historian: *Candide*

When a man says he wants to work, what he means is that he wants wages.
BISHOP RICHARD WHATELY (1787–1863)

Work is the refuge of people who have nothing better to do.
OSCAR WILDE (1856–1900), Irish poet, dramatist and wit

Work is the curse of the drinking classes.
OSCAR WILDE

FINANCE & INSTITUTIONS

Finance is vital to the functioning of business. Opinions vary, however, on the morality of borrowing and profit-making, as the quotations in this section show. The quotations here also reveal a range of attitudes on the role of institutions such as banks, the law, and government, from the humorous 'A bank is a place that will lend you money if you can prove that you don't need it' (Bob Hope), through the descriptive '*Owning* capital is not a productive activity' (Joan Robinson), to the sobering 'Be content with your wages' (The Bible).

BANKING

A banker is a man who lends you an umbrella when the weather is fair, and takes it away from you when it rains.
Anon

O Gold! I still prefer thee unto paper Which makes bank credit like a bank of *vapour*.
LORD BYRON, George Gordon Byron, 6th Baron Byron of Rochdale (1788–1824), English poet: *Don Juan*

Political Ravishment, or, The Old Lady of Threadneedle Street.
JAMES GILRAY (1757–1815), British caricaturist: *Title of cartoon*

Put not your trust in money, but put your money in trust.
OLIVER WENDELL HOLMES, SR (1809–94), American physician, professor, and author: *The Autocrat of the Breakfast Table*

A bank is a place that will lend you money if you can prove that you don't need it.
BOB HOPE (1904–), English-born American comedian and comic actor, quoted in Alan Harrington, *Life in the Crystal Palace*

Banking establishments are more dangerous than standing armies.
THOMAS JEFFERSON (1743–1826), U.S. statesman and president: *Letter to Elbridge Gerry, 26 January 1799*

It is better that a man should tyrannize over his bank balance than over his fellow citizens.
JOHN MAYNARD KEYNES, 1st Baron (1883–1946), English economist: *General Theory of Employment*

Bankers Are Just Like Anybody Else, Except Richer.
OGDEN NASH (1902–71), American humorous poet: *I'm a Stranger Here Myself*

A banker is a person who is willing to make a loan if you present sufficient evidence to show you don't need it.
HERBERT V. PROCHNOW (1897–), quoted in Robert W. Kent, *Money Talks*

There have been three great inventions since the beginning of time: fire, the wheel, and central banking.
WILL(IAM PENN ADAIR) ROGERS (1879–1935), American actor and humorist, quoted in P.A. Samuelson, *Economics*

BORROWING & LENDING

In God we trust
All others pay cash.
Anon

In our modern economy it seems unlikely that the middle-class morality about money will be able to survive. I, for example, was brought up never to buy anything until I had the cash to pay for it. If everyone did the same, i.e. bought nothing on credit, our economy would go smash.
W(YSTAN) H(UGH) AUDEN (1907–73), English poet, dramatist, critic, and librettist: *A Certain World*

The borrower is servant to the lender.
The Bible, Authorized (King James) Version, Proverbs 22:7

Live within your income, even if you have to borrow money to do so.
JOSH BILLINGS (Henry Wheeler Shaw) (1818–85)

Neither borrow money of a friend; but of a mere stranger; where, paying for it, thou shalt hear of it no more: otherwise thou shalt eclipse thy credit, lose thy friend, and yet pay as dear as to another.
WILLIAM CECIL, 1st Baron Burghley (1520–98), English statesman: *Advice to his son*

Lend money to an enemy, and thou'lt gain him; to a friend, and thou'lt lose him.
BENJAMIN FRANKLIN (1706–90), American statesman, scientist, and author: *Poor Richard's Almanac*

Better give a shilling than lend and lose half a crown.
THOMAS FULLER (1654–1734), English physician, writer, and compiler: *Gnomologia*

Borrowed garments never fit well.
THOMAS FULLER, *as above*

Would you know what money is, go borrow some.
GEORGE HERBERT (1593–1633),
English metaphysical poet: *Outlandish Proverbs*

The human species, according to the best theory I can form of it, is composed of two distinct races, *the men who borrow*, and *the men who lend*.
CHARLES (ELIA) LAMB (1775–1834),
English essayist: *Essays of Elia, The Two Races of Men*

A pig bought on credit is forever grunting.
Proverb

Borrowed garments never fit well.
Proverb

He that lends, gives.
Proverb

A borrowed cloak does not keep one warm.
Arabic proverb

A small loan makes a debtor; a great one, an enemy.
PUBLILIUS SYRUS (1st c. BC), Latin writer of mimes: *Moral Sayings*

First payments is what made us think we were prosperous, and the other nineteen is what showed us we were broke.
WILL(IAM PENN ADAIR) ROGERS (1879–1935), American actor and humorist: *The Autobiography of Will Rogers*

Polonius
Neither a borrower nor a lender be; For loan oft loses both itself and friend, And borrowing dulls the edge of husbandry.
WILLIAM SHAKESPEARE (1564–1616),
English dramatist and poet: *Hamlet, Act 1*

Words pay no debts.
WILLIAM SHAKESPEARE, *Troilus and Cressida, Act 3*

BUREAUCRACY

A memorandum is written not to inform the reader but to protect the writer.
DEAN ACHESON (1893–1971),
American politician

The perfect bureaucrat everywhere is the man who manages to make no decisions and escape all responsibility.
(JUSTIN) BROOKS ATKINSON (1894–),
American dramatic critic and essayist:
Once Around the Sun

I think we have more machinery of government than is necessary, too many parasites living on the labor of the industrious.
THOMAS JEFFERSON (1743–1826),
U.S. statesman and president: *Letter to William Ludlow*

The only governments, not representative, in which high political skill and ability have been other than exceptional, whether under

monarchical or aristocratic forms, have been essentially bureaucracies. The work of government has been in the hands of governors by profession; which is the essence and meaning of bureaucracy.
JOHN STUART MILL (1806–73), English philosopher and economist: *Representative Government*

It's all papers and forms, the entire Civil Service is like a fortress made of papers, forms and red tape.
ALEXANDER NIKOLAYEVICH OSTROVSKY (1823–86), Russian playwright: *The Diary of a Scoundrel*

Bureaucracy defends the status quo long past the time when the quo has lost its status.
DR LAURENCE J. PETER (1919–), Canadian educator

Bureaucracy is not an obstacle to democracy but an inevitable complement to it.
JOSEPH ALOIS SCHUMPETER (1883–1950), Austrian-born American economist: *Capitalism, Socialism and Democracy*, chapter 18

CAPITAL

Capital is a result of labor, and is used by labor to assist it in further production. Labor is the active and initial force, and labor is therefore the employer of capital.
HENRY GEORGE (1839–97), American economist: *Progress and Poverty, book 3*

Each needs the other: capital cannot do without labor, nor labor without capital.
POPE LEO XIII (Gioacchino Pecci) (1810–1903): *Rerum novarum, 15 May 1891*

Labor is prior to, and independent of, capital. Capital is only the fruit of labor, and could never have existed if labor had not first existed. Labor is the superior of capital, and deserves much the higher consideration.
ABRAHAM LINCOLN (1809–65), U.S. statesman and president: *Message to Congress, 3 December 1861*

Capital consists in a great part of knowledge and organisation: and of this some part is private property and other part is not.
ALFRED MARSHALL (1842–1924), English classical economist: *Principles of Economics, book 4*

Capital is dead labour that, vampire-like, lives only by sucking living labour, and lives the more, the more labour it sucks.
KARL MARX (1818–83), German founder of modern communism: *Capital*

In bourgeois society capital is independent and has individuality, while the living person is dependent and has no individuality.
KARL MARX and FRIEDRICH ENGELS (1820–95), German socialist leader: *The Communist Manifesto*

Industry is limited by capital.
JOHN STUART MILL (1806–73), English
philosopher and economist: *Principles of
Political Economy, book 1*

**Capital is that part of the wealth of
a country which is employed in
production, and consists of food,
clothing, tools, raw materials,
machinery, etc., necessary to give
effect to labour.**
DAVID RICARDO (1772–1823), English
economist: *Principles of Political
Economy*

***Owning* capital is not a productive
activity.**
JOAN VIOLET ROBINSON (1903–83),
English economist: *An Essay on Marxian
Economics, chapter 3*

**Parsimony, and not industry, is the
immediate cause of the increase of
capital. Industry, indeed, provides
the subject which parsimony
accumulates. But whatever industry
might acquire, if parsimony did not
save and store up, the capital would
never be the greater.**
ADAM SMITH (1723–90), Scottish
economist and philosopher: *The Wealth
of Nations*

CURRENCY &
DEVALUATION

**The crown has the sole right to
issue money.**
*Decision of the English Privy Council,
1603*

**There is no subtler, no surer means
of overturning the existing basis of
society than to debauch the
currency. The process engages all
the hidden forces of economic law
on the side of destruction, and does
it in a manner which not one man in
a million is able to diagnose.**
JOHN MAYNARD KEYNES, 1st Baron
(1883–1946), English economist: *The
Economic Consequences of the Peace*

**A currency, to be perfect, should be
absolutely invariable in value.**
DAVID RICARDO (1772–1823), English
economist: *Works, volume 4*

**Devaluation, whether of sterling, or
the dollar, or both, would be a
lunatic, self-destroying operation.**
SIR (JAMES) HAROLD WILSON, Lord
Wilson of Rievaulx (1916–), English
statesman and prime minister: *Speech,
1963*

**From now, the pound is worth 14
per cent or so less in terms of other
currencies. It does not mean, of
course, that the pound here in
Britain, in your pocket or purse or in
your bank, has been devalued.**
SIR (JAMES) HAROLD WILSON, *Speech
after devaluation of the pound,
20 November 1967*

FINANCE & THE ECONOMY

Rags make Paper
Paper makes Money
Money makes Banks
Banks make Loans
Loans make Beggars
Beggars make Rags
Anon

Finance
The art or science of managing revenues and resources for the best advantage of the manager.
AMBROSE (GWINETT) BIERCE (1842–?1914), American journalist and humorist: *The Devil's Dictionary*

A mixed economy is essential to social democracy.
ANTHONY CROSLAND (1918–77), British politician, quoted in *The Daily Telegraph, 25 January 1979*

The private sector is that part of the economy the Government controls and the public sector is the part that nobody controls.
SIR JAMES GOLDSMITH (1933–), British businessman: *Observer, 'Sayings of the Year', 30 December 1979*

Booms and slumps are simply the expression of the results of an oscillation of the terms of credit about their equilibrium position.
JOHN MAYNARD KEYNES (1883–1946), English economist: *A Treatise on Money, volume 1*

A financier is a pawnbroker with imagination.
SIR ARTHUR WING PINERO (1855–1934), English dramatist: *The Second Mrs Tanqueray*

Our analysis leads us to believe that recovery is sound only if it does come of itself. For any revival which is merely due to artificial stimulus leaves part of the work of depressions undone and adds, to an undigested remnant of maladjustment, new maladjustments of its own.
JOSEPH ALOIS SCHUMPETER (1883–1950), Austrian-born American economist: *Essays*

All these financiers, all the little gnomes of Zürich and the other financial centres, about whom we keep on hearing.
SIR (JAMES) HAROLD WILSON, Lord Wilson of Rievaulx (1916–), English statesman and prime minister: *Speech, House of Commons, 12 November 1956*

GAMBLING

Whoever plays deep must necessarily lose his money or his character.
LORD CHESTERFIELD, Philip Dormer Stanhope, 4th Earl of (1694–1773), English statesman and writer: *Letters to his godson*

Gambling
The sure way of getting nothing for something.
WILSON MIZNER (1876–1933), American dramatist

Gambling is the child of avarice and the father of despair.
Proverb

The best throw of the dice is to throw them away.
Proverb

There is no moral difference between gambling at cards or in lotteries or on the race track and gambling in the stock-market. One method is just as pernicious to the body politic as the other kind, and in degree the evil worked is far greater.
THEODORE ROOSEVELT (1858–1919), U.S. statesman and president: *Message to Congress, 31 January 1908*

In gambling the many must lose in order that the few may win.
GEORGE BERNARD SHAW (1856–1950), Irish dramatist and critic: *Fabian Essays, 'The Economic Basis of Socialism'*

Adventure upon all the tickets in the lottery, and you lose for certain; and the greater the number of your tickets the nearer your approach to this certainty.
ADAM SMITH (1723–90), Scottish economist and philosopher: *The Wealth of Nations, volume 1*

He that puts confidence in . . . dice, cards, balls, bowls, or any game lawful or unlawful doth adventure to be laughed at for a fool, or die a beggar unpitied.
JOHN TAYLOR (1580–1653), English writer: *A Kicksey Winsey*

GOVERNMENT & INSTITUTIONS

The divine science of government is social happiness, and the blessings of society depend entirely on the constitutions of government.
JOHN ADAMS (1735–1826), U.S. president: *Discourses on Davila*

A democracy is a government in the hands of men of low birth, no property, and vulgar employments.
ARISTOTLE (384–322 BC), Greek philosopher and scientist: *Politics*

Democracy means government by discussion but it is only effective if you can stop people talking.
CLEMENT RICHARD ATTLEE, 1st Earl Attlee (1883–1967), English statesman and prime minister: *Anatomy of Britain*

All Governments like to interfere; it elevates their position to make out that they can cure the evils of mankind.
WALTER BAGEHOT (1826–77), English economist and journalist: *Economic Studies*

This island is almost made of coal and surrounded by fish. Only an organizing genius could produce a shortage of coal and fish in Great Britain at the same time.
ANEURIN BEVAN (1897–1960), British statesman: *Speech, 1945*

The trouble in modern democracy is that men do not approach to leadership until they have lost the desire to lead anyone.
LORD BEVERIDGE, William Henry Beveridge, 1st Baron Beveridge, (1879–1963), British economist: *Observer*, 'Sayings of the Week', *15 April 1934*

The State is, or can be, master of money; but in a free society it is master of very little else.
LORD BEVERIDGE, quoted in Jonathon Green, *A Dictionary of Contemporary Quotations*

All government, – indeed, every human benefit and enjoyment, every virtue and every prudent act, – is founded on compromise and barter.
EDMUND BURKE (1729–97), British statesman, orator, and writer: *Speech, 'On Conciliation with the American Colonies', 22 March 1775*

Government is a contrivance of human wisdom to provide for human wants. Men have a right that these wants should be provided for by this wisdom.
EDMUND BURKE, *Reflections on the Revolution in France*

And having looked to government for bread, on the very first scarcity they will turn and bite the hand that fed them.
EDMUND BURKE, *Thoughts and Details on Scarcity*

All modern revolutions have ended in a reinforcement of the power of the State.
ALBERT CAMUS (1913–60), French philosopher and writer: *The Rebel*

Government is emphatically a machine: to the discontented a 'taxing machine,' to the contented a 'machine for securing property.'
THOMAS CARLYLE (1795–1881), Scottish essayist and historian: *Signs of the Times*

It has been said that Democracy is the worst form of government except all those other forms that have been tried from time to time.
SIR WINSTON LEONARD SPENCER CHURCHILL (1874–1965), English statesman, writer, and prime minister: *Speech, House of Commons, November 1947*

In a country well governed poverty is something to be ashamed of. In a country badly governed wealth is something to be ashamed of.
CONFUCIUS (Kong Zi) (551–479 BC), Chinese philosopher: *Analects*

Every time the government attempts to handle our affairs, it costs more and the results are worse than if we had handled them ourselves.
BENJAMIN CONSTANT (Henri Benjamin Constant de Rebecque) (1767–1830), French writer and politician: *Cours de politique constitutionnelle*

Most people favour an incomes policy – provided it doesn't apply to them.
FRANK COUSINS (1904–), English trade union leader: *Observer, 'Sayings of the Decade', 28 December 1969*

A good government produces citizens distinguished for courage, love of justice, and every other good quality; a bad government makes them cowardly, rapacious, and the slaves of every foul desire.
DIONYSIUS OF HALICARNASSUS (?40–8 BC), Greek historian and rhetorician: *Antiquities of Rome*

Individuals may form communities, but it is institutions alone that can create a nation.
BENJAMIN DISRAELI, 1st Earl of Beaconsfield (1804–81), English statesman, prime minister, and novelist: *Speech, Manchester, 1866*

The State is made for man, not man for the State.
ALBERT EINSTEIN (1879–1955), German-Swiss-American physicist: *The World As I See It*

We do not make a world of our own, but fall into institutions already made, and have to accommodate ourselves to them to be useful at all.
RALPH WALDO EMERSON (1803–82), American poet, essayist, and philosopher: *Journals, 1832*

Those who govern, having much business on their hands, do not generally like to take the trouble of considering and carrying into execution new projects. The best

public measures are therefore seldom adopted from previous wisdom, but forced by the occasion.
BENJAMIN FRANKLIN (1706–90), American statesman, scientist, and author: *Autobiography*

Governments never learn. Only people learn.
MILTON FRIEDMAN (1912–), American economist: *Observer, 'Sayings of the Year', 28 December 1980*

In a community where public services have failed to keep abreast of private consumption things are very different. Here in an atmosphere of private opulence and public squalor, the private goods have full sway.
JOHN KENNETH GALBRAITH (1908–), Canadian-born American economist, diplomat, and writer: *The Affluent Society*

The government that is big enough to give you all you want is big enough to take it all away.
BARRY (MORRIS) GOLDWATER (1909–), American politician: *Speech, 1964*

Government after all is a very simple thing.
WARREN G(AMALIEL) HARDING (1865–1923), U.S. politician and president

No government can save the country unless the country is determined to save itself.
EDWARD (RICHARD GEORGE) HEATH (1916–), British statesman and prime minister: *Observer, 'Sayings of the Year', 29 December 1974*

We are gradually moving towards a situation where everybody is subsidising everybody else.
H.S. HOUTHAKKER: *The Economics of Federal Subsidy Programmes, May 1972*

Agriculture, manufactures, commerce, and navigation, the four pillars of our prosperity, are the most thriving when left most free to individual enterprise.
THOMAS JEFFERSON (1743–1826), U.S. statesman and président: *Message to Congress, 1801*

I would not give half a guinea to live under one form of Government rather than another. It is of no moment to the happiness of an individual.
SAMUEL JOHNSON (1709–84), English lexicographer, essayist, and poet: Boswell, *Life of Johnson*

I sometimes think that given half a chance politicians would like to give extra tax and social security concessions to marginal constituencies only.
WILLIAM KEEGAN: *Observer, 17 September 1978*

That this nation, under God, shall have a new birth of freedom; and that government of the people, by the people, and for the people, shall not perish from the earth.
ABRAHAM LINCOLN (1809–65), U.S. statesman and president: *Address at Dedication of National Cemetery, Gettysburg, 19 November 1863*

It is perfectly true that that government is best which governs least. It is equally true that that government is best which provides most.
WALTER LIPPMANN (1889–), American teacher, editor, and journalist: *A Preface to Politics, 'The Red Herring'*

Thrift should be the guiding principle in our government expenditure.
MAO TSE-TUNG, (Mao Ze Dong) (1893–1976), Chinese Communist leader: *Quotations from Chairman Mao Tse-tung*

The worst government is the most moral. One composed of cynics is often very tolerant and human. But when fanatics are on top there is no limit to oppression.
HENRY LOUIS MENCKEN (1880–1956), American philologist, editor, and satirist: *Notebooks, 'Minority Report'*

The art of governing consists in not allowing men to grow old in their jobs.
NAPOLEON I, Napoleon Bonaparte (1769–1821), French emperor and general: *Maxims*

Government, even in its best state, is but a necessary evil; in its worst state, an intolerable one.
THOMAS PAINE (1737–1809), English philosopher and writer: *Common Sense, chapter 1*

All money nowadays seems to be produced with a natural homing instinct for the Treasury.
PRINCE PHILIP, Duke of Edinburgh (1921–): *Observer, 'Sayings of the Week', 26 May 1963*

Public money is like holy water; everyone helps himself.
Italian proverb

The business of government is to keep the government out of business – that is, unless business needs government aid.
WILL(IAM PENN ADAIR) ROGERS (1879–1935), American actor and humorist

Wise and prudent men – intelligent conservatives – have long known

ALL MONEY NOWADAYS SEEMS TO BE PRODUCED WITH A NATURAL HOMING INSTINCT FOR THE TREASURY.

that in a changing world worthy institutions can be conserved only by adjusting them to the changing time.
FRANKLIN DELANO ROOSEVELT (1882–1945), U.S. statesman and president: *Speech, Syracuse, New York, 29 September 1936*

What institution of government could tend so much to promote the happiness of mankind as the general prevalence of wisdom and virtue? All government is but an imperfect remedy for the deficiency of these.
ADAM SMITH (1723–90), Scottish economist and philosopher: *The Theory of Moral Sentiments*

Whenever you have an efficient government you have a dictatorship.
HARRY S. TRUMAN (1884–1972), U.S. statesman and president: *Lecture, Columbia University, 1959*

The Treasury could not, with any marked success, run a fish and chip shop.
SIR (JAMES) HAROLD WILSON, Lord Wilson of Rievaulx (1916–), English statesman and prime minister: *Observer, 'Sayings of the Year', 30 December 1984*

INTEREST

Interest works night and day, in fair weather and in foul. It gnaws at a man's substance with invisible teeth.
HENRY WARD BEECHER (1813–87), American clergyman, editor, and writer: *Proverbs from Plymouth Pulpit*

The Theory of Interest, As Determined by IMPATIENCE to Spend Income and OPPORTUNITY to Invest It.
IRVING FISHER (1867–1947), American mathematician and economist: *Title of book*

Interest springs from the power of increase which the reproductive forces of nature give to capital. It is not an arbitrary, but a natural thing; it is not the result of a particular social organization, but of laws of the universe which underlie society. It is, therefore, just.
HENRY GEORGE (1839–97), American economist: *Progress and Poverty*

High interest arises from *three* circumstances: a great demand for borrowing, little riches to supply that demand, and great profits arising from commerce.
DAVID HUME (1711–76), Scottish philosopher and historian: *Essays, 'Of Interest'*

No law can reduce the common rate of interest below the lowest ordinary market rate at the time when that law is made.
ADAM SMITH (1723–90), Scottish economist and philosopher: *The Wealth of Nations*

There are three forms of usury: interest on money, rent of land and houses, and profit in exchange. Whoever is in receipt of any of these is a usurer.
BENJAMIN R. TUCKER (1854–1939), American anarchist: *Instead of a Book*

Every half-year's interest costs half a year of life.
HORACE WALPOLE, 4th Earl of Orford (1717–97), English writer and historian: *Letter to the Countess of Upper Ossory, 10 November 1793*

INVESTMENT

The best investments are often those that looked dead wrong when they were made.
Anon

The purchase and quick resale of stocks is not any more gambling than the purchase and quick resale of lots, and the length of time a man may hold stocks or lots depends largely upon the temperament and ability of the man.
BISHOP JAMES CANNON, JR: *Unspotted From the World, 3 August 1929*

There is no finer investment for any community than putting milk into babies.
SIR WINSTON LEONARD SPENCER CHURCHILL (1874–1965), English statesman, writer, and prime minister: *Radio Broadcast, 21 March 1943*

'Tis money that begets money.
THOMAS FULLER (1654–1734), English physician, writer, and compiler: *Gnomologia*

Of all the mysteries of the stock exchange there is none so impenetrable as why there should be a buyer for everyone who seeks to sell.
JOHN KENNETH GALBRAITH (1908–), Canadian-born American economist, diplomat, and writer: *The Great Crash, 1929, chapter 6*

The best investment on *earth* is earth.
LOUIS GLICKMAN (1933–), quoted in *New York Post, 3 September 1957*

Both public and private investment should be carried out only to the extent to which they are considered useful. If the effective demand thus generated fails to provide full employment, the gap should be filled by increasing consumption and not by piling up unwanted public or private capital equipment.
M. KALECKI (1899–1970): *The Economics of Full Employment, 'Three Ways to Full Employment'*

Speculators may do no harm as bubbles on a steady stream of enterprise. But the position is serious when enterprise becomes the bubble on a whirlpool of speculation. When the capital development of the country becomes a by-product of the

activities of a casino, the job is likely to be ill-done.
JOHN MAYNARD KEYNES (1883–1946), English economist: *The General Theory of Employment Interest and Money*, book 4

The fact that so many opportunities for the profitable investment of resources in the development of human potentialities are neglected, and so many wasteful investments of the same kind made, is perhaps one of the most serious criticisms of existing society.
FRANK H. KNIGHT (1885–1972), Professor of Economics: *Risk, Uncertainty and Profit*

Let every man divide his money into three parts, and invest a third in land, a third in business, and a third let him keep by him in reserve.
Hebrew proverb

There are two times in a man's life when he should not speculate: when he can't afford it, and when he can.
MARK TWAIN (Samuel Langhorne Clemens) (1835–1910), American novelist and humorist: *Following the Equator*

October. This is one of the peculiarly dangerous months to speculate in stocks in. The others are July, January, September, April, November, May, March, June, December, August, and February.
MARK TWAIN, *Pudd'nhead Wilson*, chapter 13

LAW

Riches without law are more dangerous than is poverty without law.
HENRY WARD BEECHER (1813–87), American clergyman, editor, and writer: *Proverbs from Plymouth Pulpit*

We do not get good laws to restrain bad people. We get good people to restrain bad laws.
G(ILBERT) K(EITH) CHESTERTON (1874–1936), English essayist, novelist, poet, and critic: *All Things Considered*

The good of the people is the chief law.
MARCUS TULLIUS CICERO (106–43 BC), Roman statesman and orator: *De Legibus*

The Law of England is a very strange one; it cannot compel anyone to tell the truth . . . But what the Law can do is to give you seven years for not telling the truth.
CHARLES JOHN DARLING, 1st Baron (1849–1936), English judge, D. Walker-Smith, *Lord Darling*

'If the law supposes that,' said Mr Bumble . . . , 'the law is a ass – a idiot.'
CHARLES (JOHN HUFFAM) DICKENS (1812–70), English novelist: *Oliver Twist*, chapter 51

People say law but they mean wealth.
RALPH WALDO EMERSON (1803–82), American poet, essayist, and philosopher: *Journals, 1839*

As in law so in war, the longest purse finally wins.
MAHATMA GANDHI, (Mohandas Karamchand Gandhi) (1869–1948), Hindu nationalist leader: *Paper read to the Bombay Provincial Co-operative Conference, 17 September 1917*

Lord Chancellor
The Law is the true embodiment
Of everything that's excellent.
It has no kind of fault or flaw,
And I, my lords, embody the Law.
SIR WILLIAM SCHWENK GILBERT (1836–1911), English parodist and librettist: *Iolanthe, Act 1*

Laws grind the poor, and rich men rule the law.
OLIVER GOLDSMITH (?1728–74), Irish dramatist, novelist, and poet: *The Traveller*

Men are not hanged for stealing Horses, but that Horses may not be stolen.
HALIFAX, 1st Marquis of, Sir George Savile (1633–95), English statesman, writer, and orator: *Political Thoughts and Reflections: Of Punishment*

The main foundations of every state, new states as well as ancient or composite ones, are good laws and good arms . . . you cannot have good laws without good arms, and where there are good arms, good laws inevitably follow.
NICCOLÒ MACHIAVELLI (1469–1527), Italian statesman and political philosopher: *The Prince, chapter 12*

Who saves his country violates no law.
NAPOLEON I, Napoleon Bonaparte (1769–1821), French emperor and general: *Maxims*

Laws were made to be broken.
CHRISTOPHER NORTH (John Wilson) (1785–1854), Scottish poet, essayist, and critic: *Noctes Ambrosianae, 24 May 1830*

The first of all laws is to respect the laws: the severity of penalties is only a vain resource, invented by little minds in order to substitute terror for that respect which they have no means of obtaining.
JEAN-JACQUES ROUSSEAU (1712–78), Swiss-born French philosopher and writer: *A Discourse on Political Economy*

Ignorance of the law excuses no man; not that all men know the law, but because 'tis an excuse every man will plead, and no man can tell how to confute him.
JOHN SELDEN (1584–1654), English historian and antiquary: *Table Talk*

Let all the laws be clear, uniform and precise; to interpret laws is almost always to corrupt them.
VOLTAIRE (François Marie Arouet) (1694–1778), French writer, philosopher, and historian: *Philosophical Dictionary*

MEDIA

What the mass media offer is not popular art, but entertainment which is intended to be consumed like food, forgotten, and replaced by a new dish.
W(YSTAN) H(UGH) AUDEN (1907–73), English poet, dramatist, critic, and librettist: *The Dyer's Hand, 'The Poet and the City'*

The printing-press is either the greatest blessing or the greatest curse of modern times, one sometimes forgets which.
SIR JAMES MATTHEW BARRIE (1860–1937), Scottish novelist and dramatist: *Sentimental Tommy*

I read the newspaper avidly. It is my one form of continuous fiction.
ANEURIN BEVAN (1897–1960), British statesman (Attributed)

TV is an evil medium. It should never have been invented. But since we have to live with it, let's try to do something about it.
RICHARD (JENKINS) BURTON (1925–84), British stage and film actor: *Observer, 'Sayings of the Decade', 28 December 1969*

Journalism largely consists in saying 'Lord Jones Dead' to people who never knew Lord Jones was alive.
G(ILBERT) K(EITH) CHESTERTON (1874–1936), English essayist, novelist, poet, and critic

Television is more interesting than people. If it were not, we should have people standing in the corners of our rooms.
ALAN COREN (1938–), British humorist

Television
It is a medium of entertainment which permits millions of people to listen to the same joke at the same time, and yet remain lonesome.
T(HOMAS) S(TEARNS) ELIOT (1888–1965), American-born British poet, dramatist, and critic: *New York Post, 22 September 1963*

A newspaper consists of just the same number of words, whether there be any news in it or not.
HENRY FIELDING (1707–54), English novelist and dramatist, *Tom Jones*

Why should people go out and pay money to see bad films when they can stay at home and see bad television for nothing?
SAMUEL GOLDWYN (1882–1974), American film producer: *Observer, 'Sayings of the Week', 9 September 1956*

The medium is the message. This is merely to say that the personal and social consequences of any medium ... result from the new scale that is introduced into our affairs by each extension of ourselves or by any new technology.
(HERBERT) MARSHALL McLUHAN (1911–80), Canadian educator, author, and media expert: *Understanding Media, chapter 1*

The new electronic interdependence recreates the world in the image of a global village.
(HERBERT) MARSHALL McLUHAN, *The Medium is the Message*

Journalism
A profession whose business it is to explain to others what it personally does not understand.
LORD NORTHCLIFFE, Alfred Charles William Harmsworth, 1st Viscount (1865–1922), Irish-born British newspaper proprietor

All the news that's fit to print.
ADOLPH S(IMON) OCHS (1858–1935), American publisher and editor: *New York Times, motto*

Early in life I had noticed that no event is ever correctly reported in a newspaper.
GEORGE ORWELL (Eric Arthur Blair) (1903–50), English novelist and essayist: *Collected Essays, Journalism and Letters*

Don't believe everything you read in the newspapers.
Saying

Television? No good will come of this device. The word is half Greek and half Latin.
C(HARLES) P(RESTWICH) SCOTT (1846–1932), Editor, Manchester Guardian (Attributed)

An editor is one who separates the wheat from the chaff and prints the chaff.
ADLAI (EWING) STEVENSON (1900–68), American statesman

On the start of British commercial television
A stake in commercial television is the equivalent of having a licence to print money.
LORD THOMSON, KENNETH ROY, 2nd Baron Thomson of Fleet (1923–), British newspaper proprietor

We write frankly and freely but then we 'modify' before we print.
MARK TWAIN (Samuel Langhorne Clemens) (1835–1910), American novelist and humorist: *Life on the Mississippi*

News is what a chap who doesn't care much about anything wants to read. And it's only news until he reads it. After that it's dead.
EVELYN (ARTHUR ST JOHN) WAUGH (1903–66), English novelist: *Scoop*

Newspapers have degenerated. They may now be absolutely relied upon.
OSCAR WILDE (1856–1900), Irish poet, dramatist, and wit: *The Decay of Lying*

NATIONAL DEBT

Nothing is so well calculated to produce a death-like torpor in the country as an extended system of taxation and a great national debt; and, therefore, all Ministers who, like Mr Pitt, have no notion of governing but by means of the

baser passions, have regarded a public debt as a public blessing.
WILLIAM COBBETT (1762–1835), English farmer, social reformer, and writer: *Letter to W. Windham, 10 February 1804*

Public credit means the contracting of debts which a nation never can pay.
WILLIAM COBBETT, *Advice to Young Men*

A national debt, if it is not excessive, will be to us a national blessing.
ALEXANDER HAMILTON (?1757–1804), American politician: *Letter to Robert Morris, 30 April 1781*

Blessed are the young, for they shall inherit the national debt.
HERBERT (CLARK) HOOVER (1894–1964), U.S. statesman and president

It is incumbent on every generation to pay its own debts as it goes – a principle which, if acted on, would save one-half the wars of the world.
THOMAS JEFFERSON (1743–1826), U.S. statesman and president: *Letter to Destutt Tracy, 1820*

A nation is not in danger of financial disaster merely because it owes itself money.
ANDREW WILLIAM MELLON (1855–1937), American financier: *Remark, 1933*

No nation ought to be without a debt. A national debt is a national bond.
THOMAS PAINE (1737–1809), English philosopher and writer: *Common Sense, 'Of the Present Ability of America'*

PAYMENT & WAGES

Be content with your wages.
The Bible, Authorized (King James) Version, Luke 3:14

A fair day's wages for a fair day's work: it is as just a demand as governed men ever made of governing.
THOMAS CARLYLE (1795–1881), Scottish essayist and historian: *Past and Present*

It is but a truism that labor is most productive where its wages are largest. Poorly paid labor is inefficient labor, the world over.
HENRY GEORGE (1839–97), American economist: *Progress and Poverty*

We're overpaying him but he's worth it.
SAMUEL GOLDWYN (1882–1974), American film producer

The theory of the determination of wages in a free market is simply a special case of the general theory of value. Wages are the price of labour.
SIR JOHN RICHARD HICKS (1904–), British economist: *The Theory of Wages, Part 1*

It is an economic axiom as old as the hills that goods and services can be paid for only with goods and services.
ALBERT J. NOCK (1873–1945): *Memoirs of a Superfluous Man*

A good paymaster never wants workmen.
Proverb

He who pays the piper may call the tune.
Proverb

If you pay peanuts, you get monkeys.
Proverb

Everything is worth what its purchaser will pay for it.
PUBLILIUS SYRUS (1st c. BC), Latin writer of mimes: *Moral Sayings*

Wages should be left to the fair and free competition of the market, and should never be controlled by the interference of the legislature.
DAVID RICARDO (1772–1823), English economist: *Principles of Political Economy*

No business which depends for existence on paying less than living wages to its workers has any right to continue in this country. By business I mean the whole of commerce as well as the whole of industry; by workers I mean all workers – the white-collar class as well as the man in overalls; and by living wages I mean more than a bare subsistence level – I mean the wages of decent living.
FRANKLIN DELANO ROOSEVELT (1882–1945), U.S. statesman and president: *Address, 16 June 1933*

If you do things by the job, you are perpetually driven: the hours are scourges. If you work by the hour, you gently sail on the stream of Time, which is always bearing you on to the haven of Pay, whether you make any effort, or not.
CHARLES DUDLEY WARNER (1829–1900), American essayist, editor, and novelist: *My Summer in a Garden*

For two days' labour, you ask two hundred guineas?
No, I ask it for the knowledge of a lifetime.
JAMES ABBOTT McNEILL WHISTLER (1834–1903), American painter: D.C. Seitz, *Whistler Stories*

One man's wage rise is another man's price increase.
SIR (JAMES) HAROLD WILSON, Lord Wilson of Rievaulx (1916–), English statesman and prime minister: *Observer*, 'Sayings of the Week', 11 January 1970

PROFIT & LOSS

I think the railways can be made to pay. This is the first time I have said this so flat-footedly.
LORD BEECHING, Dr Richard Beeching (1913–), Chairman, British Railways Board: *Observer*, 'Sayings of the Decade', 28 December 1969

It is a socialist idea that making profits is a vice; I consider the real vice is making losses.
SIR WINSTON LEONARD SPENCER CHURCHILL (1874–1965), English statesman, writer, and prime minister

Civilization and profits go hand in hand.
(JOHN) CALVIN COOLIDGE (1872–1933), U.S. president

What is a man if he is not a thief who openly charges as much as he can for the goods he sells?
MAHATMA GANDHI (Mohandas Karamchand Gandhi) (1869–1948), Hindu nationalist leader: *Non-Violence in Peace and War*

The smell of profit is clean
And sweet, whatever the source.
JUVENAL (Decimus Junius Juvenalis) (?60–?140), Roman satirist: *Satires*

Even genius is tied to profit.
PINDAR (?518–?438 BC), Greek lyric poet: *Odes*

There are occasions when it is undoubtedly better to incur loss than to make gain.
TITUS MACCIUS PLAUTUS (?254–?184 BC), Roman comic dramatist: *The Captives*

Profit is better than fame.
Proverb

Where profit is, loss is hidden near by.
Japanese proverb

The loss which is unknown is no loss at all.
PUBLILIUS SYRUS (1st c. BC), Latin writer of mimes: *Moral Sayings*

When wages are low profits must be high.
DAVID RICARDO (1772–1823), English economist: *Works, volume 2, 'Notes on Malthus'*

Nothing contributes so much to the prosperity and happiness of a country as high profits.
DAVID RICARDO, *On Protection to Agriculture*

He that is robbed, not wanting what is stol'n,
Let him not know't, and he's not robbed at all.
WILLIAM SHAKESPEARE (1564–1616), English dramatist and poet: *Othello, Act 3*

The earnings of an entrepreneur sometimes represent nothing but the spoliation of the workmen. A profit is made not because the industry produces much more than it costs, but because it fails to give to the workman sufficient compensation for his toil. Such an industry is a social evil.
JEAN CHARLES LÉONARD SIMONDE DE SISMONDI (1773–1842), Swiss historian and economist: *Nouveaux Principes d'Économie politique, volume 1*

The trouble with the profit system has always been that it was highly unprofitable to most people.
E(LWYN) B(ROOKS) WHITE (1899–), American humorist and essayist: *One Man's Meat*

SAVING

Men are divided between those who are as thrifty as if they would live forever, and those who are as extravagant as if they were going to die the next day.
ARISTOTLE (384–322 BC), Greek philosopher and scientist, quoted in Diogenes Laertius, *Lives and Opinions of Eminent Philosophers*

Economy
Purchasing the barrel of whiskey that you do not need for the price of the cow that you cannot afford.
AMBROSE (GWINETT) BIERCE (1842–?1914), American journalist and humorist: *The Devil's Dictionary*

Mere parsimony is not economy . . . Expense, and great expense, may be an essential part of true economy. Economy is a distributive virtue, and consists not in saving but selection. Parsimony requires no providence, no sagacity, no powers of combination, no comparison, no judgment.
EDMUND BURKE (1729–97), British statesman, orator, and writer: *Letter to a Noble Lord*

Saving is a very fine thing. Especially when your parents have done it for you.
SIR WINSTON LEONARD SPENCER CHURCHILL (1874–1965), English statesman, writer, and prime minister (Attributed)

It is better to have a hen tomorrow than an egg today.
THOMAS FULLER (1654–1734), English physician, writer, and compiler: *Gnomologia*

Whenever you save five shillings, you put a man out of work for a day.
JOHN MAYNARD KEYNES (1883–1946), English economist: *Essays in Persuasion, 'Inflation and Deflation'*

A good saver is a good server.
Proverb

I shall cut my coat after my cloth.
Proverb

Take care of the pence, and the pounds will take care of themselves.
Proverb

It is not economical to go to bed early to save the candles if the results are twins.
Chinese proverb

What is annually saved is as regularly consumed as what is annually spent, and nearly in the same time too; but it is consumed by a different set of people.
ADAM SMITH (1723–90), Scottish economist and philosopher: *The Wealth of Nations, volume 1*

To recommend thrift to the poor is both grotesque and insulting. It is like advising a man who is starving to eat less.
OSCAR WILDE (1856–1900), Irish poet, dramatist, and wit: *The Soul of Man under Socialism*

ECONOMICS & BACKGROUND SCIENCES

In this section we consider economics and other related social sciences, together with some of the distinctive political teachings and theories. The quotations indicate widely ranging – and at times conflicting – opinions on these significant subjects that determine different approaches to business and economics. We move from the more familiar 'Politics is the art of the possible' (R.A. Butler), 'The unpleasant and unacceptable face of capitalism' (Edward Heath), and 'The theory of Communism may be summed up in one sentence: Abolish all private property' (Marx and Engels) to the less well-known 'The Communist is a Socialist in a violent hurry' (G.W. Gough) and 'Other Things Being Equal . . . you can generally tell whether a man is an economist by the number of times he uses this particular phrase' (William Davis).

CAPITALISM

There is a good deal of solemn cant about the common interests of capital and labor. As matters stand, their only common interest is that of cutting each other's throat.
(JUSTIN) BROOKS ATKINSON (1894–), American dramatic critic and essayist: *Once Around the Sun*

The inherent vice of capitalism is the unequal sharing of blessings; the inherent virtue of socialism is the equal sharing of miseries.
SIR WINSTON LEONARD SPENCER CHURCHILL (1874–1965), English statesman, writer, and prime minister

The unpleasant and unacceptable face of capitalism.
EDWARD (RICHARD GEORGE) HEATH (1916–), English statesman and prime minister: *Speech, House of Commons, 15 May 1973*

Labour, under capitalism, is doubly enslaved. It is directed towards ends which it has not chosen by means which are forced upon it.
JEAN LÉON JAURÈS (1859–1914), French politician and writer: *Études socialistes*

Imperialism is the monopoly stage of capitalism.
NIKOLAI LENIN (Vladimir Ilyich Ulyanov) (1870–1924), Russian statesman and Marxist theoretician: *Imperialism, the Highest Stage of Capitalism*

Capitalists are no more capable of self-sacrifice than a man is capable of lifting himself by his own bootstraps.
NIKOLAI LENIN, *Letters from Afar*

Under capitalism we have a state in the proper sense of the word, that is, a special machine for the suppression of one class by another.
NIKOLAI LENIN, *The State and Revolution*

The basic law of capitalism is you or I, not both you and I.
KARL LIEBKNECHT (1871–1919), German socialist leader: *Speech before the Fourth Socialist Young People's Conference, Stuttgart 1907*

You show me a capitalist, I'll show you a bloodsucker.
MALCOLM X, (Malcolm Little) (1925–65), U.S. Negro leader: *Malcolm X Speaks*

There is a serious tendency towards capitalism among the well-to-do peasants.
MAO TSE-TUNG (Mao Ze Dong) (1893–1976), Chinese Communist leader: *Quotations from Chairman Mao Tse-tung*

Capitalist production begets, with the inexorability of a law of nature, its own negation.
KARL MARX (1818–83), German founder of modern Communism: *Capital, chapter 15*

The conflict between capitalism and democracy is inherent and continuous; it is often hidden by misleading propaganda and by the outward forms of democracy, such as parliaments, and the sops that the owning classes throw to the other classes to keep them more or less contented.
JAWAHARLAL NEHRU (1889–1964), Indian politician and prime minister: *Glimpses of World History*

Man is born perfect, it is the capitalist system which corrupts him.
ARTHUR SCARGILL (1938–), British trade unionist: *Debate, Wakefield, 20 November 1981*

Under fully developed Capitalism civilization is always on the verge of revolution. We live as in a villa on Vesuvius.
GEORGE BERNARD SHAW (1856–1950), Irish dramatist and critic: *The Intelligent Woman's Guide to Socialism, Capitalism, Sovietism and Fascism, chapter 66*

Capitalism was doomed ethically before it was doomed economically, a long time ago.
ALEXANDER ISAYEVICH SOLZHENITSYN (1918–), Exiled Russian novelist: *Cancer Ward, Part 2*

Industrial crisis, unemployment, waste, widespread poverty, these are the incurable diseases of capitalism.
JOSEPH STALIN (Iosif Vissarionovich Dzhugashvili) (1879–1953), Russian leader: *Speech before the conference of managers of the Soviet industry, 4 February 1931*

ECONOMICS & BACKGROUND SCIENCES

Marxian economics is essentially the economics of capitalism, while 'capitalist' economics is in a very real sense the economics of socialism.
PAUL M. SWEEZY: *Economic Forum, Spring 1935, 'Economics and the Crisis of Capitalism'*

You can't be a feminist and a capitalist.
RUTH WALLSGRQVE: *Spare Rib*, quoted in *Observer, 'Sayings of 1982', 2 January 1983*

The Protestant Ethic and the Spirit of Capitalism.
MAX WEBER (1864–1920), German economist and sociologist: *Title of essay*

CLASS AND RANK

The rich man in his castle,
The poor man at his gate,
God made them, high or lowly,
And order'd their estate.
CECIL FRANCES ALEXANDER (1818–95), Irish hymn-writer: *All Things Bright and Beautiful*

Inferiors revolt in order that they may be equal and equals that they may be superior. Such is the state of mind which creates revolutions.
ARISTOTLE (384–322 BC), Greek philosopher and scientist: *Politics*

There are three classes of citizens. The first are the rich, who are indolent and yet always crave more. The second are the poor, who have nothing, are full of envy, hate the rich, and are easily led by demagogues. Between the two extremes lie those who make the state secure and uphold the laws.
EURIPIDES (?480–406 BC), Greek tragic dramatist: *The Suppliant Women*

All the world over, I will back the masses against the classes.
WILLIAM EWART GLADSTONE (1809–98), English statesman and prime minister: *Speech, Liverpool, 28 June 1886*

One man is born with a silver spoon in his mouth, and another with a wooden ladle.
OLIVER GOLDSMITH (?1728–74), Irish dramatist, novelist, and poet: *The Citizen of the World*

We are, by our occupations, education and habits of life, divided almost into different species, which regard one another, for the most part, with scorn and malignity.
SAMUEL JOHNSON (1709–84), English lexicographer, essayist, and poet: *The Rambler, 28 September 1751*

There is merit without rank, but there is no rank without some merit.
FRANÇOIS LA ROCHEFOUCAULD, Duc de la Rochefoucauld (1613–80), French writer: *Maxims*

Those who hold and those who are without property have ever formed distinct interests in society. Those who are creditors, and those who are debtors, fall under a like discrimination. A landed interest, a

manufacturing interest, a mercantile interest, a moneyed interest, with many lesser interests, grow up of necessity in civilized nations, and divide them into different classes, actuated by different sentiments and views.
JAMES MADISON (1751–1836), U.S. statesman and president: *The Federalist*

In class society everyone lives as a member of a particular class, and every kind of thinking, without exception, is stamped with the brand of a class.
MAO TSE-TUNG (Mao Ze Dong) (1893–1976), Chinese Communist leader: *Quotations from Chairman Mao Tse-tung*

The history of all hitherto existing society is the history of class struggles.
KARL MARX (1818–83), German founder of modern communism and FRIEDRICH ENGELS (1820–95), German socialist leader: *The Communist Manifesto*

A THRONE IS ONLY A BENCH COVERED WITH VELVET.

The most grinding poverty is a trifling evil compared with the inequality of classes.
WILLIAM MORRIS (1834–96), English writer and social reformer: *Letter to Andreas Scheu, 5 September 1883*

A throne is only a bench covered with velvet.
NAPOLEON I, Napoleon Bonaparte (1769–1821), French emperor and general: *Maxims*

A cat can look at a king.
Proverb

We must be thoroughly democratic and patronize everybody without distinction of class.
GEORGE BERNARD SHAW (1856–1950), Irish dramatist and critic: *Heartbreak House, Act 4*

It is impossible, in our condition of society, not to be sometimes a Snob.
WILLIAM MAKEPEACE THACKERAY (1811–63), English novelist: *The Book of Snobs, chapter 3*

COMMUNISM & MARXISM

A communist is one who has nothing and wishes to share it with the world.
Anon

Virtually the whole British establishment has been, at least until recently, educated without any real knowledge of Marxism, and is determined to see that these ideas do not reach the public ... Anyone today who speaks of class in the context of politics runs the risk of excommunication and outlawry.
ANTHONY (NEIL) WEDGWOOD BENN (1925–), English politician: *Marx Memorial Lecture, London 1982*

There is not one single social or economic principle or concept in the philosophy of the Russian Bolshevik which has not been realized, carried into action, and enshrined in immutable laws a million years ago by the white ant.
SIR WINSTON LEONARD SPENCER CHURCHILL (1874–1965), English statesman, writer, and prime minister, quoted in Bill Adler, *The Churchill Wit, 'Politics'*

What is a Communist? One who hath yearnings
For equal division of unequal earnings.
Idler or bungler, or both, he is willing,
To fork out his copper and pocket your shilling.
EBENEZER ELLIOTT (1781–1849), English poet: *Epigram*

The Communist is a Socialist in a violent hurry.
G.W. GOUGH: *The Economic Consequences of Socialism*

Far from being a classless society, Communism is governed by an elite as steadfast in its determination to

maintain its prerogatives as any oligarchy known to history.
ROBERT FRANCIS KENNEDY (1925–68), U.S. statesman: *The Pursuit of Justice*

Communists who believed we could completely alter the economic form of society in three years were visionaries. I say it will take at least a century.
NIKOLAI LENIN (Vladimir Ilyich Ulyanov) (1870–1924), Russian statesman and Marxist theoretician: *Observer, 'Sayings of the Week,' 7 April 1921*

We Communists are like seeds and the people are like the soil. Wherever we go, we must unite with the people, take root and blossom among them.
MAO TSE-TUNG, (Mao Ze Dong) (1893–1976), Chinese Communist leader: *Quotations from Chairman Mao Tse-tung*

There may be thousands of principles of Marxism, but in the final analysis they can be summed up in one sentence: Rebellion is justified.
MAO TSE-TUNG quoted in *The Times, 31 October 1966*

The theory of Communism may be summed up in one sentence: Abolish all private property.
KARL MARX (1818–83), German founder of modern communism and FRIEDRICH ENGELS (1820–95), German socialist leader: *The Communist Manifesto*

What is thine is mine, and all of mine is thine.
TITUS MACCIUS PLAUTUS (?254–?184 BC), Roman comic dramatist: *Trinummus*

Communism is inequality, but not as property is. Property is exploitation of the weak by the strong. Communism is exploitation of the strong by the weak.
PIERRE JOSEPH PROUDHON (1809–65), French political theorist: *What is Property?*

Marxism flourishes but in countries where capitalism is least successful.
JOAN VIOLET ROBINSON (1903–83), English economist: *Marx, Marshall and Keynes*

Communism is like Prohibition, it's a good idea but it won't work.
WILL(IAM PENN ADAIR) ROGERS (1879–1935), American actor and humorist: *The Autobiography of Will Rogers*

What's mine is yours and what is yours is mine.
WILLIAM SHAKESPEARE (1564–1616), English dramatist and poet: *Measure for Measure, Act 5*

Of the Communist party
As soon as classes have been abolished, and the dictatorship of the proletariat has been done away with, the party will have fulfilled its mission and can be allowed to disappear.
JOSEPH STALIN (Iosif Vissarionovich Dzhugashvili) (1879–1953), Russian leader: *Speech at Sverdloff University, April 1924*

In reply to a question on whether Communism had failed

It depends on the way you measure the concept of good, bad, better, worse, because, if you choose the example of what we Polish have in our pockets and in our shops, then I answer that Communism has done very little for us. If you choose the example of what is in our souls, instead, I answer that Communism has done very much for us. In fact our souls contain exactly the contrary of what they wanted. They wanted us not to believe in God and our churches are full. They wanted us to be materialistic and incapable of sacrifices: we are anti-materialistic, capable of sacrifice. They wanted us to be afraid of the tanks, of the guns, and instead we don't fear them at all.
LECH WALESA (1943–), Polish trade-union leader: *The Sunday Times,* *22 March 1981*

ECONOMICS & ECONOMISTS

'**Do you have anything on economics?**', asked a colleague in his local bookshop. '**Over there,**' replied the assistant, '**beyond fiction.**'
Anon, quoted in *Financial Times,* *9 November 1981*

But the age of chivalry is gone. That of sophisters, economists, and calculators, has succeeded; and the

glory of Europe is extinguished for ever.
EDMUND BURKE (1729–97), British statesman, orator, and writer: *Reflections on the Revolution in France*

Of political economy
Respectable Professors of the Dismal Science.
THOMAS CARLYLE (1795–1881), Scottish essayist and historian: *Latter-Day Pamphlets, 1, 'The Present Time'*

Others Things Being Equal – One of the old-time greats in economics; you can generally tell whether a man is an economist by the number of times he uses this particular phrase.
WILLIAM DAVIS (1933–), Author, columnist and broadcaster

In all recorded history there has not been one economist who has had to worry about where the next meal would come from.
PETER F. DRUCKER (1909–), American management expert

It takes a certain brashness to attack the accepted economic legends but none at all to perpetuate them. So they are perpetuated.
JOHN KENNETH GALBRAITH (1908–), Canadian-born American economist, diplomat, and writer: *The Liberal Hour*

All races have produced notable economists, with the exception of the Irish who doubtless can protest their devotion to higher arts.
JOHN KENNETH GALBRAITH, *The Age of Uncertainty, chapter 1*

Perhaps it is a sense of history that divides good economics from bad.
JOHN KENNETH GALBRAITH, *as above, broadcast version*

There is much of economic theory which is pursued for no better reason than its intellectual attraction; it is a good game. We have no reason to be ashamed of that, since the same would hold for many branches of mathematics.
SIR JOHN RICHARD HICKS (1904–), British economist: *Causality in Economics*

Please find me a one-armed economist so we will not always hear, 'On the other hand . . .'
HERBERT (CLARK) HOOVER (1894–1964), U.S. statesman and president (Attributed)

The theory of economics must begin with a correct theory of consumption.
WILLIAM STANLEY JEVONS (1835–82), English economist and logician: *Theory of Political Economy, chapter 3*

If economists were any good at business, they would be rich men instead of advisers to rich men.
KIRK KERKORIAN (1917–), quoted in Robert W. Kent, *Money Talks*

But . . . do not let us overestimate the importance of the economic problem, or sacrifice to its supposed necessities other matters of greater and more permanent significance. It should be a matter for specialists – like dentistry. If economists could manage to get themselves thought of as humble, competent people, on a level with dentists, that would be splendid!
JOHN MAYNARD KEYNES (1883–1946), English economist: *Essays in Persuasion, Part 5*

The ideas of economists and political philosophers, both when they are right and when they are wrong, are more powerful than is commonly understood. Indeed the world is ruled by little else. Practical men, who believe themselves to be quite exempt from any intellectual influences, are usually the slaves of some defunct economist.
JOHN MAYNARD KEYNES, *General Theory of Employment, book 6*

Economics is a subject that does not greatly respect one's wishes.
NIKITA (SERGEYEVICH) KHRUSHCHEV (1894–1971), Russian statesman and premier of Soviet Union

An economist is an expert who will know tomorrow why the things he predicted yesterday didn't happen today.
DR LAURENCE J. PETER (1919–), Canadian educator: *Peter's Quotations*

If all economists were laid end to end, they would not reach a conclusion.
GEORGE BERNARD SHAW (1856–1950), Irish dramatist and critic (Attributed)

Prime Minister
Yes. It's all very simple. I want you to abolish economists . . . Yes, all of them. They never agree on anything. They just fill the heads of politicians

with all sorts of curious notions, like the more you spend, the richer you get.
MARGARET (HILDA) THATCHER (1925–), English politician and prime minister: *Yes (Prime) Minister sketch, The National Viewers' and Listeners' Association Award Presentation, 20 January 1984*

The economists are generally right in their predictions, but generally a good deal out in their dates.
SIDNEY (JAMES) WEBB, Baron Passfield (1859–1947), English economist and social historian: *Observer, 'Sayings of the Week', 25 February 1924*

MATERIALISM

Materialism is decadent and degenerate only if the spirit of the nation has withered and if individual people are so unimaginative that they wallow in it.
(JUSTIN) BROOKS ATKINSON (1894–), American dramatic critic and essayist: *Once Around The Sun*

Ye cannot serve God and mammon.
The Bible, Authorized (King James) Version, Matthew 6:24

Our life on earth is, and ought to be, material and carnal. But we have not yet learned to manage our materialism and carnality properly; they are still entangled with the desire for ownership.
EDWARD MORGAN FORSTER (1879–1970), English novelist: *Abinger Harvest*

When this terrible conflict is over, a wave of materialism will sweep over the land. Nothing will count but machinery and output. I am all for output, and I have done my best to improve machinery and increase output. But that is not all. There is nothing more fatal to a people than that it should narrow its vision to the material needs of the hour. National ideals without imagination are but as the thistles of the wilderness, fit neither for food nor fuel.
DAVID LLOYD GEORGE, 1st Earl Lloyd George of Dwyfor (1863–1945), British politician and prime minister: *Speech, Aberystwyth National Eisteddfod, 17 August 1916*

Some men worship rank, some worship heroes, some worship power, some worship God, and over these ideals they dispute – but they all worship money.
MARK TWAIN (Samuel Langhorne Clemens) (1835–1910), American novelist and humorist: *Notebook*

MATHEMATICS

Of decimal points
I never could make out what those damned dots meant.
LORD RANDOLPH SPENCER CHURCHILL (1849–95), English statesman, quoted in W.S. Churchill, *Lord Randolph Churchill, volume 1*

To count is a modern practice, the ancient method was to guess; and

when numbers are guessed they are always magnified.
SAMUEL JOHNSON (1709–84), English lexicographer, essayist and poet: *A Journey to the Western Islands of Scotland*

The chief use of pure mathematics in economic questions seems to be in helping a person to write down quickly, shortly and exactly, some of his thoughts for his own use: and to make sure that he has enough and only enough premises for his conclusions (i.e. that his equations are neither more nor less in number than his unknowns).
ALFRED MARSHALL (1842–1924), English classical economist: *Principles of Economics*

Mathematics contains much that will neither hurt one if one does not know it nor help one if one does know it.
J.B. MENCKEN: *De charlataneria eruditorum*

Moriarty
How are you at Mathematics?
H.S.
I speak it like a native.
SPIKE MILLIGAN (1918–), Irish comedian: *The Goon Show, 'Dishonoured'*

Mathematics, rightly viewed, possesses not only truth, but supreme beauty – a beauty cold and austere, like that of sculpture.
BERTRAND (ARTHUR WILLIAM) RUSSELL, 3rd Earl Russell (1872–1970), English philosopher and mathematician: *Mysticism and Logic, chapter 4*

Mathematics may be defined as the subject in which we never know what we are talking about, nor whether what we are saying is true.
BERTRAND (ARTHUR WILLIAM) RUSSELL, *as above*

POLITICS & POLITICIANS

A politician is an animal who can sit on a fence and yet keep both ears to the ground.
Anon

Man is by nature a political animal.
ARISTOTLE (384–322 BC), Greek philosopher and scientist: *Politics*

Nowadays, for the sake of the advantage which is to be gained from the public revenues and from office, men want to be always in office.
ARISTOTLE, *as above*

To exploit and *to govern* mean the same thing . . . Exploitation and government are two inseparable expressions of what is called politics.
MIKHAIL BAKUNIN (1814–76), Russian anarchist and writer: *The Knouto-Germanic Empire and the Social Revolution*

Politics is the art of looking for trouble, finding it whether it exists

or not, diagnosing it incorrectly, and applying the wrong remedy.
SIR ERNEST BENN, quoted in *Observer*, *1930*

Politics
A strife of interests masquerading as a contest of principles. The conduct of public affairs for private advantage.
AMBROSE (GWINETT) BIERCE (1842–?1914), American journalist and humorist: *The Devil's Dictionary*

Politics is the art of the possible.
R(ICHARD) A(USTEN) BUTLER, Baron Butler of Saffron Walden (1902–84), British politician: *The Art of the Possible, Epigraph*

If you take yourself seriously in politics, you've had it.
LORD CARRINGTON (1919–), British statesman

I remain just one thing, and one thing only – and that is a clown. It places me on a far higher plane than any politician.
SIR CHARLES CHAPLIN (1889–1977), English comedian, film actor, and director: *Observer, 'Sayings of the Week', 17 June 1960*

Political skill
. . . is the ability to foretell what is going to happen tomorrow, next week, next month, and next year. And to have the ability afterwards to explain why it didn't happen.
SIR WINSTON LEONARD SPENCER CHURCHILL (1874–1965), English statesman, writer, and prime minister, Bill Adler, *The Churchill Wit*

Of Lord Charles Beresford
He is one of those orators of whom it was well said, 'Before they get up they do not know what they are going to say; when they are speaking, they do not know what they are saying; and when they sit down, they do not know what they have said.'
SIR WINSTON LEONARD SPENCER CHURCHILL (1874–1965), *Speech, House of Commons, 20 December 1912*

Everything that steel achieves in war can be won in politics by eloquence.
DEMETRIUS OF PHALERUM (ca. 345–ca. 280 BC), Greek orator and statesman, quoted in Diogenes Laertius, *Lives and Opinions of Eminent Philosophers*

For Politicians neither love nor hate.
JOHN DRYDEN (1631–1700), English poet and dramatist: *Absalom and Achitophel, I*

That fabulous animal formally called 'economic policy' and more familiarly called political interference.
G.A. DUNCAN: *Economic Journal, December 1961*

Government has come to be a trade, and is managed solely on commercial principles. A man plunges into politics to make his fortune, and only cares that the world shall last his days.
RALPH WALDO EMERSON (1803–82), American poet, essayist, and philosopher: *Letter to Thomas Carlyle, 7 October 1835*

The first mistake in public business is the going into it.
BENJAMIN FRANKLIN (1706–90), American statesman, scientist, and author: *Poor Richard's Almanac*

There are times in politics when you must be on the right side and lose.
JOHN KENNETH GALBRAITH (1908–), Canadian-born American economist, diplomat, and writer: *Observer, 'Sayings of the Year', 29 December 1968*

Politics is not the art of the possible. It consists in choosing between the disastrous and the unpalatable.
JOHN KENNETH GALBRAITH, *Ambassador's Journal*

There are two problems in my life. The political ones are insoluble and the economic ones are incomprehensible.
SIR ALEC DOUGLAS-HOME, Lord Home of Hirsel (1903–), British statesman and prime minister

Doing what's right isn't the problem. It's knowing what's right.
LYNDON B(AINES) JOHNSON (1908–), U.S. statesman and president

There is a holy, mistaken zeal in politics, as well as religion. By persuading others we convince ourselves.
JUNIUS, pseudonym of an anonymous writer to the London Public Advertiser, 1768–1772: *Letter 35, 19 December 1769*

Politicians are the same all over. They promise to build a bridge even when there's no river.
NIKITA (SERGEYEVICH) KHRUSHCHEV (1894–1971), Russian statesman and premier of Soviet Union: *Remark at Glen Cove, New York, 1960*

Politics is who gets what, when, how.
HAROLD LASSWELL (1902–), American political economist: *Politics: Who gets What, When, How*

A politician must often talk and act before he has thought and read. He may be very ill-informed respecting a question; all his notions about it may be vague and inaccurate; but speak he must; and if he is a man of talents, of tact, and of intrepidity, he soon finds that, even under such circumstances, it is possible to speak successfully.
THOMAS BABINGTON MACAULAY (1800–59), English historian, essayist, and statesman: *Edinburgh Review, April 1839, 'Gladstone on Church and State'*

Politics offers yesterday's answers to today's problems.
(HERBERT) MARSHALL McLUHAN (1911–80), Canadian educator, author, and media expert

When you're abroad, you're a statesman; when you're at home, you're just a politician.
SIR (MAURICE) HAROLD MACMILLAN, Earl of Stockton (1894–1986), British statesman and prime minister

Coffee which makes the politician wise,
And see through all things with his half-shut eyes.
ALEXANDER POPE (1688–1744), English poet and satirist: *The Rape of the Lock, III*

Lear
**Get thee glass eyes,
And, like a scurvy politician, seem
To see the things thou dost not.**
WILLIAM SHAKESPEARE (1564–1616), English dramatist and poet: *King Lear, Act 4*

He knows nothing and he thinks he knows everything. That points clearly to a political career.
GEORGE BERNARD SHAW (1856–1950), Irish dramatist and critic: *Major Barbara*

Politics is perhaps the only profession for which no preparation is thought necessary.
ROBERT LOUIS BALFOUR STEVENSON (1850–94), Scottish writer

Whoever could make two ears of corn or two blades of grass to grow upon a spot of ground where only one grew before would deserve better of mankind and do more essential service to his country than the whole race of politicians put together.
JONATHAN SWIFT (1667–1745), Anglo-Irish satirist and churchman: *Gulliver's Travels, Voyage to Brobdingnag*

Politics, as the word is commonly understood, are nothing but corruptions.
JONATHAN SWIFT, *Thoughts on Various Subjects*

Political principles resemble military tactics; they are usually designed for a war which is over.
R(ICHARD) H(ENRY) TAWNEY (1880–1962), English economic historian: *Equality*

A politician is a man who understands government, and it takes a politician to run a government. A statesman is a politician who's been dead ten or fifteen years.
HARRY S. TRUMAN (1884–1972), U.S. statesman and president, quoted in *New York World Telegram and Sun, 12 April 1958*

A week is a long time in politics.
SIR (JAMES) HAROLD WILSON, Lord Wilson of Rievaulx (1916–), English statesman and prime minister

SOCIALISM

Under capitalism man exploits man, under socialism, it's just the opposite.
Anon

Never confuse socialism with trade unionism.
ANEURIN BEVAN (1897–1960), British statesman, quoted by Paul Johnson, *Observer, 11 September 1977*

Capitalism is using its money; we socialists throw it away.
FIDEL CASTRO (RUZ) (1927–), Cuban statesman, quoted in *Observer, 'Sayings of the Year', 27 December 1964*

We are all Socialists nowadays.
EDWARD VII (1841–1910), King of the United Kingdom: *Speech, Mansion House, London, 1895*

The Third Theory is founded upon socialism . . . With the Communist system on one side and the capitalist system on the other, we must try to find a 'Third System' which would be equally different from either. For while capitalism, by handing over the reins to the individual without any restraints, has transformed society into a sort of circus, communism's claim to solve economic problems by the total and final abolishing of private property has ended by turning individual human beings into sheep.
MOAMAR AL GADDAFI, (1942–), Libyan army officer and statesman, quoted in M. Bianco, *Gadafi, Voice from the Desert, Part 3*

The purpose of the socialist society is the happiness of man, which can be realised only through material and spiritual freedom. Attainment of such freedom depends on the extent of man's ownership of his needs, ownership that is personal and sacredly guaranteed.
MOAMAR AL GADDAFI, *The Green Book*

There is a popular cliché, deeply beloved by conservatives, that socialism and communism are the cause of a low standard of living. It is much more nearly accurate to say that a low and simple standard of living makes socialism and communism feasible.
JOHN KENNETH GALBRAITH (1908–), Canadian-born American economist, diplomat, and writer: *American Capitalism, chapter 12*

The ideal of Socialism is grand and noble; and it is, I am convinced, possible of realization; but such a state of society cannot be manufactured – it must grow. Society is an organism, not a machine.
HENRY GEORGE (1839–97), American economist: *Progress and Poverty*

We are all Socialists now.
SIR WILLIAM HARCOURT (1827–1904), British statesman: *Speech*

Can you imagine lying in bed on a Sunday morning with the love of your life, a cup of tea and a bacon sandwich, and all you had to read was the *Socialist Worker*?
DEREK JAMESON (1929–), Journalist and broadcaster

The main tenet of Socialism, namely, the community of goods, must be rejected without qualification, for it would injure those it pretends to benefit, it would be contrary to the natural rights of man, and it would introduce

confusion and disorder into the commonwealth.
POPE LEO XIII (Gioacchino Pecci) (1810–1903), pope: *Rerum novarum, 15 May 1891*

To the ordinary working man, the sort you would meet in any pub on Saturday night, Socialism does not mean much more than better wages and shorter hours and nobody bossing you about.
GEORGE ORWELL (Eric Arthur Blair) (1903–50), English novelist and essayist: *The Road to Wigan Pier*

Socialism means equality of income or nothing.
GEORGE BERNARD SHAW (1856–1950), Irish dramatist and critic: *The Intelligent Woman's Guide to Socialism, Capitalism, Sovietism and Fascism, Appendix*

Socialism is nothing but the capitalism of the lower classes.
OSWALD SPENGLER (1880–1936), German philosopher of history

The temporary victory of Socialism in one country alone is possible, but its lasting victory in one country alone is impossible: that demands the victory of the revolution in other lands as well.
JOSEPH STALIN (Iosif Vissarionovich Dzhugashvili) (1879–1953), Russian leader: *Leninism*

STATISTICS

Any figure that looks interesting is probably wrong.
Anon

If you just torture the data long enough, they will confess.
Anon

Statistician
A man who can go directly from an unwarranted assumption to a preconceived conclusion.
Anon

On the reason for the War Office's keeping three sets of figures
One to mislead the public, another to mislead the Cabinet, and the third to mislead itself.
HERBERT HENRY ASQUITH, 1st Earl of Oxford and Asquith (1852–1928), English statesman and prime minister, quoted in Alastair Horne, *The Price of Glory*

A witty statesman said, you might prove anything by figures.
THOMAS CARLYLE (1795–1881), Scottish essayist and historian: *Chartism*

Statistics is a science which ought to be honourable, the basis of many most important sciences; but it is not to be carried on by steam, this science, any more than others are; a wise head is requisite for carrying it on. Conclusive facts are inseparable from inconclusive except by a head that already understands and knows.

THOMAS CARLYLE, *as above*

It is now proved beyond doubt that smoking is one of the leading causes of statistics.

FLETCHER KNEBEL (1911–), American journalist and writer, quoted in *Reader's Digest, December 1961*

You cannot feed the hungry on statistics.

DAVID LLOYD GEORGE, 1st Earl Lloyd George of Dwyfor (1863–1945), Welsh politician and British prime minister: *Speech, 1904*

There are two kinds of statistics, the kind you look up and the kind you make up.

REX STOUT (1886–1975): *Death of a Doxy*

There are three kinds of lies: lies, damned lies, and statistics.

MARK TWAIN (Samuel Langhorne Clemens) (1835–1910), American novelist and humorist: *Autobiography*

TRADE & COMMERCE

'The average man finds life very uninteresting as it is. And I think that the reason why . . . is that he is always waiting for something to happen to him instead of setting to wôrk to make things happen' (A.A. Milne). How can you make the most of opportunities that present themselves? What is the 'established wisdom' on selling? What are the effects of monopoly or competition? In this section we turn to quotations on the market-place: to buying and selling, international trade, and the laws of supply and demand: 'A fair price . . . is whatever you can get plus ten per cent' (Dr Ali Ahmed Attiga), the proverbial 'The customer is always right', and 'While the sand is yet on your feet, sell' (The Talmud).

AGRICULTURE

Farming looks mighty easy when your plow is a pencil, and you're a thousand miles from the corn field.
DWIGHT D(AVID) EISENHOWER (1890–1969), U.S. general and president: *Speech, Peoria, Illinois, 25 September 1956*

The agricultural class is the least of all disposed to innovation, and the most peculiarly attached to ancient customs and routine.
JOHN RAMSEY MACCULLOCH (1789–1864), Scottish economist, statistician, and writer: *Principles of Political Economy, Part 3*

I know of no pursuit in which more real and important services can be rendered to any country than by improving its agriculture, its breed of useful animals, and other branches of a husbandman's cares.
GEORGE WASHINGTON (1732–99), U.S. statesman and president: *Letter to John Sinclair, 20 July 1794*

Each equal additional quantity of work bestowed on agriculture, yields an actual diminished return.
SIR EDWARD WEST (1782–1828): *Essay on the Application of Capital to Land*

A good farmer is nothing more nor less than a handy man with a sense of humus.
E(LWYN) B(ROOKS) WHITE (1899–), American humorist and essayist: *One Man's Meat, 'The Practical Farmer'*

BARGAINS

Here's the rule for bargains: 'Do other men, for they would do you.' That's the true business precept.
CHARLES (JOHN HUFFAM) DICKENS (1812–70), English novelist: *Martin Chuzzlewit*

A bargain is something you have to find a use for once you have bought it.
BENJAMIN FRANKLIN (1706–90), American statesman, scientist, and author (Attributed)

Looking at bargains from a purely commercial point of view, someone is always cheated, but looked at with the simple eye both seller and buyer always win.
DAVID GRAYSON (Ray Stannard Baker) (1870–1946), American journalist, biographer, and essayist: *Adventures in Contentment*

Bargains made in speed are commonly repented at leisure.
GEORGE PETTIE (1548–89), English writer: *Petite Palace of Pettie His Pleasure*

A miser and a liar bargain quickly.
Proverb

Bargain like a gipsy, but pay like a gentleman.
Proverb

It takes two to make a bargain.
Proverb

It's a bad bargain where nobody gains.
Proverb

No bargain without wine.
Latin proverb

BUYING & SELLING

Anyone who has to ask the cost can't afford it.
Anon

As a writer I have always been keenly interested in the very impressive phenomenon of the big departmental store, regarded either as a picturesque spectacle, or as a living organism, or as a sociological portent. I am all in favour of the department store, I cannot keep my eyes off its window-displays, its crowds of customers, its army of employees.
ENOCH ARNOLD BENNETT (1867–1931), English novelist

There is no such thing as 'soft sell' and 'hard sell'. There is only 'smart sell' and 'stupid sell'.
CHARLES (HENDRICKSON) BROWER (1901–), American advertising executive: *News reports, 20 May 1958*

It is well known what a middleman is: he is a man who bamboozles one party and plunders the other.
BENJAMIN DISRAELI, 1st Earl of Beaconsfield (1804–81), English statesman, prime minister, and novelist: *Speech, 11 April 1845*

A budget tells us what we can't afford, but it doesn't keep us from buying it.
WILLIAM FEATHER (1889–), American businessman: *The Business of Life*

Man does not only sell commodities, he sells himself and feels himself to be a commodity.
ERICH FROMM (1900–80), German-born American psychoanalyst and philosopher: *Escape from Freedom*

BARGAINS MADE IN SPEED ARE COMMONLY REPENTED AT LEISURE.

When a man is trying to sell you something, don't imagine he is that polite all the time.
EDGAR WATSON HOWE (1853–1937), American journalist, novelist, and essayist: *Country Town Sayings*

The farmer is the only man in our economy who buys everything he buys at retail, sells everything he sells at wholesale, and pays the freight both ways.
JOHN FITZGERALD KENNEDY (1917–63), U.S. statesman and president: *Speech, 22 September 1960*

Caveat emptor.
Let the buyer beware.
Maxim

A man must sell his ware after the rates of the market.
Proverb

It is no sin to sell dear, but a sin to give ill measure.
Proverb

There are more fools among buyers than among sellers.
Proverb

When you go to buy use your eyes, not your ears.
Proverb

A man without a smiling face must not open a shop.
Chinese proverb

When you go to buy, don't show your silver.
Chinese proverb

Every one lives by selling something.
ROBERT LOUIS BALFOUR STEVENSON (1850–94), Scottish writer: *Across the Plains*

While the sand is yet on your feet, sell.
The Talmud

Because I cannot 'afford to buy' a thing it does not follow that I have less need of it or less desire to have it than another man who can and does afford it.
PHILIP H. WICKSTEED (1844–1927): *Alphabet of Economic Science*

CHOICE

The strongest principle of growth lies in human choice.
GEORGE ELIOT (Mary Ann Evans) (1819–90), English novelist: *Daniel Deronda*

It is your own conviction which compels you; that is, choice compels choice.
EPICTETUS (?50–?120 AD), Greek philosopher: *Discourses*

Of the colours available on the Model T Ford car
Any color, so long as it's black.
HENRY FORD (1863–1947), American car manufacturer (Attributed)

No choice among stinking fish.
THOMAS FULLER (1654–1734), English physician, writer, and compiler: *Gnomologia*

Beggars cannot be choosers.
Proverb

You pays your money and you takes your choice.
Punch, 1846

Partisanship is our great curse. We too readily assume that everything has two sides and that it is our duty to be on one or the other.
JAMES HARVEY ROBINSON (1863–1936), American historian and educator: *The Mind in the Making*

Commerce is the agency by which the power of choice is obtained.
JOHN RUSKIN (1819–1900), English art critic and social reformer: *Munera Pulveris*

Even children learn in growing up that 'both' is not an admissible answer to a choice of 'Which one?'
PAUL ANTHONY SAMUELSON (1915–), American economist: *Economics*

COMMERCE & TRADE

Money is the measure of commerce.
NICHOLAS BARBON (?–1698): *Discourse Concerning Coining the New Money Lighter*

The commerce of the world is conducted by the strong, and usually it operates against the weak.
HENRY WARD BEECHER (1813–87), American clergyman, editor, and writer: *Proverbs from Plymouth Pulpit*

Commerce
A kind of transaction in which A plunders from B the goods of C, and for compensation B picks the pocket of D of money belonging to E.
AMBROSE (GWINETT) BIERCE (1842–?1914), American journalist and humorist: *The Devil's Dictionary*

Commerce is the grand panacea, which, like a beneficent medical discovery, will serve to inoculate with the healthy and saving taste for civilisation all the nations of the world.
RICHARD COBDEN (1804–65), English economist and statesman: *England, Ireland and America*

No nation was ever ruined by trade.
BENJAMIN FRANKLIN (1706–90), American statesman, scientist, and author: *Thoughts on Commercial Subjects*

Honour sinks where commerce long prevails.
OLIVER GOLDSMITH (?1728–74), Irish dramatist, novelist, and poet: *The Traveller*

Commerce is the art of exploiting the need or desire someone has for something.
EDMOND (LOUIS ANTOINE HUOT) DE GONCOURT (1822–96) and JULES (ALFRED HUOT) DE GONCOURT (1830–70), French writers and collaborators: *Journal, July 1864*

Trade could not be managed by those who manage it if it had much difficulty.
SAMUEL JOHNSON (1709–84), English lexicographer, essayist, and poet: *Letter to Hester Thrale, 16 November 1779*

Wealth depends upon commerce, and commerce depends upon circulation.
JOHN LAW (1671–1729), Scottish financier: *Money and Trade Considered*

In the pre-capitalist stages of society, commerce rules industry. The reverse is true of modern society.
KARL MARX (1818–83), German founder of modern communism: *Capital*

Trade is the mother of money.
Proverb

He's a man. I know him: his principles are thoroughly commercial.
GEORGE BERNARD SHAW (1856–1950), Irish dramatist and critic: *Man and Superman, Act 4*

In democracies, nothing is more great or more brilliant than commerce: it attracts the attention of the public, and fills the imagination of the multitude; all energetic passions are directed towards it.
ALEXIS (CHARLES HENRI MAURICE CLÉREL) DE TOCQUEVILLE (1805–59), French politician and political writer: *Democracy in America*

I am a bad Englishman, because I think the advantages of commerce are dearly bought for some by the lives of many more.
HORACE WALPOLE, 4th Earl of Orford (1717–97), English writer and historian: *Letter to Horace Mann, 26 May 1762*

COMPETITION

Free competition tends to give to labor what labor creates, to capitalists what capital creates, and to entrepreneurs what the coordinating function creates.
JOHN BATES CLARK (1847–1938), American economist and professor: *The Distribution of Wealth*

Planning and competition can be combined only by planning for competition, but not by planning against competition.
FRIEDRICH AUGUST VON HAYEK (1899–), Czech economist: *The Road to Serfdom, chapter 3*

Competition means decentralized planning by many separate persons.
FRIEDRICH AUGUST VON HAYEK, *The Use of Knowledge in Society, in Individualism and Economic Order*

Potter is potter's enemy, and craftsman is craftsman's rival; tramp is jealous of tramp, and singer of singer.
HESIOD (ca. 700 BC), Greek poet: *Works and Days*

Price-cutting and rebating, collecting information on the trade of competitors, the operation of companies under other names to obviate prejudice or secure an advantage, or for whatever reason, are all legitimate methods of competition, whatever moral criticism they may justify. There is no rule of fairness or reasonableness which regulates competition.
JOHN G. JOHNSON and JOHN G. MILBURN: *Brief for the Standard Oil Company, filed in the U.S. Circuit Court, St Louis, 1909*

The very essence of competitive commerce is waste; the waste that comes of the anarchy of war.
WILLIAM MORRIS (1834–96), English writer and social reformer: *Art under Plutocracy*

Free competition, though within its limits it is productive of good results, cannot be the ruling principle of the economic world. It is necessary that economic affairs be brought once more into subjection to a true and effective guiding principle.
POPE PIUS XI, (Achille Ratti) (1857–1939), Italian ecclesiastic and pope: *Quadragesimo anno, 15 May 1931*

Monopolies, trade unions, political parties, arise out of the very process of competition and prevent it from being effective as a mechanism for ensuring the general good.
JOAN VIOLET ROBINSON (1903–83), English economist: *Marx, Marshall and Keynes*

CONSUMERS & CONSUMPTION

The customer is an object to be manipulated, not a concrete person whose aims the businessman is interested to satisfy.
ERICH FROMM (1900–80), German-born American psychoanalyst and philosopher: *Escape from Freedom*

The urge to consume is fathered by the value system which emphasizes the ability of the society to produce.
JOHN KENNETH GALBRAITH (1908–), Canadian-born American economist, diplomat, and writer: *The Affluent Society*

Consumer wants can have bizarre, frivolous, or even immoral origins, and an admirable case can still be made for a society that seeks to satisfy them. But the case cannot stand if it is the process of satisfying wants that creates the wants.
JOHN KENNETH GALBRAITH, *as above*

The root-evil of depressed trade is under-consumption.
JOHN ATKINSON HOBSON (1858–1940), British economist and author: *The Evolution of Modern Capitalism, chapter 11*

The consumer today is the victim of the manufacturer who launches on him a regiment of products for which he must make room in his soul.
MARY (THERESE) McCARTHY (1912–), American novelist and critic: *On the Contrary*

Consumption, in the sense in which the word is used in this science, is synonymous with use; and is, in fact, the great end and object of industry.
JOHN RAMSEY MACCULLOCH (1789–1864), Scottish economist, statistician, and writer: *Principles of Political Economy, Part 4*

The customer is always right.
Proverb

If men ceased to consume, they would cease to produce.
DAVID RICARDO (1772–1823), English economist: *Principles of Political Economy and Taxation, chapter 21*

The consumer, so it is said, is the king ... each is a voter who uses his money as votes to get the things done that he wants done.
PAUL ANTHONY SAMUELSON (1915–), American economist: *Economics*

We have no more right to consume happiness without producing it than to consume wealth without producing it.
GEORGE BERNARD SHAW (1856–1950), Irish dramatist and critic: *Candida, Act 1*

To found a great empire for the sole purpose of raising up a people of customers may at first sight appear a project fit only for a nation of shopkeepers. It is, however, a project altogether unfit for a nation of shopkeepers; but extremely fit for a nation that is governed by shopkeepers.
ADAM SMITH (1723–90), Scottish economist and philosopher: *The Wealth of Nations*

CORPORATIONS

Corporation
An ingenious device for obtaining individual profit without individual responsibility.
AMBROSE (GWINETT) BIERCE (1842–?1914), American journalist and humorist: *The Devil's Dictionary*

A nearly ideal condition would be that in which, in every department of industry, there should be one great corporation, working without friction and with enormous economy, and compelled to give to the public the full benefit of that economy.
JOHN BATES CLARK (1847–1938), American economist and professor: *The Control of Trusts*

Corporations cannot commit treason, nor be outlawed nor excommunicate, for they have no souls.
SIR EDWARD COKE (1552–1634), English jurist: *Case of Sutton's Hospital*

Corporations are invisible, immortal and have no soul.
ROGER MANWOOD, Chief baron of the English Exchequer (Attributed)

A corporation is an artificial being, invisible, intangible, and existing only in contemplation of the law.
JOHN MARSHALL (1755–1835), American jurist and Chief Justice of U.S. Supreme Court: *Trustees of Dartmouth College v Woodward, U.S. Supreme Court*

History proves that, owing to a change in social conditions, functions that were once performed by small bodies can be performed today only by large corporations. Nevertheless, just as it is wrong to take from the individual and commit to the community functions that private enterprise and industry can perform, so it is an injustice, a grave evil and a violation of right order for a large organization to arrogate to itself functions which could be performed efficiently by smaller ones.
POPE PIUS XI, (Achille Ratti) (1857–1939), Italian ecclesiastic and pope: *Quadragesimo anno, 15 May 1931*

Did you ever expect a corporation to have a conscience, when it has no soul to be damned, and no body to be kicked?
LORD THURLOW, Edward, 1st Baron of (1731–1806), English lawyer and Lord Chancellor (Attributed)

INTERNATIONAL RELATIONS & FREE TRADE

If we take care of our imports, our exports will take care of themselves.
Anon

Alliance
In international politics, the union of two thieves who have their hands so deeply inserted in each other's pocket that they cannot separately plunder a third.
AMBROSE (GWINETT) BIERCE (1842–?1914), American journalist and humorist: *The Devil's Dictionary*

Diplomacy
The patriotic art of lying for one's country.
AMBROSE (GWINETT) BIERCE, *as above*

The call for free trade is as unavailing as the cry of a spoiled child for the moon. It never has existed; it never will exist.
HENRY CLAY (1777–1852), American statesman: *Speech in the Senate, 2 February 1832*

I am a citizen of the world.
DIOGENES THE CYNIC (ca. 412–ca. 323 BC), Greek philosopher, quoted in Diogenes Laertius, *Lives and Opinions of Eminent Philosophers*

Conferences at the top level are always courteous. Name-calling is left to the foreign ministers.
W(ILLIAM) AVERELL HARRIMAN (1891–), American businessman and diplomat: *News summaries, 1 August 1955*

I am for free commerce with all nations.
THOMAS JEFFERSON (1743–1826), U.S. statesman and president: *Letter to Elbridge Gerry, 1799*

Free trade, one of the greatest blessings which a government can confer on a people, is in almost every country unpopular.
THOMAS BABINGTON MACAULAY (1800–59), English historian, essayist, and statesman: *Essay on Mitford's History of Greece*

There are many things which free trade does passably. There are none which it does absolutely well; for competition is as rife in the career of fraudulent practice as in that of real excellence.
JOHN STUART MILL (1806–73), English philosopher and economist: *Dissertations and Discussions, volume 4, 'Endowments'*

Of the United States
It is not possible for this nation to be at once politically inter-nationalist and economically isolationist. This is just as insane as asking one Siamese twin to high dive while the other plays the piano.
ADLAI (EWING) STEVENSON (1900–68), American statesman: *Speech, New Orleans, Louisiana, 10 October 1952*

An ambassador is an honest man sent to lie abroad for the commonwealth.
SIR HENRY WOTTON (1568–1639), English traveller, diplomatist, and poet: *Christopher Fleckmore's autograph album*

THE MARKET AND SUPPLY & DEMAND

The market is totally impartial.
Anon

Good ware makes quick markets.
NICOLAS BRETON (ca. 1555–ca. 1625), English poet and satirist: *Crossing of Proverbs*

Supply-and-demand, – alas! For what noble work was there ever yet any audible demand in that poor sense? The man of Macedonia, speaking in vision to an Apostle Paul, 'Come over and help us,' did not specify what rate of wages he would give.
THOMAS CARLYLE (1795–1881), Scottish essayist and historian: *Past and Present*

A friend in the market is better than money in the chest.
THOMAS FULLER (1654–1734), English physician, writer, and compiler: *Gnomologia*

The market is the best garden.
GEORGE HERBERT (1593–1633),
English metaphysical poet: *Outlandish
Proverbs*

**In the usual and ordinary course of
things, the demand for all
commodities precedes their supply.**
DAVID RICARDO (1772–1823), English
economist: *Principles of Political
Economy and Taxation, chapter 32*

**Free enterprise ended in the United
States a good many years ago. Big
oil, big steel, big agriculture avoid
the open market place. Big corporations fix prices among themselves
and drive out the small entrepreneur. In their conglomerate
forms, the huge corporations have
begun to challenge the legitimacy
of the State.**
GORE (EUGENE LUTHER) VIDAL
(1925–), American novelist and
playwright

MONOPOLY

**How come there's only one
Monopolies Commission?**
Anon

**Monopolistic combination is
common enough in all parts of the
economic system; very much the
same motives which drive business
men to form rings and cartels drive
their employees to form unions.
The one, as much as the other, is a**

**natural product of a gregarious
animal.**
SIR JOHN RICHARD HICKS (1904–),
British economist: *The Theory of Wages,
Part 2*

**It is better to abolish monopolies in
all cases than not to do it in any.**
THOMAS JEFFERSON (1743–1826),
U.S. statesman and president: *Letter to
James Madison, 1788*

**Like many businessmen of genius
he learned that free competition
was wasteful, monopoly efficient.**
MARIO PUZO: *The Godfather*

**A monopoly granted either to an
individual or to a trading company
has the same effect as a secret in
trade or manufactures. The
monopolists, by keeping the
market constantly understocked,
by never fully supplying the effectual
demand, sell their commodities
much above the natural price, and
raise their emoluments, whether
they consist in wages or profit,
greatly above their natural rate.**
ADAM SMITH (1723–90), Scottish
economist and philosopher: *The Wealth
of Nations, volume 1*

**It is not competition, but monopoly,
that deprives labor of its product.
Wages, inheritance, gifts and
gambling aside, every process by
which men acquire wealth rests
upon a monopoly, a prohibition, a
denial of liberty.**
BENJAMIN R. TUCKER (1854–1939),
American anarchist: *Why I Am an
Anarchist*

OPPORTUNITIES

The gods help them that help themselves.
AESOP (ca. 620–564 BC), Greek fabulist: *Fables, 'Hercules and the Waggoner'*

I would rather be an opportunist and float than go to the bottom with my principles round my neck.
STANLEY BALDWIN (1867–1947), British statesman (Attributed)

It is always good
When a man has two irons in the fire.
FRANCIS BEAUMONT (1584–1616) and JOHN FLETCHER (1579–1625), English dramatists: *The Faithful Friends*

You never know till you try to reach them how accessible men are; but you must approach each man by the right door.
HENRY WARD BEECHER (1813–87), American clergyman, editor, and writer: *Proverbs from Plymouth Pulpit*

Go around asking a lot of damfool questions and taking chances. Only through curiosity can we discover opportunities, and only by gambling can we take advantage of them.
CLARENCE BIRDSEYE (1886–1956), American industrialist

It is folly for a man to pray to the gods for that which he has the power to obtain for himself.
EPICURUS (341–270 BC), Greek philosopher: *Vatican Sayings*

Gather ye rosebuds while ye may.
ROBERT HERRICK (1591–1674), English poet: *Hesperides*

There is one disadvantage which the man of philosophical habits of mind suffers, as compared with the man of action. While he is taking an enlarged and rational view of the matter before him, he lets his chance slip through his fingers.
OLIVER WENDELL HOLMES, SR (1809–94), American physician, professor, and author: *The Professor at the Breakfast Table*

When one door of happiness closes, another opens; but often we look so long at the closed door that we do not see the one which has been opened for us.
HELEN (ADAMS) KELLER (1880–1968), American author and lecturer: *We Bereaved*

All of us do not have equal talent, but all of us should have an equal opportunity to develop our talents.
JOHN FITZGERALD KENNEDY (1917–63), U.S. statesman and president: *Address, San Diego State College, California, 6 June 1963*

In great affairs we ought to apply ourselves less to creating chances than to profiting from those that offer.
FRANÇOIS LA ROCHEFOUCAULD, Duc de la Rochefoucauld (1613–80), French writer: *Maxims*

The average man finds life very uninteresting as it is. And I think that the reason why . . . is that he is

always waiting for something to happen to him instead of setting to work to make things happen.
ALAN ALEXANDER MILNE (1882–1956), English writer and dramatist: *If I May: The Future*

An occasion lost cannot be redeemed.
Proverb

Make hay while the sun shines.
Proverb

Opportunity seldom knocks twice.
Proverb

Strike while the iron is hot.
Proverb

When one door shuts, another opens.
Proverb

While we stop to think, we often miss our opportunity.
PUBLILIUS SYRUS (1st c. BC), Latin writer of mimes: *Sententiae*

I was seldom able to see an opportunity until it had ceased to be one.
MARK TWAIN (Samuel Langhorne Clemens) (1835–1910), American novelist and humorist

---

PRICES & VALUE

Nothing that costs only a dollar is worth having.
ELIZABETH ARDEN (1884–1966), American cosmetician, quoted in *Fortune*, 1973

A fair price for oil is whatever you can get plus ten per cent.
DR ALI AHMED ATTIGA (1931–), Saudi Arabian delegate to OPEC, quoted in *Observer*, 'Sayings of the Year,' 29 December 1974

But the market is the best judge of value: for by the concourse of buyers and sellers, the quantity of wares, and the occasion for them are best known. Things are just worth so much, as they can be sold for, according to the old rule *Valet Quantum Veni Potest*.
NICHOLAS BARBON (?–1698): *A Discourse of Trade*

That which cost little is less valued.
MIGUEL DE CERVANTES (SAAVEDRA) (1547–1616), Spanish writer: *Don Quixote*

This would, at a stroke, reduce the rise in prices, increase productivity and reduce unemployment.
Conservative Party Press Release, 16 June 1970

If the choice lies between the production or purchase of two commodities, the value of one is measured by the sacrifice of going without the other.
H.J. DAVENPORT (1862–1931), *Journal of Political Economy*, 'The Formula of Sacrifice'

What is a man if he is not a thief who openly charges as much as he can for the goods he sells?
MAHATMA GANDHI (Mohandas Karamchand Gandhi) (1869–1948), Hindu nationalist leader: *Non-Violence in Peace and War*

The value of a thing is the amount of laboring or work that its possession will save the possessor.
HENRY GEORGE (1839–97), American economist: *The Science of Political Economy*

Question
What's two and two?
Grade
Buying or selling?
LORD GRADE (1906–), British television mogul: *Observer, 1962*

As in other things, so in men, not the seller but the buyer determines the price. For let a man (as most men do) rate themselves at the highest value they can; yet their true value is no more than it is esteemed by others.
THOMAS HOBBES (1588–1679), English political philosopher: *Leviathan*

The value or worth of a man is . . . his price – that is to say, so much as would be given for the use of his power.
THOMAS HOBBES, *as above*

It has long been recognised, by the business world and by economists alike, that a period of rising prices acts as a stimulus to enterprise and is beneficial to business men.
JOHN MAYNARD KEYNES (1883–1946), English economist: *A Tract on Monetary Reform, chapter 1*

Ad valorem.
According to the value.
Latin phrase

Cheat me in price, but not in the goods I purchase.
Proverb

Value is the life-giving power of anything; cost, the quantity of labour required to produce it; price, the quantity of labour which its possessor will take in exchange for it.
JOHN RUSKIN (1819–1900), English art critic and social reformer: *Munera Pulveris*

Every man has his price.
Saying

The word *value* . . . has two different meanings, and sometimes expresses the utility of some particular object, and sometimes the power of purchasing other goods which the possession of that object conveys. The one may be called 'value in use'; the other, 'value in exchange'.
ADAM SMITH (1723–90), Scottish economist and philosopher: *The Wealth of Nations, volume 1*

The market price of every particular commodity is regulated by the proportion between the quantity which is actually brought to market and the demand of those who are willing to pay the natural price of the commodity.
ADAM SMITH, *as above*

The real price of every thing, what every thing really costs to the man who wants to acquire it, is the toil and trouble of acquiring it.
ADAM SMITH, *as above*

All those men have their price.
SIR ROBERT WALPOLE, 1st Earl of
Orford (1676–1745), English statesman
(Attributed)

It is not that pearls fetch a high price *because* men have dived for them; but on the contrary, men dive for them because they fetch a high price.
BISHOP RICHARD WHATELY (1787–1863), *Introductory Lectures on Political Economy*

SPENDING

Annual income twenty pounds, annual expenditure nineteen nineteen six, result happiness. Annual income twenty pounds, annual expenditure twenty pounds ought and six, result misery.
CHARLES (JOHN HUFFAM) DICKENS (1812–70), English novelist: *David Copperfield, chapter 12*

Everybody is always in favour of general economy and particular expenditure.
SIR (ROBERT) ANTHONY EDEN, 1st Earl of Avon (1897–1977), British statesman and prime minister: *Observer, 'Sayings of the Week', 17 June 1956*

The workers spend what they get and the capitalists get what they spend.
M. KALECKI (1899–1970) (Attributed)

Cut your coat according to your cloth.
Proverb

Don't spoil the ship for a ha'porth of tar.
Proverb

Easy come, easy go.
Proverb

Spend, and God will send.
Proverb

To a good spender, God is the treasurer.
Proverb

All decent people live beyond their incomes nowadays, and those who aren't respectable live beyond other people's. A few gifted individuals manage to do both.
SAKI (Hector Hugh Munro) (1870–1916), English novelist and short-story writer: *The Match Maker*

UTILITY & EXPEDIENCY

By the principle of utility is meant that principle which approves or disapproves of every action what-soever according to the tendency which it appears to have to augment or diminish the happiness of the party whose interest is in question.
JEREMY BENTHAM (1748–1832), English philosopher: *The Principles of Morals and Legislation*

A stronger incentive will be required to induce a person to pay a given price for anything if he is poor than if he is rich. A shilling is the measure of less pleasure, or satisfaction of any kind, to a rich man than to a poor one.
ALFRED MARSHALL (1842–1924), English classical economist: *Principles of Economics, book 1*

You can't learn too soon that the most useful thing about a principle is that it can always be sacrificed to expediency.
W(ILLIAM) SOMERSET MAUGHAM (1874–1965), English writer: *The Circle, Act 3*

Actions are right in proportion as they tend to promote happiness; wrong as they tend to produce the reverse of happiness. By happiness is intended pleasure, and the absence of pain; by unhappiness, pain, and the privation of pleasure.
JOHN STUART MILL (1806–73), English philosopher and economist: *Utilitarianism*

No man is justified in doing evil on the ground of expediency.
THEODORE ROOSEVELT (1858–1919), U.S. statesman and president: *The Strenuous Life*

Utility is the great idol of the age, to which all powers must do service and all talents swear allegiance.
(JOHANN CHRISTOPH) FRIEDRICH VON SCHILLER (1759–1805), German playwright, poet, and historian: *On the Aesthetic Education of Man*

HUMAN RESOURCES

'To be successful, a woman has to be better at her job than a man' (Golda Meir).
'Management by objectives works if you know the objectives.
Ninety percent of the time you don't' (Peter Drucker). 'I think it's ludicrous that
it takes seventeen unions to build a motor car in Britain' (Lord Scanlon).
The quotations in this section consider the essential business asset of people.
We see widely varying opinions of businessmen and businesswomen,
the art of delegation and good management, and the roles of trade unions and
public relations. We also look at what it's like to live in a city and trace the path
of careers through promotion up to old age and retirement.

BUSINESSMEN & BUSINESSWOMEN

Executive
An ulcer with authority.
FRED ALLEN (John F. Sullivan) (1894–
1956), American comedian

**A woman who strives to be like a
man lacks ambition.**
Anon

**If you want something done, give it
to a busy man . . . and he'll have his
secretary do it.**
Anon

Speaking to her husband
**Dear, never forget one little point.
It's my business. You just work here.**
ELIZABETH ARDEN (1884–1966),
American cosmetician, quoted in J. Fisk
and R. Barron, *Great Business Quotations*

**Men of business have a solid
judgement – a wonderful guessing
power of what is going to happen –
each in his own trade; but they have
never practised themselves in
reasoning out their judgements and
in supporting their guesses by
argument: probably if they did so
some of the finer and correcter
parts of their anticipations would
vanish.**
WALTER BAGEHOT (1826–77), English
economist and journalist: *Economic
Studies*

No matter who reigns, the merchant reigns.
HENRY WARD BEECHER (1813–87), American clergyman, editor, and writer: *Proverbs from Plymouth Pulpit*

When asked the secret of his success with women
I treat the charwomen like duchesses, and the duchesses like charwomen.
GEORGE BRYAN BRUMMELL (Beau Brummell) (1778–1840), English dandy

Brigands demand your money or your life; women require both.
SAMUEL BUTLER (1835–1902), English author, painter, and musician (Attributed)

Few people do business well who do nothing else.
LORD CHESTERFIELD, Philip Dormer Stanhope, 4th Earl of (1694–1773), English statesman and writer: *Letters, 7 August 1749*

IF YOU WANT SOMETHING DONE, GIVE IT TO A BUSY MAN ... AND HE'LL HAVE HIS SECRETARY DO IT.

Don't ever wear artistic jewellery; it wrecks a woman's reputation.
SIDONIE GABRIELLE CLAUDINE COLETTE (1873–1954), French novelist: *Gigi*

A businessman needs three umbrellas – one to leave at the office, one to leave at home and one to leave on the train.
PAUL DICKSON (1939–), American writer: *Playboy, 1978*

A man of straw is worth more than a woman of gold.
JOHN FLORIO (?1553–?1625), English lexicographer: *Second Frutes*

These men of the technostructure are the new and universal priesthood. Their religion is business success; their test of virtue is growth and profit. Their bible is the computer printout; their communion bench is the committee room. The sales force carries their message to the world, and a message is what it is often called.
JOHN KENNETH GALBRAITH (1908–), Canadian-born American economist, diplomat, and writer: *The Age of Uncertainty*

The decisive economic contribution of women in the developed industrial society is rather simple . . . It is, overwhelmingly, to make possible a continuing and more or less unlimited increase in the sale and use of consumer goods.
JOHN KENNETH GALBRAITH, *Annals of an Abiding Liberal*

Every director bites the hand that lays the golden egg.
SAMUEL GOLDWYN (1882–1974), American film producer (Attributed)

Women's liberation, if it abolishes the patriarchal family, will abolish a necessary substructure of the authoritarian state, and once that withers away Marx will have come true willy-nilly, so let's get on with it.
GERMAINE GREER (1939–), Australian writer and feminist: *The Female Eunuch*

Man has his will, – but woman has her way.
OLIVER WENDELL HOLMES, SR (1809–94), American physician, professor, and author: *The Autocrat of the Breakfast Table*

The appointment of a woman to office is an innovation for which the public is not prepared, nor am I.
THOMAS JEFFERSON (1743–1826), U.S. statesman and president: *Letter to Albert Gallatin, January 1807*

For the female of the species is more deadly than the male.
(JOSEPH) RUDYARD KIPLING (1865–1936), English novelist, poet, and short-story writer: *The Female of the Species*

The silliest woman can manage a clever man; but it needs a very clever woman to manage a fool.
(JOSEPH) RUDYARD KIPLING, *Plain Tales from the Hills*, 'Three and – an Extra'

The businessman has the same fundamental psychology as the artist, inventor, or statesman. He has set himself at a certain work and the work absorbs and becomes himself. It is the expression of his personality; he lives in its growth and perfection according to his plans.
FRANK H. KNIGHT (1885–1972), Professor of Economics: *Risk, Uncertainty and Profit*

If a woman is sufficiently ambitious, determined *and* gifted – there is practically nothing she can't do.
HELEN LAWRENSON, American journalist: *Esquire, 1971*

Damn the great executives, the men of measured merriment, damn the men with careful smiles, damn the men that run the shops, oh, damn their measured merriment.
(HARRY) SINCLAIR LEWIS (1885–1951), American novelist: *Arrowsmith*

There is only one political career for which women are perfectly suited: diplomacy.
CLARE BOOTHE LUCE (1903–), American diplomat

Men and women must receive equal pay for equal work in production. Genuine equality between the sexes can only be realized in the process of the socialist transformation of society as a whole.
MAO TSE-TUNG (Mao Ze Dong) (1893–1976), Chinese Communist leader

To be successful, a woman has to be better at her job than a man.
GOLDA MEIR (1898–1978), Russian-born Israeli stateswoman and prime minister

Let woman then go on – not asking favors, but claiming as a right the removal of all hindrances to her elevation in the scale of being – let her receive encouragement for the proper cultivation of her powers, so that she may enter profitably into the active business of life.
LUCRETIA MOTT (1793–1880), *Speech, 17 December 1849*

A man in business must put up many affronts if he loves his own quiet.
WILLIAM PENN (1644–1718), English Quaker and founder of Pennsylvania: *Some Fruits of Solitude*

A man who is always ready to believe what is told him will never do well, especially a businessman.
PETRONIUS GAIUS also known as Petronius Arbiter (? –65 AD), Roman writer: *Satyricon*

The best executive is the one who has sense enough to pick good men to do what he wants done, and self-restraint enough to keep from meddling with them while they do it.
THEODORE ROOSEVELT (1858–1919), U.S. statesman and president

In their hearts women think that it is men's business to earn money and theirs to spend it.
ARTHUR SCHOPENHAUER (1788–1860), German pessimist philosopher: *Parerga and Paralipomena, 'On Women'*

The business man has failed in politics as he has in citizenship. Why? Because politics is business. That's what's the matter with everything – art, literature, religion, journalism, law, medicine – they're all businesses, and all – as you see them. Make politics a sport, as they do in England, or a profession, as they do in Germany, and we'll have – well, something else than we have now – if we want it, which is another question.
LINCOLN STEFFENS (1866–1936), American writer and editor: *The Shame of the Cities*

Whilst there is a world 'tis woman that will govern it.
SIR JOHN VANBRUGH (1664–1726), English dramatist and baroque architect: *The Provok'd Wife*

On liberated women
They have a right to work wherever they want to – as long as they have dinner ready when you get home.
JOHN WAYNE (Marion Michael Morrison) (1907–79), American film star

A great society is a society in which its men of business think greatly of their functions.
ALFRED NORTH WHITEHEAD (1861–1947), English mathematician and philosopher: *Adventures in Ideas*

Even when the path is nominally open – when there is nothing to prevent a woman from being a doctor, a lawyer, a civil servant – there are many phantoms and obstacles, I believe, looming in her way.
(ADELINE) VIRGINIA WOOLF (1882–1941), English novelist and critic: *Women and Wanting*

CAREERS & PROMOTION

You've forgotten the grandest moral attribute of a Scotsman, Maggie, that he'll do nothing which might damage his career.
SIR JAMES MATTHEW BARRIE (1860–1937), Scottish novelist and dramatist: *What Every Woman Knows*, Act 2

If you aspire to the highest place, it is no disgrace to stop at the second, or even the third, place.
MARCUS TULLIUS CICERO (106–43 BC), Roman statesman and orator: *On Oratory*

Sir Joseph Porter
When I was a lad I served a term As office boy to an Attorney's firm. I cleaned the windows and I swept the floor, And I polished up the handle of the big front door. I polished up that handle so carefullee

That now I am the Ruler of the Queen's Navee!
SIR WILLIAM SCHWENK GILBERT (1836–1911), English parodist and librettist: *HMS Pinafore, Act 1*

Your levellers wish to level down as far as themselves; but they cannot bear levelling up to themselves. They would all have some people under them; why not then have some people above them?
SAMUEL JOHNSON (1709–84), English lexicographer, essayist, and poet: Boswell, *Life of Johnson*

Be nice to people on your way up because you'll meet 'em on your way down.
WILSON MIZNER (1876–1933), American dramatist

The Peter Principle
In a Hierarchy Every Employee Tends to Rise to his Level of Incompetence.
Work is accomplished by those employees who have not yet reached their level of incompetence. Competence, like truth, beauty and contact lenses, is in the eye of the beholder.
DR LAURENCE J. PETER (1919–), Canadian educator and RAYMOND HULL (1919–): *The Peter Principle*

He who would climb the ladder must begin at the bottom.
Proverb

Do not despise the bottom rungs in the ascent to greatness.
PUBLILIUS SYRUS (1st c. BC), Latin writer of mimes: *Moral Sayings*

CITIES

To some extent, if you've seen one city slum you've seen them all.
SPIRO T. AGNEW (1918–), U.S. vice-president: *Speech, Detroit, 18 October 1968*

A great city is not to be confounded with a populous one.
ARISTOTLE (384–322 BC), Greek philosopher and scientist: *Politics*

The building of cities is one of man's greatest achievements. The form of his city always has been and always will be a pitiless indicator of the state of his civilisation.
EDMUND N. BACON (1910–): *Contemporary Architects*

It is much more difficult to develop a city than to send a man to the moon.
PROFESSOR COLIN BUCHANAN (1907–), Transport and planning consultant: *Observer, 'Sayings of the Decade', 28 December 1969*

Of Los Angeles
A city with all the personality of a paper cup.
RAYMOND CHANDLER (1888–1959), American thriller writer

In great cities men are more callous both to the happiness and the misery of others . . . for they are constantly in the habit of seeing both extremes.
CHARLES CALEB COLTON (?1780–1832), English clergyman and writer: *Lacon*

If you would be known, and not know, vegetate in a village; if you would know, and not be known, live in a city.
CHARLES CALEB COLTON, *as above*

New York, New York! It's a wonderful town! The west side of the island was rich in façades not unlike the possibilities of a fairy princess with syphilis.
RICHARD CONDON (1915–), American novelist: *The Manchurian Candidate*, chapter 11

No city should be too large for a man to walk out of in a morning.
CYRIL (VERNON) CONNOLLY (1903–74), English essayist, critic, and novelist: *The Unquiet Grave, chapter 1*

God made the country, and man made the town.
WILLIAM COWPER (1731–1800), English poet: *The Task*

GOD MADE THE COUNTRY, AND MAN MADE THE TOWN.

Cities give us collision. London and New York take the nonsense out of man.
RALPH WALDO EMERSON (1803–82), American poet, essayist, and philosopher: *The Conduct of Life*

'Tis the men, not the houses, that make the city.
THOMAS FULLER (1654–1734), English physician, writer, and compiler: *Gnomologia*

Of London
Crowds without company, and dissipation without pleasure.
EDWARD GIBBON (1737–94), English historian: *Autobiography*

In the country we forget the town, and in town we despise the country.
WILLIAM HAZLITT (1778–1830), English essayist: *Table Talk, 'On Going a Journey'*

**Great cities seldom rest: if there be none
T'invade from far, they'll find worse foes at home.**
ROBERT HERRICK (1591–1674), English poet: *Hesperides*

You find no man, at all intellectual, who is willing to leave London. No, Sir, when a man is tired of London, he is tired of life; for there is in London all that life can afford.
SAMUEL JOHNSON (1709–84), English lexicographer, essayist, and poet: Boswell, *Life of Johnson*

The city has a face, the country a soul.
JACQUES DE LACRETELLE (1888–), French novelist: *Idées dans un chapeau*

I have an affection for a great city. I feel safe in the neighborhood of man, and enjoy the sweet security of the streets.
HENRY WADSWORTH LONGFELLOW (1807–82), American poet and translator: *Driftwood*

I'd rather wake up in the middle of nowhere than in any city on earth.
STEVE McQUEEN (1932–80), American film actor

In great cities men are like a lot of stones thrown together in a bag; their jagged corners are rubbed off till in the end they are as smooth as marbles.
W(ILLIAM) SOMERSET MAUGHAM (1874–1965), English writer: *The Summing Up*

Towered cities please us then, And the busy hum of men.
JOHN MILTON (1608–74), English poet: *L'Allegro*

**A commuter is one who never knows
how a show comes out because he has to leave early to catch a train to get him back to the country in time to catch a train to bring him back to the city.**
OGDEN NASH (1902–71), American humorous poet: *Versus, 'The Banker's Special'*

Of Los Angeles
Seventy-two suburbs in search of a city.
DOROTHY (ROTHSCHILD) PARKER (1893–1967), American writer

Any city, however small, is in fact divided into two, one the city of the poor, the other of the rich; these are at war with one another.
PLATO (?427–?347 BC), Greek philosopher. *The Republic*

Cities are the abyss of the human species. At the end of a few generations in them races perish or degenerate, and it is necessary to renew them. This renewal always comes from the country.
JEAN-JACQUES ROUSSEAU (1712–78), Swiss-born French philosopher and writer: *Émile*

The people are the city.
WILLIAM SHAKESPEARE (1564–1616), English dramatist and poet: *Coriolanus, Act 3*

A city is like a magnet – the bigger it is, the greater the drawing power.
SAMUEL TENENBAUM, American academic: *New York Times, 1971*

DELEGATION

And Moses chose able men out of all Israel, and made them heads over the people, rulers of thousands, rulers of hundreds, rulers of fifties, and rulers of tens. And they judged the people at all seasons: the hard causes they brought unto Moses, but every small matter they judged themselves.
The Bible, Authorized (King James) Version, Exodus 18:25–26

What is worth doing is worth the trouble of asking somebody to do it.
AMBROSE (GWINETT) BIERCE (1842–?1914), American journalist and humorist: *The Devil's Dictionary*

He who does a thing through an agent does it himself.
Maxim

Life is too short to do anything for oneself that one can pay others to do for one.
W(ILLIAM) SOMERSET MAUGHAM (1874–1965), English writer: *The Summing Up*

If you want a thing done well, do it yourself.
NAPOLEON I (Napoleon Bonaparte) (1769–1821), French emperor and general: *Maxims*

Nothing is impossible for the man who doesn't have to do it himself.
A.H. WEILER, American newspaperman and editor: *New York Times, privately circulated memorandum*

INDUSTRIAL RELATIONS

Strike while your employer has a big contract.
Anon

There is no right to strike against the public safety by anybody, anywhere, anytime.
(JOHN) CALVIN COOLIDGE (1872–1933), U.S. president: *Telegram to the president of the American Federation of Labor, 14 September 1919*

Of Stanley Baldwin
His motto in the fierce crises in industrial relations was 'not to fire the first shot'. That did not prevent him from firing the last, but it was, at worst, only designed to graze.
SIR COLIN R. COOTE, 14 July 1967, quoted in Frank S. Pepper, *Contemporary Biographical Quotations*

Industrial relations are like sexual relations. It's better between two consenting parties.
LORD VIC FEATHER (1908–76), General secretary of the TUC, quoted in *Guardian Weekly, 8 August 1976*

An occasional strike is an indication that countervailing power is being employed in a sound context where the costs of any wage increase cannot readily be passed along to someone else. It should be an occasion for mild rejoicing in the conservative press. The *Daily Worker*, eagerly contemplating the downfall of capitalism, should regret this manifestation of the continued health of the system.
JOHN KENNETH GALBRAITH (1908–), Canadian-born American economist, diplomat, and writer: *American Capitalism, chapter 9*

Industrial Relations are human relations.
EDWARD (RICHARD GEORGE) HEATH (1916–), British statesman and prime minister (Attributed)

Another fact of life that will not have escaped you is that, in this country, the twenty-four-hour strike is like the twenty-four-hour flu. You have to reckon on it lasting at least five days.
DENIS NORDEN (1922–), British humorist: *You Can't Have Your Kayak and Heat It, 'Great Expectations'*

Industrial relations are much more like a marriage relationship than anything else. You do not want the courts. When you do it means you are finished.
GEORGE WOODCOCK (1904–79), General secretary of the TUC: *Observer, 'Sayings of 1968', 29 December 1968*

LEADERSHIP & MANAGEMENT

Management is the art of getting other people to do all the work.
Anon

The Leaders of Industry, if Industry is ever to be led, are virtually the Captains of the World . . . Captains of Industry are the true Fighters, henceforth recognisable as the only true ones.
THOMAS CARLYLE (1795–1881), Scottish essayist and historian: *Past and Present, book 4*

British management doesn't seem to understand the importance of the human factor.
CHARLES, Prince of Wales (1948–), heir to throne of United Kingdom: *Speech, Parliamentary and Scientific Committee lunch, 21 February 1979*

The man who commands efficiently must have obeyed others in the past, and the man who obeys dutifully is worthy of being some day a commander.
MARCUS TULLIUS CICERO (106–43 BC), Roman statesman and orator: *De Legibus*

Management by objectives works if you know the objectives. Ninety percent of the time you don't.
PETER F. DRUCKER (1909–), American management expert

So much of what we call management consists in making it difficult for people to work.
PETER F. DRUCKER

I tell you, sir, the only safeguard of order and discipline in the modern world is a standardized worker with interchangeable parts. That would solve the entire problem of management.
JEAN GIRAUDOUX (1882–1944), French dramatist: *The Madwoman of Chaillot*

The first myth of management is that it exists. The second myth of management is that success equals skill.
ROBERT HELLER (1919–), American writer: *The Great Executive Dream*

You don't have to be intellectually bright to be a competent leader.
SIR EDMUND HILLARY (1919–), New Zealand explorer and mountaineer

If you can keep your head when all about you are losing theirs, it's just possible you haven't grasped the situation.
JEAN KERR (1923–), American essayist and playwright: *Please Don't Eat the Daisies*

Chief executives repeatedly fail to recognize that for communication to be effective, it must be two-way: *there has to be feedback to ascertain the extent to which the message has actually been understood, believed, assimilated, and accepted.* **This is a step few companies ever take (perhaps because they fear to learn how little of the message has actually been transmitted).**
ROBERT N. McMURRY (1901–): *Harvard Business Review, 1965, 'Clear Communications for Chief Executives'*

The real leader has no need to lead – he is content to point the way.
HENRY MILLER (1891–1980), American writer: *The Wisdom of the Heart*

The ordinary man is involved in action, the hero acts. An immense difference.
HENRY MILLER, *The Books in My Life*

People ask the difference between a leader and a boss . . . The leader works in the open, and the boss in

covert. **The leader leads, and the boss drives.**
THEODORE ROOSEVELT (1858–1919), U.S. statesman and president: *Speech, New York, 24 October 1910*

Monopoly . . . is a great enemy to good management.
ADAM SMITH (1723–90), Scottish economist and philosopher: *The Wealth of Nations, volume 1*

PUBLIC RELATIONS

Some are born great, some achieve greatness, and some hire public relations officers.
DANIEL J. BOORSTIN (1914–), American educator and writer: *The Image*

Public-relations specialists make flower arrangements of the facts, placing them so that the wilted and less attractive petals are hidden by sturdy blooms.
ALAN HARRINGTON (1919–), American writer: *Life in the Crystal Palace*

There are a million definitions of public relations. I have found it to be the craft of arranging the truth so that people will like you.
ALAN HARRINGTON, *as above*

Of Anthony Eden
They asked for a leader and were given a public relations officer; here is the news and this is Anthony Eden reading it.
MALCOLM MUGGERIDGE (1903–), English editor and writer: *Tread Softly for You Tread on My Jokes*

RETIREMENT & OLD AGE

Retirement means twice as much husband on half as much money.
Anon

There is no such thing as 'on the way out'. As long as you are still doing something interesting and good, you're in business because you're still breathing.
(DANIEL) LOUIS ARMSTRONG nickname Satchmo (1900–71), American jazz trumpeter and bandleader

Age will not be defied.
FRANCIS BACON, 1st Baron Verulam, Viscount St Albans (1561–1626), English writer, philosopher, and statesman: *Essays, 'Of Regiment of Health'*

The old repeat themselves and the young have nothing to say. The boredom is mutual.
JACQUES BAINVILLE (1879–1936), French historian, journalist, and essayist: *Lectures, 'Charme de la conversation'*

I will never be an old man. To me, old age is always fifteen years older than I am.
BERNARD MANNES BARUCH (1870–1965), American financier and statesman: *Observer, 'Sayings of the Week', 21 August 1955*

The role of a retired person is no longer to possess one.
SIMONE DE BEAUVOIR (1908–86), French existentialist novelist and feminist: *The Coming of Age*

In the morning, we carry the world like Atlas; at noon, we stoop and bend beneath it; and at night, it crushes us flat to the ground.
HENRY WARD BEECHER (1813–87), American clergyman, editor, and writer: *Proverbs from Plymouth Pulpit*

They shall grow not old, as we that are left grow old:
Age shall not weary them, nor the years condemn.
At the going down of the sun and in the morning
We will remember them.
LAURENCE ROBERT BINYON (1869–1943), English poet: *For the Fallen (1914–1918)*

Happy is the man who, ignored by the world, lives contented with himself in some retired nook.
NICOLAS BOILEAU (-DESPRÉAUX) (1636–1711), French poet and critic: *Épîtres*

Retirement at sixty-five is ridiculous. When I was sixty-five, I still had pimples.
GEORGE BURNS (1896–), American comedian

Going away: I can generally bear the separation, but I don't like the leave-taking.
SAMUEL BUTLER (1835–1902), English author, painter, and musician: *Note-Books, 'Higgledy-Piggledy'*

'You are old, Father William,' the young man said,
'And your hair has become very white;
And yet you incessantly stand on your head –
Do you think at your age, it is right?'
LEWIS CARROLL (Charles Lutwidge Dodgson) (1832–98), English writer and mathematician: *Alice's Adventures in Wonderland, chapter 5*

I prefer old age to the alternative.
MAURICE CHEVALIER (1888–1972), French singer and film actor: *Remark, 1962*

Youth is a blunder; manhood a struggle; old age a regret.
BENJAMIN DISRAELI, 1st Earl of Beaconsfield (1804–81), English statesman, prime minister, and novelist: *Coningsby*

I grow old . . . I grow old . . .
I shall wear the bottoms of my trousers rolled.
T(HOMAS) S(TEARNS) ELIOT (1888–1965), American-born British poet, dramatist, and critic: *The Love Song of J. Alfred Prufrock*

Si jeunesse savait; si vieillesse pouvait.
If only youth knew; if only age could.
HENRI ESTIENNE (1528–98), French scholar and editor: *Les Prémices*

In general we must reduce and eventually remove subsidies of all kinds which distort the relative cost of different forms of energy, and which stimulate wasteful consumption . . . But the best way to help

pensioners is to increase pensions, not to sell fuel to everybody far below its cost.
DENIS (WINSTON) HEALEY (1917–), English politician: *Budget Speech, House of Commons, 12 November 1974*

Retirement is the ugliest word in the language.
ERNEST HEMINGWAY (1899–1961), American novelist and short-story writer

I don't feel eighty. In fact I don't feel *anything* till noon. Then it's time for my nap.
BOB HOPE (1904–), English-born American comedian and comic actor

You know you're getting old when the candles cost more than the cake.
BOB HOPE

Whenever a man's friends begin to compliment him about looking young, he may be sure that they think he is growing old.
WASHINGTON IRVING (1783–1859), American essayist, biographer, and historian: *Bracebridge Hall, 'Bachelors'*

The love of retirement has, in all ages, adhered closely to those minds which have been most enlarged by knowledge, or elevated by genius.
SAMUEL JOHNSON (1709–84), English lexicographer, essayist, and poet: *The Rambler, 10 April 1750*

Pension
An allowance made to anyone without an equivalent. In England it is generally understood to mean

pay given to a state hireling for treason to his country.
SAMUEL JOHNSON, *Dictionary of the English Language*

The first years of man must make provision for the last.
SAMUEL JOHNSON, *Rasselas*

I am Retired Leisure. I am to be met with in trim gardens. I am already come to be known by my vacant face and careless gesture, perambulating at no fixed pace nor with any settled purpose. I walk about; not to and from.
CHARLES (ELIA) LAMB (1775–1834), English essayist: *Last Essays of Elia, 'The Superannuated Man'*

Old age has its pleasures, which, though different, are not less than the pleasures of youth.
W(ILLIAM) SOMERSET MAUGHAM (1874–1965), English writer: *The Summing Up*

One of the many pleasures of old age is giving things up.
MALCOLM MUGGERIDGE (1903–), English editor and writer

Few men of action have been able to make a graceful exit at the appropriate time.
MALCOLM MUGGERIDGE, *The Most of Malcolm Muggeridge, 'Twilight of Greatness'*

I have made noise enough in the world already, perhaps too much,

and am now getting old, and want retirement.
NAPOLEON I (Napoleon Bonaparte) (1769–1821), French emperor and general: *To Barry E. O'Meara at St Helena, 1 October 1816*

My second fixed idea is the useless-ness of men above 60 years of age, and the incalculable benefit it would be in commercial, political and professional life if, as a matter of course, men stopped work at this age.
SIR WILLIAM OSLER (1849–1919), Canadian physician: *Speech, Baltimore, 22 February 1905*

If you wish good advice, consult an old man.
Proverb

It is better to wear out than to rust out.
Proverb

Old age comes stealing on.
Proverb

There's no fool like an old fool.
Proverb

Young men think old men fools, and old men know young men to be so.
Proverb

So little done, so much to do.
CECIL JOHN RHODES (1853–1902), English colonial financier and statesman in South Africa: *Last words*

Every parting gives a foretaste of death; every coming together again a foretaste of the resurrection. This is why even people who were indifferent to each other rejoice so much if they come together again after twenty or thirty years' separation.
ARTHUR SCHOPENHAUER (1788–1860), German pessimist philosopher: *Parerga and Paralipomena, 'Further Psychological Observations'*

Jacques
All the world's a stage,
And all the men and women merely players;
They have their exits and their entrances;
And one man in his time plays many parts,
His acts being seven ages.
WILLIAM SHAKESPEARE (1564–1616), English dramatist and poet: *As You Like It, Act 2*

The pension system is only an alternative to paying a higher salary to those rendering existing services and leaving them subsequently to look after their own superannuation allowance.
SIR JOSIAH STAMP (1880–1941): *Wealth and Taxable Capacity, chapter 2*

When asked what she wanted to be remembered for
Everything.
MAE WEST (1892–1980), American stage and film actress

TRADE UNIONS

Trade unions are islands of anarchy in a sea of chaos.
ANEURIN BEVAN (1897–1960), British statesman

Not a penny off the pay,
not a second on the day.
ARTHUR COOKE (1885–1931), English trade unionist: *Slogan before miners' strike of 1926*

With all their faults, trade-unions have done more for humanity than any other organization of men that ever existed. They have done more for decency, for honesty, for education, for the betterment of the race, for the developing of character in man, than any other association of men.
CLARENCE SEWARD DARROW (1857–1938), American lawyer, reformer, and writer: *The Railroad Trainman, November 1909*

If trade unionists failed to register their protest by striking, their silence would be regarded as an admission that they acquiesced in the pre-eminence of economic forces over human welfare. Such acquiescence would be a recognition of the right of the middle classes to exploit the workers when business was flourishing and to let the workers go hungry when business was slack.
FRIEDRICH ENGELS (1820–95), German socialist leader and political philosopher: *The Condition of the Working Class in England in 1844,* chapter 9

A whole new way of life started after the dispute with the government in 1971. It seemed as if trade unions suddenly became aware of their position and their potential. Whereas in the 1960s, we in the Trade Union movement used to bemoan our inertia. I remember us complaining, 'Well, we are really passive.' 'We observe only from the sidelines.' 'We do not affect politics very much.' Now all that has changed!
LORD GORMLEY, Joseph, Lord of Ashton-in-Makefield (1917–), British trade unionist, quoted in Cary L. Cooper and Peter Hingley, *The Change Makers*

Trade unions are the only means by which workmen can protect themselves from the tyranny of those who employ them. But the moment that trade unions become tyrants in their turn they are engines for evil: they have no right to prevent people from working on any terms that they choose.
MR JUSTICE LINDLEY: *Judgment in Lyons v Wilkins, 1896*

Trade unionism has enabled skilled artisans, and even many classes of unskilled workers, to enter into negotiations with their employers

with the same gravity, self-restraint, dignity and forethought as are observed in the diplomacy of great nations. It has led them generally to recognise that a simply aggressive policy is a foolish policy, and that the chief use of military resources is to preserve an advantageous peace.
ALFRED MARSHALL (1842–1924), English classical economist: *Principles of Economics, book 6*

In the first place, trade unions are about individuals, and the right of a man to answer back to his boss.
LIONEL (LEN) MURRAY, Baron Murray of Epping Forest (1922–), British trade unionist

It is one of the characteristics of a free and democratic modern nation that it have free and independent labor unions.
FRANKLIN DELANO ROOSEVELT (1882–1945), U.S. statesman and president: *Address, Teamsters' Union convention, Washington DC, 11 September 1940*

It is essential that there should be organizations of labor. This is an era of organization. Capital organizes and therefore labor must organize.
THEODORE ROOSEVELT (1858–1919), U.S. statesman and president: *Speech, Milwaukee, 14 October 1912*

I think it's ludicrous that it takes seventeen unions to build a motor car in Britain.
LORD SCANLON, Hugh (1913–), British trade unionist: *Observer, 'Sayings of the Week', 30 July 1979*

Workers' control means the castration of the trade union movement.
ARTHUR SCARGILL (1938–), British trade unionist: *Observer, 'Sayings of 1978', 31 December 1978*

Facts show that politically independent trade unions do not exist anywhere. There have never been any. Experience and theory say that there never will be any.
LEON TROTSKY (Lev Davidovich Bronstein) (1879–1940), Russian revolutionary and Communist theorist: *Communism and Syndicalism, 1929*

WORKERS & THE PEOPLE

FISH: First In, Still Here.
Anon

Human labour is not an *end* but a *means*.
FRÉDÉRIC BASTIAT (1801–50): *Sophismes Économiques, chapter 2*

The people are the masters.
EDMUND BURKE (1729–97), British statesman, orator, and writer: *Speech on the Economical Reform, 11 February 1780*

We are all special cases.
ALBERT CAMUS (1913–60), French philosopher and writer

I am for people. I can't help it.
SIR CHARLES CHAPLIN (1889–1977),
English comedian, film actor, and
director: *Observer, 'Sayings of the Week',
28 September 1952*

Mankind is not a tribe of animals to which we owe compassion. Mankind is a club to which we owe our subscription.
G(ILBERT) K(EITH) CHESTERTON
(1874–1936), English essayist, novelist,
poet, and critic: *Daily News, 10 April 1906*

I got disappointed in human nature as well and gave it up because I found it too much like my own.
JAMES PATRICK DONLEAVY (1926–),
American-born Irish novelist: *Fairy Tales
of New York*

No man is an island, entire of itself; every man is a piece of the Continent, a part of the main.
JOHN DONNE (1573–1631), English
metaphysical poet and preacher:
Devotions, 12

Jack of all trades and master of none.
MARIA EDGEWORTH (1767–1849),
English novelist: *Popular Tales*

The world is full of willing people: some willing to work, the rest willing to let them.
ROBERT FROST (1874–1963),
American poet

We cannot safely leave politics to politicians, or political economy to college professors. The people
themselves must think, because the people alone can act.
HENRY GEORGE (1839–97), American
economist: *Social Problems*

Getting results through people is a skill that cannot be learned in the classroom.
J(EAN) PAUL GETTY (1892–1976),
American financier

I don't want any yes-men around me. I want everybody to tell me the truth even if it costs them their jobs.
SAMUEL GOLDWYN (1882–1974),
American film producer (Attributed)

Every thing in the world is purchased by labour.
DAVID HUME (1711–76), Scottish
philosopher and historian: *Essays, 'Of
Commerce'*

It is a shameful and inhuman thing to treat men as mere chattels for profit, or to regard them as simply so much muscle power.
POPE LEO XIII (Gioacchino Pecci)
(1810–1903), pope: *Rerum novarum,
15 May 1891*

Labor is prior to, and independent of, capital. Capital is only the fruit of labor, and could never have existed if labor had not first existed. Labor is the superior of capital, and deserves much the higher consideration.
ABRAHAM LINCOLN (1809–65), U.S.
statesman and president: *Message to
Congress, 3 December 1861*

You can fool some of the people all the time and all the people some of

the time; but you can't fool all the people all the time.
ABRAHAM LINCOLN (Attributed)

The power of population is indefinitely greater than the power in the earth to produce subsistence for man. Population, when unchecked, increases in a geometrical ratio. Subsistence only increases in an arithmetical ratio. A slight acquaintance with numbers will show the immensity of the first power in comparison with the second.
THOMAS ROBERT MALTHUS (1766–1834), English economist: *An Essay on the Principle of Population, chapter 1*

The people, and the people alone, are the motive force in the making of world history.
MAO TSE-TUNG (Mao Ze Dong) (1893–1976), Chinese Communist leader: *Quotations from Chairman Mao Tse-tung*

The workers have nothing to lose but their chains. They have a world to gain. Workers of the world, unite!
KARL MARX (1818–83), German founder of modern communism and, FRIEDRICH ENGELS (1820–95), German socialist leader: *The Communist Manifesto, closing words*

I've always been interested in people, but I've never liked them.
W(ILLIAM) SOMERSET MAUGHAM (1874–1965), English writer: *Observer, 'Sayings of the Week', 28 August 1949*

The bad workmen who form the majority of the operatives in many branches of industry are decidedly of opinion that bad workmen ought to receive the same wages as good.
JOHN STUART MILL (1806–73), English philosopher and economist: *On Liberty*

When white-collar people get jobs, they sell not only their time and energy, but their personalities as well. They sell by the week, or month, their smiles and their kindly gestures, and they must practice that prompt repression of resentment and aggression.
C(HARLES) WRIGHT MILLS (1916–62), American sociologist: *White Collar*

Cloth must be cheaper made, when one cards, another spins, another weaves, another draws, another dresses, another presses and packs; than when all the operations above-mentioned, were clumsily performed by the same hand.
SIR WILLIAM PETTY (1623–87), English economist: *Political Arithmetick*

A bad workman always blames his tools.
Proverb

Labour, like all other things which are purchased and sold, and which may be increased or diminished in quantity, has its natural and its market price. The natural price of labour is that price which is necessary to enable the labourers, one with another, to subsist and perpetuate their race, without either increase or diminution.
DAVID RICARDO (1772–1823), English economist: *On the Principles of Political Economy and Taxation, chapter 1*

_We_ are an indispensable team; _you_ are overmanned; _they_ are redundant.
ANTHONY SAMPSON (1926–), English journalist and biographer: *Observer, 1981*

I love mankind, it's people I can't stand.
CHARLES (MONROE) SCHULZ (1922–), American cartoonist: *Go Fly a Kite, Charlie Brown*

Hamlet
What a piece of work is a man! How noble in reason! how infinite in faculties! in form and moving, how express and admirable! in action, how like an angel! in apprehension, how like a god! the beauty of the world! the paragon of animals! And yet, to me, what is this quintessence of dust? Man delights not me – no, nor woman neither.
WILLIAM SHAKESPEARE (1564–1616), English dramatist and poet: *Hamlet, Act 2*

IT IS ABSURD TO DIVIDE PEOPLE INTO GOOD AND BAD. PEOPLE ARE EITHER CHARMING OR TEDIOUS.

You're not a man, you're a machine.
GEORGE BERNARD SHAW (1856–1950), Irish dramatist and critic: *Arms and the Man, Act 3*

People are always blaming their circumstances for what they are. I don't believe in circumstances. The people who get on in this world are the people who get up and look for the circumstances they want, and, if they can't find them, make them.
GEORGE BERNARD SHAW, *Mrs Warren's Profession*

The greatest improvement in the productive powers of labour, and the greater part of the skill, dexterity and judgement with which it is any where directed, or applied, seem to have been the effects of the division of labour.
ADAM SMITH (1723–90), Scottish economist and philosopher: *The Wealth of Nations, volume 1*

I remember your name perfectly, but I just can't think of your face.
WILLIAM ARCHIBALD SPOONER (1844–1930), English clergyman and academic (Attributed)

The really efficient laborer will be found not to crowd his day with work, but will saunter to his task surrounded by a wide halo of ease and leisure.
HENRY DAVID THOREAU (1817–62), American essayist and poet: *Journal, 1841*

You can fool too many of the people too much of the time.
JAMES (GROVER) THURBER (1894–1961), American humorist and cartoonist: *The Thurber Carnival*

Lord Darlington
It is absurd to divide people into good and bad. People are either charming or tedious.
OSCAR WILDE (1856–1900), Irish poet, dramatist, and wit: *Lady Windermere's Fan, Act 1*

TIME

Sometimes life seems to be a battle against time.
There are often too many things to fit into the day. The quotations here
remind us that 'Time is money', but their scope is much wider than this.
We see what can be learnt from the past, and also how to plan for – and cope
with – the future, while not forgetting John Maynard Keynes' famous quote,
'In the long run we are all dead.' And since our time isn't just spent working, we
consider how we occupy our time off, at home or on holiday . . .
although, as Noël Coward puts it, 'Work is much more fun than fun.'

FUTURE & PLANNING

Forecasting is very difficult,
especially if it is about the future.
Anon

The future is not what it was.
Anon

The future is . . . black.
JAMES (ARTHUR) BALDWIN (1924–),
American novelist and essayist: Observer,
'Sayings of the Week', 25 August 1963

In developing our industrial
strategy for the period ahead, we
have had the benefit of much
experience. Almost everything has
been tried at least once.
ANTHONY (NEIL) WEDGWOOD BENN
(1925–), English politician: Observer,
'Sayings of the Week', 17 March 1974

Future
That period of time in which our
affairs prosper, our friends are true
and our happiness is assured.
AMBROSE (GWINETT) BIERCE (1842–
?1914), American journalist and
humorist: The Devil's Dictionary

You can never plan the future by the
past.
EDMUND BURKE (1729–97), British
statesman, orator, and writer: Letter to a
Member of the National Assembly

A trend is a trend is a trend
But the question is, will it bend?
Will it alter its course
Through some unforeseen force
And come to a premature end?
SIR ALEC CAIRNCROSS (1911–),
Scottish economist: Economic Journal,
December 1969, 'Economic Forecasting'

You never reach the promised land. You can march towards it.
(LEONARD) JAMES CALLAGHAN (1912–), English statesman and prime minister: *Observer, 'Sayings of 1978', 31 December 1978*

Red Queen
The rule is, jam tomorrow and jam yesterday – but never jam today.
LEWIS CARROLL (Charles Lutwidge Dodgson) (1832–98), English writer and mathematician: *Through the Looking-Glass, chapter 5*

It is a mistake to look too far ahead. Only one link of the chain of destiny can be handled at a time.
SIR WINSTON LEONARD SPENCER CHURCHILL (1874–1965), English statesman, writer, and prime minister: *Speech, House of Commons, 27 February 1945*

It is always wise to look ahead, but difficult to look farther than you can see.
SIR WINSTON LEONARD SPENCER CHURCHILL, *Observer, 'Sayings of the Week', 27 July 1952*

There is a perverse failure to make the actual demand of yesterday a basis for the production of today, or to make the demand of last year a basis for the production of this year.
JOHN BATES CLARK (1847–1938), American economist and professor, K. Rodbertus, *Overproduction and Crises*

Study the past, if you would divine the future.
CONFUCIUS (Kong Zi) (551–479 BC), Chinese philosopher: *Analects*

I never think of the future. It comes soon enough.
ALBERT EINSTEIN (1879–1955), German-Swiss-American physicist: *Interview, 1930*

If a man carefully examine his thoughts he will be surprised to find how much he lives in the future. His well-being is always ahead.
RALPH WALDO EMERSON (1803–82), American poet, essayist, and philosopher: *Journals, 1827*

Remember that the future is neither ours nor wholly not ours, so that we may neither count on it as sure to come nor abandon hope of it as certain not to be.
EPICURUS (341–270 BC), Greek philosopher: *Letter to Menoeceus*

The danger of the past was that men became slaves. The danger of the future is that men may become robots.
ERICH FROMM (1900–80), German-born American psychoanalyst and philosopher: *The Sane Society*

He that fears not the future may enjoy the present.
THOMAS FULLER (1654–1734), English physician, writer, and compiler: *Gnomologia*

You cannot fight against the future. Time is on our side.
WILLIAM EWART GLADSTONE (1809–98), British statesman and prime minister: *Speech on Reform Bill, 1866*

Excessive forethought and too great solicitude for the future are often productive of misfortune; for the affairs of the world are subject to so many accidents that seldom do things turn out as even the wisest predicted; and whoever refuses to take advantage of present good from fear of future danger, provided the danger be not certain and near, often discovers to his annoyance and disgrace that he has lost opportunities full of profit and glory, from dread of dangers which have turned out to be wholly imaginary.
FRANCESCO GUICCIARDINI (1483–1540), Florentine statesman and historian: *Storia d'Italia*

The best preparation for good work tomorrow is to do good work today.
ELBERT (GREEN) HUBBARD (1856–1915), American businessman, writer, and printer: *The Note Book*

The world community can continue to pursue the arms race and build ever-larger and more deadly weapons, or it can shift and move deliberately and urgently towards the provision of the basic needs of our global family. It cannot do both. Either we invest in arms and death, or we invest in life and the future development of the people of the world.
CARDINAL (GEORGE) BASIL HUME (1923–), English Roman Catholic Benedictine monk, archbishop of Westminster

I like the dreams of the future better than the history of the past.
THOMAS JEFFERSON (1743–1826), U.S. statesman and president: *Letter to John Adams*

The importance of money essentially flows from its being a link between the present and the future.
JOHN MAYNARD KEYNES (1883–1946), English economist: *The General Theory of Employment, Interest and Money, book 5*

This *long run* is a misleading guide to current affairs. *In the long run* we are all dead. Economists set themselves too easy, too useless a task if in tempestuous seasons they can only tell us that when the storm is long past the ocean is flat again.
JOHN MAYNARD KEYNES, *A Tract on Monetary Reform, chapter 3*

The earth we abuse and the living things we kill will, in the end, take their revenge; for in exploiting their presence we are diminishing our future.
MARYA MANNES (1904–), American essayist and journalist: *More in Anger*

We are all in favour of the future.
REGINALD MAUDLING (1917–79), British politician: *Observer, 'Sayings of 1964', 27 December 1964*

If you want a picture of the future, imagine a boot stamping on the human face – forever.
GEORGE ORWELL (Eric Arthur Blair) (1903–50), English novelist and essayist

The wise man looks ahead.
Proverb

He who plants a walnut tree expects
not to eat of the fruit.
Proverb

He who can see three days ahead
will be rich for three thousand years.
Japanese proverb

The only limit to our realization of
tomorrow will be our doubts of
today.
FRANKLIN DELANO ROOSEVELT
(1882–1945), U.S. statesman and
president

Looking forward into an empty year
strikes one with a certain awe,
because one finds therein no
recognition. The years behind have
a friendly aspect, and they are
warmed by the fires we have
kindled, and all their echoes are the
echoes of our own voices.
ALEXANDER SMITH (1830–67),
Scottish poet and essayist: Dreamthorp

I consider the world as made for
me, not me for the world. It is my
maxim therefore to enjoy it while I
can, and let futurity shift for itself.
TOBIAS GEORGE SMOLLETT (1721–71),
British novelist: Roderick Random,
chapter 45

Future shock is the disorientation
that affects an individual, a corporation or a country when he or it is
overwhelmed by change and the
prospect of change. It is the
consequence of having to make too
many decisions about too many
new and unfamiliar problems in too
short a time. Future shock is more
than a metaphor. It is a form of
personal and social breakdown. We
are in collision with tomorrow.
Future shock has arrived.
ALVIN TOFFLER (1928–), American
academic: Observer, 1972

The Shape of Things to Come.
H(ERBERT) G(EORGE) WELLS (1866–
1946), English novelist, journalist, and
social philosopher: Title of book

HISTORY

History is the sum total of the
things that could have been avoided.
KONRAD ADENAUER (1876–1967),
Chancellor of West Germany

History
An account mostly false, of events
mostly unimportant, which are
brought about by rulers mostly
knaves, and soldiers mostly fools.
AMBROSE (GWINETT) BIERCE (1842–
?1914), American journalist and
humorist: The Devil's Dictionary

History is philosophy teaching by
examples.
DIONYSIUS OF HALICARNASSUS
(?40–8 BC), Greek historian and
rhetorician: Ars Rhetorica

The materialist conception of
history starts from the proposition
that the production of the means to
support human life and, next to
production, the exchange of things

produced, is the basis of all social structure ... From this point of view the final causes of all social changes and political revolutions are to be sought ... in changes in the modes of production and exchange.
FRIEDRICH ENGELS (1820–95), German socialist leader and political philosopher: *Socialism, Utopian and Scientific*

History is more or less bunk. It's tradition. We don't want tradition. We want to live in the present and the only history that is worth a tinker's dam is the history we make today.
HENRY FORD (1863–1947), American car manufacturer, quoted in *Chicago Tribune, 1916*

The marriage of economics and history produces a hybrid which regularly combines the inadequacies of both.
JOHN KENNETH GALBRAITH (1908–), Canadian-born American economist, diplomat, and writer: *The Liberal Hour*

We have all passed a lot of water since then.
SAMUEL GOLDWYN (1882–1974), American film producer, quoted in Philip French, *The Movie Moguls*

What experience and history teach is this – that people and governments never have learned anything from history, or acted on principles deduced from it.
GEORG WILHELM FRIEDRICH HEGEL (1770–1831), German philosopher: *Philosophy of History*

What we know of the past is mostly not worth knowing. What is worth knowing is mostly uncertain.
Events in the past may roughly be divided into those which probably never happened and those which do not matter.
WILLIAM RALPH INGE (1860–1954), English theologian: *Assessments and Anticipations, 'Prognostications'*

It takes a great deal of history to produce a little literature.
HENRY JAMES (1843–1916), American-born British novelist: *Life of Nathaniel Hawthorne, chapter 1*

History, Stephen said, is a nightmare from which I am trying to awake.
JAMES (AUGUSTINE ALOYSIUS) JOYCE (1882–1941), Irish novelist and short-story writer: *Ulysses*

The great events of history are often due to secular changes in the growth of population and other fundamental economic causes, which, escaping by their gradual character the notice of contemporary observers, are attributed to the follies of statesmen or the fanaticism of atheists.
JOHN MAYNARD KEYNES (1883–1946), English economist: *The Economic Consequences of the Peace, chapter 2*

History repeats itself.
Proverb

Those who cannot remember the past are condemned to repeat it.
GEORGE SANTAYANA (1863–1952), American philosopher and poet: *The Life of Reason*

History gets thicker as it approaches recent times.
A(LAN) J(OHN) P(ERCIVALE) TAYLOR (1906–), English historian: *English History 1914–1945*

Anything but history, for history must be false.
SIR ROBERT WALPOLE, 1st Earl of Orford (1676–1745), English statesman: *Walpoliana*

Honesty is the best policy, but he who acts on that principle is not an honest man.
BISHOP RICHARD WHATELY (1787–1863): *Apothegms*

HOLIDAYS & LEISURE

Sunday clears away the rust of the whole week.
JOSEPH ADDISON (1672–1719), English essayist and dramatist: *Spectator, 9 July 1711*

There can be no high civilization where there is not ample leisure.
HENRY WARD BEECHER (1813–87), American clergyman, editor, and writer: *Proverbs from Plymouth Pulpit*

Life's too short for chess.
HENRY JAMES BYRON (1834–84), English dramatist: *Our Boys, Act 1*

A single sentence will suffice for modern man: he fornicated and read the papers.
ALBERT CAMUS (1913–60), French philosopher and writer: *The Fall*

Work is much more fun than fun.
SIR NOËL (PIERCE) COWARD (1899–1973), English actor and dramatist: *Observer, 'Sayings of the Week', 21 June 1963*

Sunburn is very becoming – but only when it is even – one must be careful not to look like a mixed grill.
SIR NOËL (PIERCE) COWARD, *The Lido Beach*

What is this life if, full of care, We have no time to stand and stare?
W(ILLIAM) H(ENRY) DAVIES (1871–1940), Welsh-born English poet: *Leisure*

Rat
There is nothing – absolutely nothing – half so much worth doing as simply messing about in boats.
KENNETH GRAHAME (1859–1932), Scottish writer: *The Wind in the Willows*, chapter 1

Of cricket
It's more than a game. It's an institution.
THOMAS HUGHES (1822–96), English novelist: *Tom Brown's Schooldays*

Summer afternoon – summer afternoon; to me those have always been the two most beautiful words in the English language.
HENRY JAMES (1843–1916), American-born British novelist: *A Backward Glance (Edith Wharton)*, chapter 10

Holidays are often overrated disturbances of routine, costly and uncomfortable, and they usually need another holiday to correct their ravages.
E(DWARD) V(ERRALL) LUCAS (1868–1938), English novelist, poet, and essayist

I must confess that I am interested in leisure in the same way that a poor man is interested in money.
PRINCE PHILIP, Duke of Edinburgh (1921–)

A good holiday is one spent among people whose notions of time are vaguer than yours.
J(OHN) B(OYNTON) PRIESTLEY (1894–1984), English author

Idle folks have the least leisure.
Proverb

To be able to fill leisure intelligently is the last product of civilization.
BERTRAND (ARTHUR WILLIAM) RUSSELL, 3rd Earl Russell (1872–1970), English philosopher and mathematician: The Conquest of Happiness

Prince
If all the year were playing holidays, To sport would be as tedious as to work.
WILLIAM SHAKESPEARE (1564–1616), English dramatist and poet: Henry the Fourth, Part One, Act 1

What the banker sighs for, the meanest clown may have, – leisure and a quiet mind.
HENRY DAVID THOREAU (1817–62), American essayist and poet: Journal, 18 January 1841

HOME & FAMILY LIFE

You are a king by your own fire-side, as much as any monarch in his throne.
MIGUEL DE CERVANTES (SAAVEDRA) (1547–1616), Spanish writer: Don Quixote

A man's house is his castle.
SIR EDWARD COKE (1552–1634), English jurist: Institutes

A house is a machine for living in.
(CHARLES ÉDOUARD JEANNERET) LE CORBUSIER (1887–1965), Swiss architect: Towards an architecture

Accidents will happen in the best-regulated families.
CHARLES (JOHN HUFFAM) DICKENS (1812–70), English novelist: David Copperfield

A man builds a fine house; and now he has a master, and a task for life; he is to furnish, watch, show it, and keep it in repair the rest of his days.
RALPH WALDO EMERSON (1803–82), American poet, essayist, and philosopher: Society and Solitude

Blood's thicker than water, and when one's in trouble
Best to seek out a relative's open arms.
EURIPIDES (?480–406 BC), Greek tragic dramatist: Andromache

Marry, and with luck
It may go well. But when a marriage
fails
Then those who marry live at home
in hell.
EURIPIDES, *Orestes*

Charity begins at home, but should
not end there.
THOMAS FULLER (1654–1734), English
physician, writer, and compiler:
Gnomologia

What children hear at home soon
flies abroad.
THOMAS FULLER, *as above*

What's the good of a home, if you
are never in it?
GEORGE GROSSMITH (1847–1912),
English comedian and singer and
WALTER WEEDON GROSSMITH
(1854–1919), his brother: *The Diary of
a Nobody, chapter 1*

YOU ARE A KING BY YOUR OWN FIRE-SIDE, AS MUCH AS ANY MONARCH IN HIS
THRONE.

To be happy at home is the ultimate result of all ambition, the end to which every enterprise and labour tends, and of which every desire prompts the prosecution.
SAMUEL JOHNSON (1709–84), English lexicographer, essayist, and poet: *The Rambler*

There is no more lovely, friendly and charming relationship, communion or company than a good marriage.
MARTIN LUTHER (1483–1546), German leader of Protestant Reformation: *Table Talk*

There's no place like home.
JOHN HOWARD PAYNE (1791–1852), American writer: *Home sweet home*

Home is the girl's prison and the woman's workhouse.
GEORGE BERNARD SHAW (1856–1950), Irish dramatist and critic: *Man and Superman, Maxims for Revolutionists*

Everybody's always talking about people breaking into houses ... but there are more people in the world who want to break out of houses.
THORNTON (NIVEN) WILDER (1897–1975), American novelist and playwright: *The Matchmaker*

TIME

To choose time is to save time.
FRANCIS BACON, 1st Baron Verulam, Viscount St Albans (1561–1626), English writer, philosopher, and statesman: *Essays, 'Of Dispatch'*

Time is the greatest innovator.
FRANCIS BACON, *as above, 'Of Innovations'*

Year
A period of three hundred and sixty-five disappointments.
AMBROSE (GWINETT) BIERCE (1842–?1914), American journalist and humorist: *The Devil's Dictionary*

It is an undoubted truth, that the less one has to do, the less time one finds to do it in. One yawns, one procrastinates, one can do it when one will, and therefore one seldom does it at all.
LORD CHESTERFIELD, Philip Dormer Stanhope, 4th Earl of (1694–1773), English statesman and writer

There is time enough for everything in the course of the day if you do but one thing at once; but there is not time enough in the year if you will do two things at a time.
LORD CHESTERFIELD, *Letters to his son, 14 April 1747*

I recommend you to take care of the minutes; for hours will take care of themselves.
LORD CHESTERFIELD, *as above, 6 November 1747*

One of the great disadvantages of hurry is that it takes such a long time.
G(ILBERT) K(EITH) CHESTERTON (1874–1936), English essayist, novelist, poet, and critic: *All Things Considered*

I felt as if I were walking with destiny, and that all my past life had been but a preparation for this hour and this trial.
SIR WINSTON LEONARD SPENCER CHURCHILL (1874–1965), English statesman, writer, and prime minister: *The Gathering Storm, chapter 38*

Time is a great manager: it arranges things well.
PIERRE CORNEILLE (1606–84), French tragic dramatist: *Sertorius*

The supply of time is totally inelastic. Time is totally perishable and cannot be stored. Time is totally irreplaceable . . . there is no substitute for time.
PETER F. DRUCKER (1909–), American management expert: *The Effective Manager*

All my possessions for a moment of time.
ELIZABETH I (1533–1603), Queen of England: *Last words*

Can anybody remember when the times were not hard, and money not scarce?
RALPH WALDO EMERSON (1803–82), American poet, essayist, and philosopher: *Society and Solitude, 'Works and Days'*

Lost time is never found again.
BENJAMIN FRANKLIN (1706–90), American statesman, scientist, and author: *Poor Richard's Almanac*

Remember that time is money.
BENJAMIN FRANKLIN, *Advice to Young Tradesmen*

Do not squander time, for that is the stuff life is made of.
BENJAMIN FRANKLIN, *The Way to Wealth*

Most people work the greater part of their time for a mere living; and the little freedom which remains to them so troubles them that they use every means of getting rid of it.
JOHANN WOLFGANG VON GOETHE (1749–1832), German poet, scientist, and writer: *The Sorrows of Young Werther*

The hours we pass with happy prospects in view are more pleasing than those crowned with fruition.
OLIVER GOLDSMITH (?1728–74), Irish dramatist, novelist, and poet: *The Hermit*

Time goes by; reputation increases, ability declines.
DAG HAMMARSKJÖLD (1905–61), Swedish statesman and secretary-general of the United Nations: *Markings, '1945–1949: Towards new shores –?'*

Old time, in whose banks we deposit our notes,
Is a miser who always wants guineas for groats;
He keeps all his customers still in arrears
By lending them minutes and charging them years.
OLIVER WENDELL HOLMES, SR (1809–94), American physician, professor, and author: *Our Banker*

Carpe diem.
Seize the day.
HORACE (Quintus Horatius Flaccus) (65–8 BC), Roman poet and satirist: *Ars Poetica, I:11:8*

We must use time as a tool not as a couch.
JOHN FITZGERALD KENNEDY (1917–63), U.S. statesman and president: *Observer*, 'Sayings of the Week', *10 December 1961*

Those who make the worst use of their time are the first to complain of its brevity.
JEAN DE LA BRUYÈRE (1645–96), French moralist: *Characters*

Lives of great men all remind us We can make our lives sublime. And, departing, leave behind us Footprints on the sands of time.
HENRY WADSWORTH LONGFELLOW (1807–82), American poet and translator: *A Psalm of Life*

Time has no divisions to mark its passage, there is never a thunderstorm or blare of trumpets to announce the beginning of a new month or year. Even when a new century begins it is only we mortals who ring bells and fire off pistols.
THOMAS MANN (1875–1955), German novelist and essayist: *The Magic Mountain*

Time . . . is the centre of the chief difficulty of almost every economic problem.
ALFRED MARSHALL (1842–1924), English classical economist: *Principles of Economics*

Tempus fugit.
Time flies.
OVID (Publius Ovidius Naso) (43BC–?17AD), Roman poet: *Fasti*

Lose an hour in the morning and you'll be all day hunting for it.
Proverb

Punctuality is the soul of business.
Proverb

Take time by the forelock.
Proverb

The early bird catches the worm.
Proverb

There is a time and place for everything.
Proverb

Time and tide wait for no man.
Proverb

Time is money.
Proverb

Time lost cannot be recalled.
Proverb

Time will tell.
Proverb

What greater crime than loss of time?
Proverb

Who waits for time, loses time.
Proverb

Half our life is spent trying to find something to do with the time we have rushed through life trying to save.
WILL(IAM PENN ADAIR) ROGERS (1879–1935), American actor and humorist: *The Autobiography of Will Rogers*

We burn daylight.
WILLIAM SHAKESPEARE (1564–1616),
English dramatist and poet: *The Merry
Wives of Windsor, Act 2*

**Better three hours too soon than a
minute too late.**
WILLIAM SHAKESPEARE, *as above*

Macbeth
**Tomorrow, and tomorrow, and
tomorrow,
Creeps in this petty pace from day
to day
To the last syllable of recorded time,
And all our yesterdays have lighted
fools
The way to dusty death. Out, out,
brief candle!
Life's but a walking shadow, a poor
player,
That struts and frets his hour upon
the stage,
And then is heard no more; it is a
tale
Told by an idiot, full of sound and
fury,
Signifying nothing.**
WILLIAM SHAKESPEARE, *Macbeth, Act 5*

**Time's the king of men,
He's both their parent, and he is
their grave,
And gives them what he will, not
what they crave.**
WILLIAM SHAKESPEARE, *Pericles, Act 2*

**If Winter comes, can Spring be far
behind?**
PERCY BYSSHE SHELLEY (1792–1822),
English poet: *Ode to the West Wind*

**Time: that which man is always
trying to kill, but which ends in
killing him.**
HERBERT SPENCER (1820–1903),
English philosopher: *Definitions*

***Fugit irreparabile tempus.*
When time flies it cannot be
recalled.**
VIRGIL (Publius Vergilius Maro) (70–19
BC), Roman poet: *Georgics*

**He was always late on principle, his
principle being that punctuality is
the thief of time.**
OSCAR WILDE (1856–1900), Irish poet,
dramatist, and wit: *The Picture of Dorian
Gray*

Time is waste of money.
OSCAR WILDE, *Phrases and Philosophies
for the Use of the Young*

Procrastination is the thief of time.
EDWARD YOUNG (1683–1765), English
poet and dramatist: *Night Thoughts*

BUSINESS FACTS OF LIFE

The quotations in this section reveal differing attempts to come to terms with such realities of life as failure, poverty, bankruptcy, debt, and unemployment. On the one hand we see an approach that looks objectively at the problems, trying to find a solution, for example the Arabic proverb 'Man learns little from success, but much from failure.' On the other hand there's an approach that tries to raise morale by touches of gentle humour – for example Errol Flynn's 'If there's anyone listening to whom I owe money, I'm prepared to forget it if you are.'

BANKRUPTCY

A beggar can never be bankrupt.
JOHN CLARKE (1609–76), English writer and pioneer settler of Rhode Island: *Paroemiologia Anglo-Latina*

Micawber
Annual income twenty pounds, annual expenditure nineteen nineteen six, result happiness. Annual income twenty pounds, annual expenditure twenty pounds ought and six, result misery.
CHARLES (JOHN HUFFAM) DICKENS (1812–70), English novelist: *David Copperfield, chapter 12*

It has been long my deliberate judgment that all bankrupts, of whatsoever denomination, civil or religious, ought to be hanged.
CHARLES (ELIA) LAMB (1775–1834), English essayist: *Letter to Bernard Barton, 8 December 1829*

If the nation is living within its income its credit is good. If in some crisis it lives beyond its income for a year or two it can usually borrow temporarily on reasonable terms. But if, like the spendthrift, it throws discretion to the winds, is willing to make no sacrifice at all in spending, extends its taxing up to the limit of the people's power to pay, and continues to pile up deficits, it is on the road to bankruptcy.
FRANKLIN DELANO ROOSEVELT (1882–1945), U.S. statesman and president: *Speech, Pittsburgh, 19 October 1932*

All decent people live beyond their incomes nowadays, and those who aren't respectable live beyond other people's. A few gifted individuals manage to do both.
SAKI (Hector Hugh Munro) (1870–1916), English novelist and short-story writer: *The Match Maker*

Solvency is entirely a matter of temperament and not of income.
LOGAN PEARSALL SMITH (1865–1946), American-born English man of letters: *All Trivia*

He was a gentleman who was generally spoken of as having nothing a-year, paid quarterly.
ROBERT SMITH SURTEES (1803–64), English sporting writer: *Mr Sponge's Sporting Tour, chapter 24*

CRIME

I think crime pays. The hours are good, you travel a lot.
WOODY ALLEN (Allen Stewart Konigsberg) (1935–), American film comedian, screenwriter, and director: *Take the Money and Run*

Poverty is the parent of revolution and crime.
ARISTOTLE (348–322 BC), Greek philosopher and scientist: *Politics*

Be sure your sin will find you out.
The Bible, Authorized (King James) Version, Numbers 32:23

A crime . . . is an act committed or omitted in violation of a public law either forbidding or commanding it.
SIR WILLIAM BLACKSTONE (1723–80), English jurist: *Commentaries on the Laws of England*

How many crimes committed merely because their authors could not endure being wrong!
ALBERT CAMUS (1913–60), French philosopher and writer: *The Fall*

Stolen sweets are best.
COLLEY CIBBER (1671–1757), English actor, dramatist, and poet laureate: *The Rival Fools*

Of Professor Moriarty
He is the Napoleon of crime.
SIR ARTHUR CONAN DOYLE (1859–1930), English writer: *The Final Problem*

No man who commits a crime in secret can ever be sure that he will not be detected, even though he has escaped 10,000 times in the past.
EPICURUS (341–270 BC), Greek philosopher: *Aphorisms*

There are three ways by which an individual can get wealth – by work, by gift, and by theft. And, clearly, the reason why the workers get so little is that the beggars and thieves get so much.
HENRY GEORGE (1839–97), American economist: *Social Problems*

Mikado
My object all sublime
I shall achieve in time –
To let the punishment fit
the crime –
The punishment fit the crime.
SIR WILLIAM SCHWENK GILBERT
(1836–1911), English parodist and
librettist: *The Mikado, Act 2*

Men are not hanged for stealing
Horses, but that Horses may not be
stolen.
HALIFAX, 1st Marquis of, Sir George
Savile (1633–95), English statesman,
writer, and orator: *Political Thoughts and*
Reflections: Of Punishment

I am not a crook.
RICHARD MILHOUS NIXON (1913–),
U.S. politician and president: *Remark,*
17 November 1973

Property is theft.
PIERRE JOSEPH PROUDHON (1809–
65), French political theorist: *Qu'est-ce*
que la propriété?, chapter 1

Crime is a logical extension of the
sort of behavior that is often
considered perfectly respectable in
legitimate business.
ROBERT RICE (1916–), American
criminologist: *The Business of Crime*

Crime pays.
Saying

The faults of the burglar are the
qualities of the financier.
GEORGE BERNARD SHAW (1856–
1950), Irish dramatist and critic: *Major*
Barbara

A crowded police court docket is
the surest of all signs that trade is
brisk and money plenty.
MARK TWAIN (Samuel Langhorne
Clemens) (1835–1910), American
novelist and humorist: *Roughing it*

I came to the conclusion many years
ago that almost all crime is due to
the repressed desire for aesthetic
expression.
EVELYN (ARTHUR ST JOHN) WAUGH
(1903–66), English novelist: *Decline and*
Fall

DEBT

It is better to pay a creditor than to
give to a friend.
ARISTOTLE (384–322 BC), Greek
philosopher and scientist: *Nicomachean*
Ethics

Debt
An ingenious substitute for the
chain and whip of the slave-driver.
AMBROSE (GWINETT) BIERCE (1842–
?1914), American journalist and
humorist: *The Devil's Dictionary*

Always pay; for first or last you
must pay your entire debt.
RALPH WALDO EMERSON (1803–82),
American poet, essayist, and philosopher:
Essays, 'Compensation'

If there's anyone listening to whom
I owe *money*. I'm prepared to forget
it if you are.
ERROL FLYNN (1909–59), American
film star

Sins and debts are always more than we think them to be.
THOMAS FULLER (1654–1734), English physician, writer, and compiler: *Gnomologia*

Debt is the worst poverty.
THOMAS FULLER, *as above*

Small debts are like small shot; they are rattling on every side, and can scarcely be escaped without a wound: great debts are like cannon; of loud noise, but little danger.
SAMUEL JOHNSON (1709–84), English lexicographer, essayist, and poet: *Letter to Joseph Simpson, 1759*

Debt is better than death.
Proverb

Say nothing of my debts unless you mean to pay them.
Proverb

The debtor is always in the wrong.
Proverb

A promise made is a debt unpaid.
ROBERT W(ILLIAM) SERVICE (1874–1958), English-born Canadian writer: *The Cremation of Sam McGee*

Stephano
He that dies pays all debts.
WILLIAM SHAKESPEARE (1564–1616), English dramatist and poet: *The Tempest, Act 3*

EQUALITY & INEQUALITY

Equality is a myth – women are better.
Anon

When quarrels and complaints arise, it is when people who are equal have not got equal shares, or vice versa.
ARISTOTLE (384–322 BC), Greek philosopher and scientist: *Nicomachean Ethics*

'The removal of all social and political inequalities' is a very dubious phrase with which to replace 'the removal of all class distinctions'. There will always be *certain* inequalities in the standard of life in different countries, provinces and places. They can be reduced to a minimum, but they can never be removed.
FRIEDRICH ENGELS (1820–95), German socialist leader and political philosopher: *Letter to August Bebel, 28 March 1875*

Just as the modern mass production requires the standardization of commodities, so the social process requires standardization of man, and this standardization is called 'equality'.
ERICH FROMM (1900–80), German-born American psychoanalyst and philosopher: *The Art of Loving, chapter 2*

Though all men were made of one metal, yet they were not cast all in the same mould.
THOMAS FULLER (1654–1734), English physician, writer, and compiler: *Gnomologia*

The grocery store is the great equalizer where mankind comes to grips with the facts of life like toilet tissue.
JOSEPH GOLDBERG (1915–), American grocer, quoted in Jonathon Green, *A Dictionary of Contemporary Quotations*

That all men are equal is a proposition to which, at ordinary times, no sane individual has ever given his assent.
ALDOUS (LEONARD) HUXLEY (1894–1963), English novelist and essayist: *Proper Studies*

We hold these truths to be self-evident: that all men are created equal; that they are endowed by their Creator with inalienable rights; that among these are life, liberty, and the pursuit of happiness.
THOMAS JEFFERSON (1743–1826), U.S. statesman and president: *The Declaration of Independence*

So far is it from being true that men are naturally equal, that no two people can be half an hour together, but one shall acquire an evident superiority over the other.
SAMUEL JOHNSON (1709–84), English lexicographer, essayist, and poet: Boswell, *Life of Johnson*

We need inequality in order to eliminate poverty.
SIR KEITH JOSEPH (1918–), British politician, quoted in Audrey Hilton, *This England, 74–78*

All of us do not have equal talent, but all of us should have an equal opportunity to develop our talents.
JOHN FITZGERALD KENNEDY (1917–63), U.S. statesman and president: *Speech, 1963*

All animals are equal but some animals are more equal than others.
GEORGE ORWELL (Eric Arthur Blair) (1903–50), English novelist and essayist: *Animal Farm, chapter 10*

A cat may look at a king.
Proverb

At a round table, there's no dispute of place.
Proverb

The only real equality is in the cemetery.
Proverb

The nature of things continually tends to the destruction of equality.
JEAN-JACQUES ROUSSEAU (1712–78), Swiss-born French philosopher and writer: *Du contrat social*

The yearning after equality is the offspring of covetousness, and there is no possible plan for satisfying that yearning which can do aught else than rob A to give to B; consequently all such plans nourish some of the meanest vices

of human nature, waste capital, and overthrow civilization.
WILLIAM SUMNER (1840–1910), American political economist and sociologist: *What Social Classes Owe to Each Other*

Inequality . . . leads to the misdirection of production. For, since the demand of one income of £50,000 is as powerful a magnet as the demand of 500 incomes of £100, it diverts energy from the creation of wealth to the multiplication of luxuries.
R(ICHARD) H(ENRY) TAWNEY (1880–1962), English economic historian: *The Acquisitive Society*

So far as the natural law is concerned, all men are equal.
ULPIAM (Domitius Ulpianus) (ca. 170–ca. 228 AD), Roman jurist: *Liber singularis regularum*

Everybody should have an equal chance – but they shouldn't have a flying start.
SIR (JAMES) HAROLD WILSON, Lord Wilson of Rievaulx (1916–), English statesman and prime minister: *Observer, 'Sayings of the Year', 1963*

FAILURE

There is much to be said for failure. It is more interesting than success.
SIR MAX BEERBOHM (1872–1956), English writer and caricaturist: *Mainly on the Air, 'A Small Boy Seeing Giants'*

The world is made of people who never quite get into the first team and who just miss the prizes at the flower show.
JACOB BRONOWSKI (1908–74), English scientist and writer: *The Face of Violence*, chapter 6

He that is down needs fear no fall.
JOHN BUNYAN (1628–88), English preacher and writer: *Pilgrim's Progress*

What worries me is that we are going to end up as a fourth-rate country.
CHARLES, Prince of Wales (1948–), heir to throne of United Kingdom: *Observer, 'Sayings of the Year', 29 December 1985*

Would you ever buy a used car from me?
JOHN DE LOREAN (1924–) Motor-car entrepreneur: *Observer, 'Sayings of the Year', 30 December 1984*

If at first you don't succeed, try again. Then quit. No use being a damn fool about it.
WILLIAM CLAUDE FIELDS (William Claude Dukenfield) (1880–1946), American actor and comedian

A useless life is an early death.
JOHANN WOLFGANG VON GOETHE (1749–1832), German poet, scientist, and writer: *Iphigenie*

It's a good thing to make mistakes so long as you're found out quickly.
JOHN MAYNARD KEYNES (1883–1946), English economist (Attributed)

Men fall from great fortune because of the same shortcomings that led to their rise.
JEAN DE LA BRUYÈRE (1645–96), French moralist: *Characters*

If we had no faults of our own, we would not take so much pleasure in noticing those of others.
FRANÇOIS LA ROCHEFOUCAULD, Duc de La Rochefoucauld (1613–80), French writer: *Reflections*

Great men too make mistakes, and many among them do it so often that one is almost tempted to call them little men.
GEORG CHRISTOPH LICHTENBERG (1742–99), German physicist and writer: *Aphorisms*

Many of the job failures, nervous breakdowns, and 'battles with the bottle' almost certainly have their causes in vocational misplacement

IF WE HAD NO FAULTS OF OUR OWN, WE WOULD NOT TAKE SO MUCH PLEASURE IN NOTICING THOSE OF OTHERS.

and subsequent mishandling by well-intentioned but often unqualified personnel people.
ROBERT N. McMURRY (1901–), *Harvard Business Review, 1965, 'Clear Communications for Chief Executives'*

Failure makes people bitter and cruel. Success improves the character of the man.
W(ILLIAM) SOMERSET MAUGHAM (1874–1965), English writer: *The Summing Up*

Of a bankrupt
Failure has gone to his head.
WILSON MIZNER (1876–1933), American dramatist (Attributed)

The man who makes no mistakes does not usually make anything.
EDWARD JOHN PHELPS (1822–1900), American lawyer and diplomat: *Speech, Mansion House, London, 24 January 1899*

To err is human, to forgive, divine.
ALEXANDER POPE (1688–1744), English poet and satirist: *An Essay on Criticism*

A miss is as good as a mile.
Proverb

Failure teaches success.
Proverb

You can't win them all.
Proverb

You win some, you lose some.
Proverb

Man learns little from success, but much from failure.
Arabic proverb

The drowning man is not troubled by rain.
Persian proverb

There is no formula for success. But there is a formula for failure, and that is trying to please everybody.
NICHOLAS RAY, American film director, quoted in Jonathon Green, *A Dictionary of Contemporary Quotations*

Fortune's not content with knocking a man down; she sends him spinning head over heels, crash upon crash.
MARCUS or LUCIUS ANNAEUS SENECA (The Elder) (?55 BC–?39 AD), Roman writer on oratory and history: *Letters to Lucilius*

I would prefer even to fail with honour than win by cheating.
SOPHOCLES (?496–406 BC), Greek dramatist: *Philoctetes*

Experience is the name everyone gives to their mistakes.
OSCAR WILDE (1856–1900), Irish poet, dramatist, and wit: *Lady Windermere's Fan*

THE HAVES & THE HAVE-NOTS

The Third World is not a reality, but an ideology.
HANNAH ARENDT (1906–75), American writer: *On Violence*

The unfortunate need people who will be kind to them; the prosperous need people to be kind to.
ARISTOTLE (384–322 BC), Greek philosopher and scientist: *Nicomachean Ethics*

You cannot sift out the poor from the community. The poor are indispensable to the rich.
HENRY WARD BEECHER (1813–87), American clergyman, editor, and writer: *Proverbs from Plymouth Pulpit*

There are only two families in the world, my old grandmother used to say, The *Haves* and the *Have-Nots*.
MIGUEL DE CERVANTES (SAAVEDRA) (1547–1616), Spanish writer: *Don Quixote*

The rich man may never get into heaven, but the pauper is already serving his term in hell.
ALEXANDER CHASE (1926–), American journalist: *Perspectives*

The honest poor can sometimes forget poverty. The honest rich can never forget it.
G(ILBERT) K(EITH) CHESTERTON (1874–1936), English essayist, novelist, poet, and critic: *All Things Considered, 'Cockneys and Their Jokes'*

If rich, it is easy enough to conceal our wealth; but if poor, it is not quite so easy to conceal our poverty. It is less difficult to hide a thousand guineas than one hole in our coat.
CHARLES CALEB COLTON (?1780–1832), English clergyman and writer: *Lacon*

Two nations between whom there is no intercourse and no sympathy; who are as ignorant of each other's habits, thoughts and feelings, as if they were dwellers in different zones or inhabitants of different planets . . . the rich and the poor.
BENJAMIN DISRAELI, 1st Earl of Beaconsfield (1804–81), English statesman, prime minister, and novelist: *Sybil, book 2*

I was told that the Privileged and the People formed Two Nations.
BENJAMIN DISRAELI, *as above, book 4*

At the end of this century when we look back on the great tragedies and movements of our age, certainly this famine, which potentially will kill 100 million people, is one of the shameful things of our time and I find it an indictment of us and of a pathetic way of living that a piece of plastic 7" across with a hole in the middle is the price of someone's life this year.
BOB GELDOF (1954–), Irish rock star: *BBC News Review of the Year, 29 December 1985*

So long as all the increased wealth which modern progress brings goes but to build up great fortunes, to increase luxury and make sharper the contrast between the House of Have and the House of Want, progress is not real and cannot be permanent.
HENRY GEORGE (1839–97), American economist: *Progress and Poverty*

Development in the Third World usually means the over-development of objects and the under-development of people.
RICHARD GOTT Journalist: *Guardian, 30 November 1976*

F. Scott Fitzgerald
You know, Ernest, the rich are different from us.
Ernest Hemingway
Yes I know. They have more money than we do.
ERNEST HEMINGWAY (1889–1961), American novelist and short-story writer

If a free society cannot help the many who are poor, it cannot save the few who are rich.
JOHN FITZGERALD KENNEDY (1917–63), U.S. statesman and president: *Inaugural address, 20 January 1961*

The concessions of the privileged to the unprivileged are seldom brought about by any better motive than the power of the unprivileged to extort them.
JOHN STUART MILL (1806–73), English philosopher and economist: *The Subjugation of Women*

God help the rich; the poor can beg.
Proverb

There's one law for the rich, and another for the poor.
Proverb

The rich man thinks of the future, the poor man thinks of today.
Chinese proverb

The rich would have to eat money, but luckily the poor provide food.
Russian proverb

As long as there are rich people in the world, they will be desirous of distinguishing themselves from the poor.
JEAN-JACQUES ROUSSEAU (1712–78), Swiss-born French philosopher and writer: *Discourse on Political Economy*

Who made your millions for you? Me and my like. Whats kep us poor? Keepin you rich.
GEORGE BERNARD SHAW (1856–1950), Irish dramatist and critic: *Major Barbara, Act 2*

The poor man is ruined as soon as he begins to ape the rich.
PUBLILIUS SYRUS (1st c. BC), Latin writer of mimes: *Moral Sayings*

The world will not live in harmony so long as two-thirds of its inhabitants find difficulty in living at all.
U THANT (1909–74), Burmese diplomat, secretary-general of United Nations: *Observer, 'Sayings of the Decade', 28 December 1969*

There is only one class in the community that thinks more about money than the rich, and that is the poor.
OSCAR WILDE (1856–1900), Irish poet, dramatist, and wit: *The Soul of Man Under Socialism*

INFLATION

Inflation means that your money won't buy as much today as it did when you didn't have any.
Anon

When I first started working I used to dream of the day when I might be earning the salary I'm starving on now.
Anon

Inflation is one form of taxation that can be imposed without legislation.
MILTON FRIEDMAN (1912–), American economist

Inflation does not lubricate trade but by rescuing traders from their errors of optimism or stupidity.
JOHN KENNETH GALBRAITH (1908–), Canadian-born American economist, diplomat, and writer: *Money, chapter 2*

Inflation is like sin; every government denounces it and every government practises it.
SIR FREDERICK LEITH-ROSS (1887– 1968), quoted in *Observer, 30 June 1957*

JUSTICE & INJUSTICE

Justice is a certain rectitude of mind whereby a man does what he ought to do in the circumstances

confronting him.
SAINT THOMAS AQUINAS (1225–74), Italian theologian, scholastic philosopher, and Dominican friar: *Summa theologiae*

A false balance is abomination to the LORD: but a just weight is his delight.
The Bible, Authorized (King James) Version, Proverbs 11:1

Is not this the fast that I have chosen? to loose the bands of wickedness, to undo the heavy burdens, and to let the oppressed go free, and that ye break every yoke? Is it not to deal thy bread to the hungry, and that thou bring the poor that are cast out to thy house? when thou seest the naked, that thou cover him; and that thou hide not thyself from thine own flesh? Then shall thy light break forth as the morning, and thine health shall spring forth speedily: and thy righteousness shall go before thee; the glory of the LORD shall be thy rereward.
as above, Isaiah 58:6–8

The labourer is worthy of his hire.
as above, Luke 10:7

The fundamentals of justice are that no one shall suffer wrong, and that the public good be served.
MARCUS TULLIUS CICERO (106–43 BC), Roman statesman and orator: *De officiis*

Let justice be done, though the world perish.
FERDINAND I (1503–64), Holy Roman Emperor (Attributed)

Justice is the end of government. It is the end of civil society. It ever has been and ever will be pursued until it be obtained, or until liberty be lost in the pursuit.
ALEXANDER HAMILTON (?1757–1804), American Federalist politician: *The Federalist*

Justice should not only be done, but should manifestly and undoubtedly be seen to be done.
GORDON HEWART, Lord Hewart (1870–1943), British lawyer and statesman: *The Chief (R. Jackson)*

If you study the history and records of the world you must admit that the source of justice was the fear of injustice.
HORACE, (Quintus Horatius Flaccus) (65–8 BC), Roman poet and satirist: *Satires*

The three fundamental rules of justice, the stability of possession, its transference by consent, and the performance of promises, are duties of princes as well as of subjects . . . Where possession has no stability, there must be per-petual war. Where property is not transferred by consent, there can be no commerce. Where promises are not observed, there can be no leagues or alliances.
DAVID HUME (1711–76), Scottish philosopher and historian: *A Treatise of Human Nature, book 3*

Love of justice in the generality of men is only the fear of suffering from injustice.
FRANÇOIS LA ROCHEFOUCAULD, Duc de La Rochefoucauld (1613–80), French writer: *Maxims*

Justice without force is impotent, force without justice is tyranny . . . Not being able to make what is just strong, we make what was strong just.
BLAISE PASCAL (1623–62), French philosopher, mathematician, and physicist: *Pensées*

Every one loves justice in the affairs of another.
Proverb

It is no sin to sell dear, but a sin to give ill measure.
Proverb

POVERTY

God loves the poor, and that is why he made so many of them.
Anon

A true test of a civilization is the way it treats its poor.
Anon

What fun it would be to be poor, as long as one was *excessively* poor! Anything in excess is most exhilarating.
JEAN ANOUILH (1910–), French dramatist: *Ring Round the Moon, Act 2*

Poverty is the parent of revolution and crime.
ARISTOTLE (384–322 BC), Greek philosopher and scientist: *The Politics, book 2*

Poverty is an anomaly to rich people. It is very difficult to make out why people who want dinner do not ring the bell.
WALTER BAGEHOT (1826–77), English economist and journalist: *Literary Studies*

Poverty is not a misfortune to the poor only who suffer it, but it is more or less a misfortune to all with whom he deals.
HENRY WARD BEECHER (1813–87), American clergyman, editor, and writer: *Speech, 16 October 1863*

For the poor always ye have with you.
The Bible, Authorized (King James) Version, John 12:8

To be poor and independent is very nearly an impossibility.
WILLIAM COBBETT (1762–1835), English farmer, social reformer, and writer: *Advice to Young Men*

Poverty is the symptom; slavery the disease.
G(EORGE) D(OUGLAS) H(OWARD) COLE (1889–1959), English economist and historian: *Self-government in Industry*

The poor man is happy: he expects no change for the worse.
DEMETRIUS OF PHALERUM (ca. 345–ca. 280 BC), Greek orator and statesman: *Fragment*

Sam Weller
Poverty and oysters always seem to go together.
CHARLES (JOHN HUFFAM) DICKENS (1812–70), English novelist: *Pickwick Papers, chapter 22*

Poverty consists in feeling poor.
RALPH WALDO EMERSON (1803–82), American poet, essayist, and philosopher: *Society and Solitude*

There's no scandal like rags, nor any crime so shameful as poverty.
GEORGE FARQUHAR (1678–1707), Irish dramatist: *The Beaux' Stratagem*

I used to think I was poor. Then they told me I wasn't poor, I was needy. Then they told me it was self-defeating to think of myself as needy. I was deprived. Then they told me that underprivileged was overused. I was disadvantaged. I still don't have a dime. But I have a great vocabulary.
JULES FEIFFER (1929–), American cartoonist: *Village Voice, 1965*

Poverty often deprives a man of all spirit and virtue.
BENJAMIN FRANKLIN (1706–90), American statesman, scientist, and author: *Poor Richard's Almanac*

He is not poor that hath not much, but he that craves much.
THOMAS FULLER (1654–1734), English physician, writer, and compiler: *Gnomologia*

It is but a truism that labor is most productive where its wages are largest. Poorly paid labor is inefficient labor, the world over.
HENRY GEORGE (1839–97), American economist: *Progress and Poverty, book 9*

Poverty is a great enemy to human happiness; it certainly destroys liberty, and it makes some virtues impracticable, and others extremely difficult.
SAMUEL JOHNSON (1709–84), English lexicographer, essayist, and poet: Boswell, *Life of Johnson*

Our purpose is not to buy friends or hire allies. Our purpose is to defeat poverty . . . Our goal is to again influence history instead of merely observing it.
JOHN FITZGERALD KENNEDY (1917–63), U.S. statesman and president: *Saturday Review, 7 December 1963, 'Ideas, Attitudes, Purposes from his Speeches and Writings'*

In other countries poverty is a misfortune – with us it is a crime.
EDWARD GEORGE EARLE LYTTON BULWER-LYTTON, 1st Baron Lytton (1803–73), English novelist, dramatist, and statesman: *England and the English*

If you are poor today you will always be poor. Only the rich now acquire riches.
MARTIAL (Marcus Valerius Martialis) (?40–?104 AD), Spanish-born epigrammatist and poet: *Epigrams*

Beggars should be abolished entirely! Verily, it is annoying to give to them and it is annoying not to give to them.
FRIEDRICH WILHELM NIETZSCHE (1844–1900), German philosopher, poet, and critic: *Thus Spoke Zarathustra, 'On the Pitying'*

Work for the elimination of concrete evils rather than for the realisation of abstract goods. Do not aim at establishing happiness by political means. Rather, aim at the elimination of poverty by direct means.
SIR KARL POPPER (1902–), Austrian-born English philosopher and biochemist: *Conjectures and Refutations, 'Utopia and Violence'*

Better die a beggar than live a beggar.
Proverb

He who is content in his poverty, is wonderfully rich.
Proverb

If you have no money, be polite.
Proverb

Poverty has no relatives.
Proverb

Poverty is not a vice.
Proverb

Poverty is the mother of crime.
Proverb

The poor sit on the front benches in Paradise.
Proverb

Lack of money is the root of all evil.
GEORGE BERNARD SHAW (1856–1950), Irish dramatist and critic: *Man and Superman*

The greatest of our evils and the worst of our crimes is poverty, and . . . our first duty, to which every other consideration should be sacrificed, is not to be poor.
GEORGE BERNARD SHAW, *Major Barbara*

I cant talk religion to a man with bodily hunger in his eyes.
GEORGE BERNARD SHAW, *as above, Act 1*

POVERTY IS NO DISGRACE TO A MAN, BUT IT IS CONFOUNDEDLY INCONVENIENT.

No complaint . . . is more common than that of a scarcity of money.
ADAM SMITH (1723–90), Scottish economist and philosopher: *The Wealth of Nations, volume 1*

No society can surely be flourishing and happy, of which the far greater part of the members are poor and miserable.
ADAM SMITH, *as above*

Poverty is no disgrace to a man, but it is confoundedly inconvenient.
SYDNEY SMITH (1771–1845), English journalist, clergyman, and wit: *His Wit and Wisdom*

TAXES

His horse went dead, and his mule went lame,
And he lost six cows in a poker game;
Then a hurricane came on a Summer day,
And blew the house where he lived away;
An earthquake came when that was gone,
And swallowed the land the house stood on.
And then the tax collector came around,
And charged him up with the hole in the ground.
Anon

Taxman
The position is that if I don't have one thousand pounds from you soon, you're going to jail.
Businessman
Now you're talking. Here's one thousand pounds in used notes.
Taxman
Let me give you a receipt.
Businessman
What, a thousand nicker in cash and you're going to put it through the books?
Anon, quoted in Fred Metcalf, *The Penguin Dictionary of Modern Humorous Quotations*

Render therefore unto Caesar the things which are Caesar's; and unto God the things that are God's.
The Bible, Authorized (King James) Version, Matthew 22:21

Tariff
A scale of taxes on imports, designed to protect the domestic producer against the greed of his consumer.
AMBROSE (GWINETT) BIERCE (1842–?1914), American journalist and humorist: *The Devil's Dictionary*

There is no such thing as a good tax.
SIR WINSTON LEONARD SPENCER CHURCHILL (1874–1965), English statesman, writer, and prime minister: *Observer, 'Sayings of the Week', 6 June 1937*

The art of taxation consists in so plucking the goose as to obtain the

largest amount of feathers with the least possible amount of hissing.
JEAN BAPTISTE COLBERT (1619–83), French statesman (Attributed)

The hardest thing in the world to understand is the income tax.
ALBERT EINSTEIN (1879–1955), German-Swiss-American physicist

The Treasury has a vested interest in trying to sustain the process by which people are encouraged to get lung cancer.
MICHAEL FOOT (1913–), English politician: *Observer, 'Sayings of the Year', 27 December 1964*

A government big enough to give us everything we want would be big enough to take from us everything we have.
GERALD FORD (1913–), U.S. president

In this world nothing can be said to be certain, except death and taxes.
BENJAMIN FRANKLIN (1706–90), American statesman, scientist, and author: *Letter to Jean Baptiste Le Roy, 13 November 1789*

The amount paid by those who drink and smoke was £715,000,000, very nearly a pre-war Budget, whereas the taxation paid by those who did not drink and smoke, on tea, coffee, and so on, was £25,000,000. Yet those citizens expect and receive precisely the same protections from the Fleet, the Army, and the police.
(SIR) A(LAN) P(ATRICK) HERBERT (1890–1971), English writer and MP: *House of Commons, 29 November 1945*

I hope a crusade will be kept up against the duty on books until those in power shall become sensible of this stain on our legislation, and shall wipe it from their code, and from the remembrance of man, if possible.
THOMAS JEFFERSON (1743–1826), U.S. statesman and president: *Letter to Jared Sparks*

A tax is a payment exacted by authority from part of the community for the benefit of the whole.
SAMUEL JOHNSON (1709–84), English lexicographer, essayist, and poet: *Taxation No Tyranny*

Tariffs today are no longer a means of safeguarding growing capitalist production against mature competitors, but a weapon in the struggle of one nationalist block against another. They do not assist industry to grow and capture the domestic market, but merely serve the cartelisation of industry, i.e. assist the struggle of capitalist *producers* against *consumers* . . . Thus a policy of tariffs is in fact no more than a means of casting *feudal interests in capitalist form*.
ROSA LUXEMBURG (1871–1919), Polish-born German socialist revolutionary: *Social Reform or Revolution*

A country cannot be expected to renounce the power of taxing foreigners, unless foreigners will in return practise towards itself the same forbearance. The only mode in which a country can save itself from being a loser by the duties imposed

by other countries on its commodities, is to impose corresponding
duties on theirs.
JOHN STUART MILL (1806–73), English
philosopher and economist: *Essays on
some Unsettled Questions of Political
Economy*

The men who collect taxes are
working in one of oldest professions
known. Archaeological evidence
dating from 1900 BC includes a clay
tablet recording a tax for public
works and a papyrus scroll which
reveals that even 4000 years ago,
taxpayers had some complaints.
Optimist Magazine

Taxation without representation is
tyranny.
JAMES OTIS (1725–83), American
revolutionary leader: *Speech to the
Superior Court of Massachusetts,
February 1761*

Almost all taxes on production fall
finally on the consumer.
DAVID RICARDO (1772–1823), English
economist: *On Protection to Agriculture*

Taxes, after all, are the dues that we
pay for the privileges of member-
ship in an organized society.
FRANKLIN DELANO ROOSEVELT
(1882–1945), U.S. statesman and
president: *Speech, Worcester, Massachusetts, 21 October 1936*

The greatest, the most important
power entrusted to the government
is the right to tax the citizens; it is
from this right that all the others
flow.
CLAUDE HENRI SAINT-SIMON, Comte de
(1760–1825), French political
economist: *Politics*

The subjects of every state ought to
contribute towards the support of
the government, as nearly as
possible, in proportion to their
respective abilities; that is, in
proportion to the revenue which
they respectively enjoy under the
protection of the state.
ADAM SMITH (1723–90), Scottish
economist and philosopher: *The Wealth
of Nations*

There is just one thing I can promise
you about the outer-space program
– your tax dollar will go farther.
WERNHER VON BRAUN (1912–77),
German-born American rocket engineer

UNEMPLOYMENT

FIFO: First In, First Out.
Anon

'I quit because the boss used
repulsive language.'
'What did he say?'
'He said, "You're fired!"'
Anon

LIFO: Last In, First Out.
Anon

The rate of unemployment is 100
per cent if it is you that is
unemployed.
Anon

A man willing to work, and unable to find work, is perhaps the saddest sight that fortune's inequality exhibits under this sun.
THOMAS CARLYLE (1795–1881), Scottish essayist and historian: *Chartism*

In order to mitigate unemployment attending business depression, we urge the enactment of legislation authorizing that construction and repair of public works be initiated in periods of acute unemployment.
U.S. Democratic National Platform, 1924

During a tour of unemployment areas in South Wales
Something must be done.
EDWARD VIII (1894–1972), King of United Kingdom

Unemployment is of vital impor-tance, particularly to the unemployed.
EDWARD (RICHARD GEORGE) HEATH (1916–), British statesman and prime minister: *Observer, 'Sayings of 1980', 28 December 1980*

WAR

Endless money forms the sinews of war.
MARCUS TULLIUS CICERO (106–43 BC), Roman statesman and orator: *Philippics*

War is the trade of kings.
JOHN DRYDEN (1631–1700), English poet and dramatist: *King Arthur*

Do you want to know the cause of war? It is capitalism, greed, the dirty hunger for dollars. Take away the capitalist and you will sweep war from the earth.
HENRY FORD (1863–1947), American car manufacturer: *Interview, Detroit News*

Non-violence is not a garment to be put on and off at will. Its seat is in the heart, and it must be an inseparable part of our very being.
MAHATMA GANDHI, (Mohandas Karamchand Gandhi) (1869–1948), Hindu nationalist leader: *Non-Violence in Peace and War*

Frankly, I'd like to see the govern-ment get out of war altogether and leave the whole field to private industry.
JOSEPH HELLER (1923–), American novelist: *Catch-22*

The most shocking fact about war is that its victims and its instruments are individual human beings, and that these individual beings are condemned by the monstrous conventions of politics to murder or be murdered in quarrels not their own.
ALDOUS (LEONARD) HUXLEY (1894–1963), English novelist and essayist: *The Olive Tree*

At the conclusion of a ten years' war, how are we recompensed for the death of multitudes and the expense of millions but by con-templating the sudden glories of paymasters and agents, contractors

and commissaries, whose equipages shine like meteors, and whose palaces rise like exhalations?
SAMUEL JOHNSON (1709–84), English lexicographer, essayist, and poet: *Thoughts Respecting Falkland's Islands*

Mankind must put an end to war or war will put an end to mankind.
JOHN FITZGERALD KENNEDY (1917–63), U.S. statesman and president: *Address, United Nations General Assembly, 25 September 1961*

Though fraud in other activities be detestable, in the management of war it is laudable and glorious, and he who overcomes an enemy by fraud is as much to be praised as he who does so by force.
NICCOLÒ MACHIAVELLI (1469–1527), Italian statesman and political philosopher: *Discorsi*

War can only be abolished through war, and in order to get rid of the gun it is necessary to take up the gun.
MAO TSE-TUNG (Mao Ze Dong) (1893–1976), Chinese Communist leader: *Quotations from Chairman Mao Tse-tung*

All are not soldiers that go to war.
Proverb

All is fair in love and war.
Proverb

I have seen war. I have seen war on land and sea. I have seen blood running from the wounded. I have seen men coughing out their gassed lungs. I have seen the dead in the mud. I have seen cities destroyed. I have seen 200 limping, exhausted men come out of the line – the survivors of a regiment of 1000 that went forward 48 hours before. I have seen children starving. I have seen the agony of mothers and wives. I hate war.
FRANKLIN DELANO ROOSEVELT (1882–1945), U.S. statesman and president: *Speech, Chautauqua, New York, 14 August 1936*

Guerre à mort.
War to the death.
French saying

In the midst of the most destructive foreign war . . . the greater part of manufacturers may frequently flourish greatly, and, on the contrary, they may decline on the return to peace.
ADAM SMITH (1723–90), Scottish economist and philosopher: *The Wealth of Nations, volume 1*

Let him who desires peace, prepare for war.
VEGETIUS (Flavius Vegetius Renatus) (ca. 374 AD), Latin writer: *Epitoma Rei Militaris*

God is always on the side of the heaviest battalions.
VOLTAIRE (François Marie Arouet) (1694–1778), French writer, philosopher, and historian: *Letter to M. de Riche, 6 February 1770*

To be prepared for war is one of the most effectual means of preserving peace.
GEORGE WASHINGTON (1732–99), U.S. statesman and president: *Speech, 8 January 1790*

Asking for a declaration of war
The world must be made safe for democracy.
(THOMAS) WOODROW WILSON (1856–1924), U.S. statesman and president: *Speech to Congress, 2 April 1917*

BUSINESS QUALITIES

What qualities lead to success in business? Does prosperity come from years of hard work or one 'lucky break', from ruthlessly pursuing a goal, asserting your rights and exploiting others, or just by being in the right place at the right time? The quotations in this final section also tackle such questions as: 'Is honesty always the best policy?', 'Do fame and wealth lead to happiness?', 'Do qualities such as loyalty still have a place in the modern business world?', and 'How do you cope with power and fame when you have reached the top?'

ABILITY

Let every man practise the profession that he knows best.
MARCUS TULLIUS CICERO (106–43 BC), Roman statesman and orator: *Tusculanae disputationes*

It is not enough to have a good mind; the main thing is to use it well.
RENÉ DESCARTES (1596–1650), French philosopher and mathematician: *Discourse on Method*

Genius is one percent inspiration and ninety-nine percent perspiration.
THOMAS ALVA EDISON (1847–1931), American inventor: *Life*

The same man cannot well be skilled in everything; each has his special excellence.
EURIPIDES (?480–406 BC), Greek tragic dramatist: *Rhesus*

One good head is better than a hundred strong hands.
THOMAS FULLER (1654–1734), English physician, writer, and compiler: *Gnomologia*

'Tis skill, not strength that governs a ship.
THOMAS FULLER, *as above*

The winds and waves are always on the side of the ablest navigators.
EDWARD GIBBON (1737–94), English historian: *Decline and Fall of the Roman Empire*

Few great men could pass Personnel.
PAUL GOODMAN (1911–72), American writer, quoted in Jonathon Green, *A Dictionary of Contemporary Quotations*

Some men are born mediocre, some men achieve mediocrity, and some men have mediocrity thrust upon them. With Major Major it had been all three.
JOSEPH HELLER (1923–), American novelist: *Catch-22, chapter 9*

If you want work well done, select a busy man: the other kind has no time.
ELBERT (GREEN) HUBBARD (1856–1915), American businessman, writer, and printer: *The Note Book*

GENIUS IS ONE PER CENT INSPIRATION AND NINETY-NINE PER CENT PERSPIRATION.

There is no substitute for talent. Industry and all the virtues are of no avail.
ALDOUS (LEONARD) HUXLEY (1894–1963), English novelist and essayist: *Point Counter Point*

A man who qualifies himself well for his calling never fails of employment.
THOMAS JEFFERSON (1743–1826), U.S. statesman and president

The height of ability in the least able consists in knowing how to submit to the good leadership of others.
FRANÇOIS LA ROCHEFOUCAULD, Duc de La Rochefoucauld (1613–80), French writer: *Maxims*

It is a great ability to be able to conceal one's ability.
FRANÇOIS LA ROCHEFOUCAULD, *as above*

We have more ability than will power, and it is often an excuse to ourselves that we imagine that things are impossible.
FRANÇOIS LA ROCHEFOUCAULD, *as above*

From each according to his ability, to each according to his needs!
KARL MARX (1818–83), German founder of modern communism: *Critique of the Gotha Programme*

It takes no more actual sagacity to carry on the everyday hawking and haggling of the world, or to ladle out its normal doses of bad medicine and worse law, than it takes to operate a taxicab or fry a pan of fish.
HENRY LOUIS MENCKEN (1880–1956), American philologist, editor, and satirist: *In Defense of Women, 'The Feminine Mind'*

I think I can recognise a real entrepreneur at 300 yards on a misty day! Like an actor he is full of self-confidence and vanity . . . He feels alone and knows that what he says matters, so being able to make and carry through his own decisions is crucial to him. Above all he has this drive to succeed and get things done.
SIR PETER PARKER (1924–), Former Chairman of British Rail, quoted in Cary L. Cooper and Peter Hingley, *The Change Makers*

Competence, like truth, beauty and contact lenses, is in the eye of the beholder.
DR LAURENCE J. PETER (1919–), Canadian educator and RAYMOND HULL (1919–): *The Peter Principle*, chapter 3

If you have great talents, industry will improve them: if you have but moderate abilities, industry will supply their deficiency.
SIR JOSHUA REYNOLDS (1723–92), English portrait painter: *Discourses*

The price of ability does not depend on merit, but on supply and demand.
GEORGE BERNARD SHAW (1856–1950), Irish dramatist and critic: *The Fortnightly Review, April 1894, 'Socialism and Superior Brains'*

Democracy substitutes election by the incompetent many for appointment by the corrupt few.
GEORGE BERNARD SHAW, *Man and Superman, Maxims for Revolutionists*

They are able because they think they are able.
VIRGIL (Publius Vergilius Maro) (70–19 BC), Roman poet: *Aeneid*

Experto credite.
Always believe the expert.
VIRGIL, *as above*

Luck is not something you can mention in the presence of self-made men.
E(LWYN) B(ROOKS) WHITE (1899–), American humorist and essayist: *One Man's Meat*

Intelligence is quickness to apprehend as distinct from ability, which is capacity to act wisely on the thing apprehended.
ALFRED NORTH WHITEHEAD (1861–1947), English mathematician and philosopher: *Dialogues*

An expert is a man who has stopped thinking. Why should he think? He is an expert.
FRANK LLOYD WRIGHT (1869–1959), American architect, quoted in *Daily Express, 1959*

AMBITION

Ambition
An overmastering desire to be vilified by enemies while living and made ridiculous by friends when dead.
AMBROSE (GWINETT) BIERCE (1842–?1914), American journalist and humorist: *The Devil's Dictionary*

Ambition, having reached the summit, longs to descend.
PIERRE CORNEILLE (1606–84), French tragic dramatist: *Cinna*

A big man has no time really to do anything but just sit and be big.
FRANCIS SCOTT (KEY) FITZGERALD (1896–1940), American novelist: *This Side of Paradise*

Who never climbed high never fell low.
THOMAS FULLER (1654–1734), English physician, writer, and compiler: *Gnomologia*

Great ambition, unchecked by principle or the love of glory, is an unruly tyrant.
ALEXANDER HAMILTON (?1757–1804), American Federalist politician: *Letter to James Bayard, 16 January 1801*

A wise man is cured of ambition by ambition itself; his aim is so exalted that riches, office, fortune, and favour cannot satisfy him.
SAMUEL JOHNSON (1709–84), English lexicographer, essayist, and poet: *Characters*

Ambition makes more trusty slaves than need.
BEN JONSON (1573–1637), English playwright and poet: *Sejanus*

We often pass from love to ambition, but we hardly ever return from ambition to love.
FRANÇOIS LA ROCHEFOUCAULD, Duc de La Rochefoucauld (1613–80), French writer: *Maxims*

Most people would succeed in small things, if they were not troubled with great ambitions.
HENRY WADSWORTH LONGFELLOW (1807–82), American poet and translator: *Driftwood, 'Table-Talk'*

A man's worth is no greater than the worth of his ambitions.
MARCUS AURELIUS ANTONINUS (121–180), Roman emperor and Stoic philosopher: *Meditations*

Men may be popular without being ambitious; but there is rarely an ambitious man who does not try to be popular.
LORD NORTH, Frederick, 2nd Earl of Guildford (1732–92), English statesman and prime minister: *House of Commons, March 1769*

He who would leap high must take a long run.
Proverb

Ambition is a vice, but it may be the father of virtue.
QUINTILIAN, Marcus Fabius Quintilianus (?35–?96 AD), Roman rhetorician and teacher: *De institutione oratoria*

Ambition often puts men upon doing the meanest offices: so climbing is performed in the same posture with creeping.
JONATHAN SWIFT (1667–1745), Anglo-Irish satirist and churchman: *Thoughts on Various Subjects*

Ambition is the last refuge of the failure.
OSCAR WILDE (1856–1900), Irish poet, dramatist, and wit: *Phrases and Philosophies for the Use of the Young*

CAUTION

Better one safe way than a hundred on which you cannot reckon.
AESOP (ca. 620–564 BC), Greek fabulist: *Fables, 'The Fox and the Cat'*

'Tis the part of a wise man to keep himself today for tomorrow, and not venture all his eggs in one basket.
MIGUEL DE CERVANTES (SAAVEDRA) (1547–1616), Spanish writer: *Don Quixote*

Delay always breeds danger.
MIGUEL DE CERVANTES (SAAVEDRA), *as above*

The cautious seldom err.
CONFUCIUS (Kong Zi) (551–479 BC), Chinese philosopher: *The Confucian Analects*

He who is not a bird should not build his nest over abysses.
FRIEDRICH WILHELM NIETZSCHE (1844–1900), German philosopher, poet and critic: *Thus Spoke Zarathustra*

Look before you leap.
Proverb

It is well to moor your ship with two anchors.
PUBLILIUS SYRUS (1st c. BC), Latin writer of mimes: *Moral Sayings*

It is a characteristic of wisdom not to do desperate things.
HENRY DAVID THOREAU (1817–62), American essayist and poet: *Walden*

CONFIDENCE & SELF-DETERMINATION

Some men are just as firmly convinced of what they think as others are of what they know.
ARISTOTLE (384–322 BC), Greek philosopher and scientist: *Nicomachean Ethics*

We have got to take the gloves off and have a bare-knuckle fight on some of the things we have to do, because we have to have an effective and prosperous industry.
SIR TERENCE BECKETT (1923–), Director General, CBI, *CBI conference 1980*

And though hard be the task, 'Keep a stiff upper lip.'
PHOEBE CARY (1824–71), American poet: *Keep a Stiff Upper Lip*

The most important thing in the Olympic Games is not winning but taking part . . . The essential thing in life is not conquering but fighting well.
BARON PIERRE DE COUBERTIN (1863–1937), French founder of the modern Olympic Games: *Speech, Banquet to Officials of Olympic Games, London, 24 July 1908*

The perfection preached in the Gospels never yet built an empire. Every man of action has a strong dose of egotism, pride, hardness, and cunning.
CHARLES ANDRÉ JOSEPH MARIE DE GAULLE (1890–1970), French general and statesman, quoted in *The New York Times Magazine, 12 May 1968*

Neither a wise man nor a brave man lies down on the tracks of history to wait for the train of the future to run over him.
DWIGHT D(AVID) EISENHOWER (1890–1969), U.S. general and president: *Time, 6 October 1952*

Nothing great was ever achieved without enthusiasm.
RALPH WALDO EMERSON (1803–82), American poet, essayist, and philosopher: *Essays, 'Circles'*

Boldness in business is the first, second, and third thing.
THOMAS FULLER (1654–1734), English physician, writer, and compiler: *Gnomologia*

You ought to take the bull between the teeth.
SAMUEL GOLDWYN (1882–1974), American film producer (Attributed)

He who would make serious use of his life must always act as though he had a long time to live and must schedule his time as though he were about to die.
(MAXIMILIEN PAUL) ÉMILE LITTRÉ (1801–81), French scholar and lexicographer: *Dictionnaire de la langue française*

Just at this moment we are suffering a national defeat comparable to any lost military campaign, and what is more it is self-inflicted ... I think it is about time we pulled our finger out.
PRINCE PHILIP, Duke of Edinburgh (1921–): *Speech to businessmen, 17 October 1961*

How to be one up – **how to make the other man feel that something has gone wrong, however slightly.**
STEPHEN POTTER (1900–69), English writer and radio producer: *Lifemanship*

Between saying and doing many a pair of shoes is worn out.
Proverb

Every man is the architect of his own fortune.
Proverb

Every man is the son of his own works.
Proverb

In our complex world, there cannot be fruitful initiative without government, but unfortunately there can be government without initiative.
BERTRAND (ARTHUR WILLIAM) RUSSELL, 3rd Earl Russell (1872–1970), English philosopher and mathematician: *Authority and the Individual, 'Control and Initiative'*

Self-determination is not a mere phrase. It is an imperative principle of action, which statesmen will henceforth ignore at their peril.
(THOMAS) WOODROW WILSON (1856–1924), U.S. statesman and president: *Speech to Congress, 11 February 1918*

COURTESY

Politeness
The most acceptable hypocrisy.
AMBROSE (GWINETT) BIERCE (1842–?1914), American journalist and humorist: *The Devil's Dictionary*

Be polite. Write diplomatically. Even in a declaration of war one observes the rules of politeness.
OTTO (EDUARD LEOPOLD) VON BISMARCK (1815–98), German statesman

Manners are of more importance than laws. Upon them, in a great measure, the laws depend. The law touches us but here and there, and now and then. Manners are what vex or soothe, corrupt or purify, exalt or debase, barbarize or refine us, by a constant, steady, uniform,

insensible operation, like that of the air we breathe in.
EDMUND BURKE (1729–97), British statesman, orator, and writer: *Letters on a Regicide Peace*

Manners maketh man. Yes, but they make woman still more.
SAMUEL BUTLER (1835–1902), English author, painter, and musician: *Note-Books*

Red Queen
It isn't etiquette to cut anyone you've been introduced to.
LEWIS CARROLL (Charles Lutwidge Dodgson) (1832–98), English writer and mathematician: *Through the Looking Glass, chapter 9*

Politeness is the chief sign of culture.
BALTASAR GRACIÁN (1601–58), Spanish prose writer and Jesuit priest: *The Art of Worldly Wisdom*

A commercial society whose members are essentially ascetic and indifferent in social ritual has to be provided with blueprints and specifications for evoking the right tone for every occasion.
(HERBERT) MARSHALL McLUHAN (1911–80), Canadian educator, author, and media expert: *The Mechanical Bride*

Impropriety is the soul of wit.
W(ILLIAM) SOMERSET MAUGHAM (1874–1965), English writer: *The Moon and Sixpence, chapter 4*

Manners make the man.
Proverb

EFFICIENCY

Our wages are lower, our holidays are shorter, our working hours are longer – simply because we produce less per man employed. Unless we put this right we risk becoming the peasants of the Western world.
SIR MICHAEL CLAPHAM (1912–), President, CBI: *Observer*, *'Sayings of the Year'*, *30 December 1973*

Desire to have things done quickly prevents their being done thoroughly.
CONFUCIUS (Kong Zi) (551–479 BC), Chinese philosopher: *Analects*

Watch out for the fellow who talks about putting things in order! Putting things in order always means getting other people under your control.
DENIS DIDEROT (1713–84), French philosopher: *Supplement to Bougainville's 'Voyage'*

Nothing is more central to an organization's effectiveness than its ability to transmit accurate, relevant, understandable information among its members. All the advantages of organizations – economy of scale, financial and technical resources, diverse talents, and contacts – are of no practical value if the organization's members are unaware of what other members require of them and why.
SAUL GELLERMAN: *The Management of Human Resources*

Celerity is the mother of good fortune. He has done much who leaves nothing over till tomorrow.
BALTASAR GRACIÁN (1601–58), Spanish prose writer and Jesuit priest: *The Art of Worldly Wisdom*

To find men capable of managing business efficiently and secure to them the positions of responsible control is perhaps the most important single problem of economic organisation on the efficiency scale.
FRANK H. KNIGHT (1885–1972), Professor of Economics

The efficiency of industry may be expected to be great, in proportion as the fruits of industry are insured to the person exerting it.
JOHN STUART MILL (1806–73), English philosopher and economist: *Principles of Political Economy, book 1*

DESIRE TO HAVE THINGS DONE QUICKLY PREVENTS THEIR BEING DONE THOROUGHLY.

173

An ounce of image is worth a pound of performance.
DR LAURENCE J. PETER (1919–), Canadian educator: *Peter's Quotations*

To do two things at once is to do neither.
PUBLILIUS SYRUS (1st c. BC), Latin writer of mimes: *Moral Sayings*

There are only two qualities in the world: efficiency and inefficiency, and only two sorts of people: the efficient and the inefficient.
GEORGE BERNARD SHAW (1856–1950), Irish dramatist and critic: *John Bull's Other Island, Act 4*

EXPLOITATION

If you allow men to use you for your own purposes, they will use you for theirs.
AESOP (ca. 620–564 BC), Greek fabulist: *Fables, 'The Horse, Hunter, and Stag'*

Under capitalism man exploits man, under socialism, it's just the opposite.
Anon

The history of all past society has consisted in the development of class antagonisms, antagonisms that assumed different forms at different epochs. But whatever form they may have taken, one fact is common to all past ages, viz., the exploitation of one part of society by the other.
KARL MARX (1818–83), German founder of modern communism and FRIEDRICH ENGELS (1820–95), German socialist leader: *The Communist Manifesto*

EXTRAVAGANCE

We deny that it is fun to be saving. It is fun to be prodigal. Go to the butterfly, thou parsimonious sluggard; consider her ways and get wise.
FRANKLIN P. ADAMS (1881–1960), American journalist and humorist: *Nods and Becks*

The road of excess leads to the palace of Wisdom.
WILLIAM BLAKE (1757–1827), English poet, painter, and engraver: *The Marriage of Heaven and Hell, 'Proverbs of Hell'*

To go beyond is as wrong as to fall short.
CONFUCIUS (Kong Zi) (551–479 BC), Chinese philosopher: *Analects*

My problem lies in reconciling my gross habits with my net income.
ERROL FLYNN (1909–59), American film star

I have not been afraid of excess: excess on occasion is exhilarating. It prevents moderation from

acquiring the deadening effect of a habit.
W(ILLIAM) SOMERSET MAUGHAM (1874–1965), English writer: *The Summing Up*

The biggest waste of water in the country by far. You spend half a pint and flush two gallons.
PRINCE PHILIP, Duke of Edinburgh (1921–): *Speech, 1965*

Enough is as good as a feast.
Proverb

He who gives his milk to his cat must drink water.
Proverb

Moderation in all things.
Proverb

Waste not, want not.
Proverb

He who buys what he needs not, sells what he needs.
Japanese proverb

A glut is an evil. It generally implies production without profit, and sometimes without even the return of the capital employed.
DAVID RICARDO (1772–1823), English economist: *Works, volume 2*

Nothing in excess.
SOLON (?638–?559 BC), Athenian statesman

Lord Illingworth
Moderation is a fatal thing, Lady Hunstanton. Nothing succeeds like excess.
OSCAR WILDE (1856–1900), Irish poet, dramatist, and wit: *A Woman of No Importance, Act 3*

FAME

A celebrity is a person who works hard all his life to become known, then wears dark glasses to avoid being recognized.
FRED ALLEN (John F. Sullivan) (1894–1956), American comedian: *Treadmill to Oblivion*

The desire for fame tempts even noble minds.
SAINT AUGUSTINE (354–430 AD), Early Christian church father and philosopher: *The City of God*

All men desire fame. I have never known a single exception to that rule, and I doubt if anyone else has.
(JOSEPH) HILAIRE (PIERRE) BELLOC (1870–1953), Anglo-French author: *The Silence of the Sea*

Famous
Conspicuously miserable.
AMBROSE (GWINETT) BIERCE (1842–?1914), American journalist and humorist: *The Devil's Dictionary*

The celebrity is a person who is known for his well-knownness.
DANIEL J. BOORSTIN (1914–), American educator and writer: *The Image, chapter 2*

Celebrity: the advantage of being known by those who don't know you.
SÉBASTIEN ROCH NICOLAS CHAMFORT (1741–94), French writer and wit: *Maximes et pensées*

I have often thought of forming a Society for the Prevention of Cruelty to Celebrities. Apparently for certain individuals, men and women in the public eye are fair game to be knocked off their balance occasionally and made to look foolish. You know, a central figure at a social function isn't always as happy as he looks.
SIR NOËL (PIERCE) COWARD (1899–1973), English actor and dramatist (Attributed)

People that seem so glorious are all show;
Underneath they're like anybody else.
EURIPIDES (?480–406 BC), Greek tragic dramatist: *Andromache*

If I'm such a legend, then why am I so lonely? . . . let me tell you, legends are all very well if you've got somebody around who loves you.
JUDY GARLAND (1922–69), American singer and film star

Nothing arouses ambition so much in the heart as the trumpet-clang of another's fame.
BALTASAR GRACIÁN (1601–58), Spanish prose writer and Jesuit priest: *The Art of Worldly Wisdom*

What is fame? an empty bubble.
JAMES GRAINGER (?1721–66), English physician and man of letters: *Solitude*

No really great man ever thought himself so.
WILLIAM HAZLITT (1778–1830), English essayist: *The Plain Speaker*

Nothing is so common-place as to wish to be remarkable.
OLIVER WENDELL HOLMES, SR (1809–94), American physician, professor, and author: *The Autocrat of the Breakfast Table*

We're more popular than Jesus Christ now.
JOHN LENNON (1940–80), English rock musician and songwriter

Fame is the spur that the clear spirit doth raise . . .
To scorn delights, and live laborious days.
JOHN MILTON (1608–74), English poet: *Lycidas*

Would you be known by everybody? Then you know nobody.
PUBLILIUS SYRUS (1st c. BC), Latin writer of mimes: *Moral Sayings*

The first test of a truly great man is his humility.
JOHN RUSKIN (1819–1900), English art critic and social reformer: *Modern Painters*

Malvolio

Some are born great, some achieve greatness, and some have greatness thrust upon 'em.
WILLIAM SHAKESPEARE (1564–1616), English dramatist and poet: *Twelfth Night, Act 2*

Fame and rest are utter opposites.
SIR RICHARD STEELE (1672–1729), Irish-born British dramatist and essayist: *The Funeral*

Fame is a vapor, popularity an accident; the only earthly certainty is oblivion.
MARK TWAIN (Samuel Langhorne Clemens) (1835–1910), American novelist and humorist: *Notebook*

GREED

The world has enough for everyone's need, but not enough for everyone's greed.
MAHATMA GANDHI (Mohandas Karamchand Gandhi) (1869–1948), Hindu nationalist leader (Attributed)

Avarice, the spur of industry.
DAVID HUME (1711–76), Scottish philosopher and historian: *Essays*

Avarice, or the desire of gain, is a universal passion, which operates at all times, at all places, and upon all persons.
DAVID HUME, *as above*

Avarice and luxury have been the ruin of every great state.
LIVY (Titus Livius) (59 BC–17 AD), Roman historian: *History of Rome*

Excess of wealth is cause of covetousness.
CHRISTOPHER MARLOWE (1564–93), English dramatist and poet: *The Jew of Malta, Act 1*

Avarice has so seized upon mankind that their wealth seems rather to possess them than they to possess their wealth.
PLINY THE YOUNGER (Gaius Plinius Caecilius Secundus) (?62–?113 AD), Roman writer and administrator: *Letters*

**Accursed greed for gold,
To what dost thou not drive the heart of man?**
VIRGIL (Publius Vergilius Maro) (70–19 BC), Roman poet: *Aeneid*

HAPPINESS

Happiness seems to require a modicum of external prosperity.
ARISTOTLE (384–322 BC), Greek philosopher and scientist: *Nicomachean Ethics*

Different men seek after happiness in different ways and by different means, and so make for themselves different modes of life and forms of government.
ARISTOTLE, *Politics*

The greatest happiness of the greatest number is the foundation of morals and legislation.
JEREMY BENTHAM (1748–1832), English philosopher: *The Commonplace Book*

Happiness
An agreeable sensation arising from contemplating the misery of another.
AMBROSE (GWINETT) BIERCE (1842–?1914), American journalist and humorist: *The Devil's Dictionary*

In every adversity of fortune, to have been happy is the most unhappy kind of misfortune.
ANICIUS MANLIUS SEVERINUS BOETHIUS (ca. 475–524), Roman statesman and philosopher: *De Consolatione Philosophiae*

Who is content with nothing possesses all things.
NICOLAS BOILEAU (-DESPRÉAUX) (1636–1711), French poet and critic: *Épîtres*

Happiness is a mystery like religion, and should never be rationalized.
G(ILBERT) K(EITH) CHESTERTON (1874–1936), English essayist, novelist, poet, and critic: *Heretics, chapter 7*

To fill the hour – that is happiness.
RALPH WALDO EMERSON (1803–82), American poet, essayist, and philosopher: *Experience*

Modern man's happiness consists in the thrill of looking at the shop windows, and in buying all that he can afford to buy, either for cash or on installments.
ERICH FROMM (1900–80), German-born American psychoanalyst and philosopher: *The Art of Loving*

Well, I've had a happy life.
WILLIAM HAZLITT (1778–1830), English essayist: *Last words*

It's pretty hard to tell what does bring happiness; poverty and wealth have both failed.
FRANK McKINNEY HUBBARD ('Kin Hubbard') (1868–1930): *Abe Martin's Broadcast*

Happiness is like coke – something you get as a by-product in the process of making something else.
ALDOUS (LEONARD) HUXLEY (1894–1963), English novelist and essayist: *Point Counter Point*

There is nothing of permanent value (putting aside a few human affections), nothing that satisfies quiet reflection, except the sense of having worked according to one's capacity and light to make things clear and get rid of cant and shams of all sorts.
THOMAS HENRY HUXLEY (1825–95), English biologist, teacher, and writer: *To W. Platt Ball, 27 October 1890*

Human life is every where a state in which much is to be endured, and little to be enjoyed.
SAMUEL JOHNSON (1709–84), English lexicographer, essayist, and poet: *Rasselas, chapter 11*

It is better that some should be unhappy, than that none should be happy, which would be the case in a general state of equality.
SAMUEL JOHNSON, Boswell, *Life of Johnson*

The great source of pleasure is variety.
SAMUEL JOHNSON, *Lives of the English Poets, Butler*

Nothing is surely a waste of time when one enjoys the day.
ARTHUR KOESTLER (1905–83), Hungarian-born British writer

We are never so happy nor so unhappy as we imagine.
FRANÇOIS LA ROCHEFOUCAULD, Duc de La Rochefoucauld (1613–80), French writer: *Reflections*

Happy is the man with a wife to tell him what to do and a secretary to do it.
LORD MANCROFT (1914–), British politician: *Observer, 1966*

Few people would assert that a man with fifty thousand a year is likely to have a very much happier life than if he had only a thousand.
ALFRED MARSHALL (1842–1924), English classical economist: *Economic Journal, March 1907, 'The Social Possibilities of Economic Chivalry'*

It is only in a very imperfect state of the world's arrangements that any one can best serve the happiness of others by the absolute sacrifice of his own.
JOHN STUART MILL (1806–73), English philosopher and economist: *Utilitarianism, chapter 2*

Our object in the construction of the state is the greatest happiness of the whole, and not that of any one class.
PLATO (?427–?347 BC), Greek philosopher: *Republic*

To be without some of the things you want is an indispensable part of happiness.
BERTRAND (ARTHUR WILLIAM) RUSSELL, 3rd Earl Russell (1872–1970), English philosopher and mathematician: *The Conquest of Happiness*

If there were in the world today any large number of people who desired their own happiness more than they desired the unhappiness of others, we could have a paradise in a few years.
BERTRAND (ARTHUR WILLIAM) RUSSELL, *Observer, 'Sayings of the Decade', 28 December 1969*

Few people can be happy unless they hate some other person, nation or creed.
BERTRAND (ARTHUR WILLIAM) RUSSELL (Attributed)

Happiness is the only sanction of life; where happiness fails, existence remains a mad and lamentable experiment.
GEORGE SANTAYANA (1863–1952), American philosopher and poet: *The Life of Reason*

The heart is great which shows moderation in the midst of prosperity.
MARCUS or LUCIUS ANNAEUS SENECA (The Elder) (?55 BC–?39 AD), Roman writer on oratory and history: *Suasoriae*

How bitter a thing it is to look into happiness through another man's eyes!
WILLIAM SHAKESPEARE (1564–1616), English dramatist and poet: *As You Like It, Act 5*

A lifetime of happiness! No man alive could bear it: it would be hell on earth.
GEORGE BERNARD SHAW (1856–1950), Irish dramatist and critic: *Man and Superman*

The most decisive mark of the prosperity of any country is the increase of the number of inhabitants.
ADAM SMITH (1723–90), Scottish economist and philosopher: *The Wealth of Nations, volume 1*

There is more felicity on the far side of baldness than young men can possibly imagine.
LOGAN PEARSALL SMITH (1865–1946), American-born English man of letters: *All Trivia*

Call no man happy until he dies; he is at best fortunate.
SOLON (?638–?559 BC), Athenian statesman: *Histories (Herodotus)*

It is not the level of prosperity that makes for happiness but the

kinship of heart to heart and the way we look at the world. Both attitudes are within our power, so that a man is happy so long as he chooses to be happy, and no one can stop him.
ALEXANDER ISAYEVICH SOLZHENITSYN (1918–), Exiled Russian novelist: *Cancer Ward, Part 1*

There is no duty we so much underrate as the duty of being happy.
ROBERT LOUIS BALFOUR STEVENSON (1850–94), Scottish writer: *Virginibus Puerisque, An Apology for Idlers*

Good friends, good books and a sleepy conscience: this is the ideal life.
MARK TWAIN (Samuel Langhorne Clemens) (1835–1910), American novelist and humorist: *Notebook*

Grief can take care of itself, but to get the full value of joy you must have somebody to divide it with.
MARK TWAIN, *as above*

Employment gives health, sobriety, and morals. Constant employment and well-paid labor produce, in a country like ours, general prosperity, content, and cheerfulness.
DANIEL WEBSTER (1782–1852), American statesman and orator: *Speech, the Senate, 25 July 1846*

After you have exhausted what there is in business, politics, conviviality, and so on – have found that none of these finally satisfy, or

BUSINESS QUALITIES

permanently wear – what remains?
Nature remains.
WALT(ER) WHITMAN (1819–92),
American poet, journalist, and essayist:
*Specimen Days, 'New Themes Entered
Upon'*

Give me the luxuries of life and I will
willingly do without the necessities.
FRANK LLOYD WRIGHT (1869–1959),
American architect, quoted in his obituary

HEALTH

Mr Woodhouse
Nobody is healthy in London,
nobody can be.
JANE AUSTEN (1775–1817), English
novelist: *Emma, chapter 12*

Never go to a doctor whose office
plants have died.
ERMA BOMBECK (1927–), American
humorist

The trouble about always trying to
preserve the health of the body is
that it is so difficult to do without
destroying the health of the mind.
G(ILBERT) K(EITH) CHESTERTON
(1874–1936), English essayist, novelist,
poet, and critic: *Come to Think of It*

The poorest man would not part
with health for money, but the
richest would gladly part with all
their money for health.
CHARLES CALEB COLTON (?1780–
1832), English clergyman and writer:
Lacon

Our health is our sound relation to
external objects; our sympathy with
external being.
RALPH WALDO EMERSON (1803–82),
American poet, essayist, and philosopher:
Journals

Study sickness while you are well.
THOMAS FULLER (1654–1734), English
physician, writer, and compiler:
Gnomologia

Anybody who goes to see a
psychiatrist ought to have his
head examined.
SAMUEL GOLDWYN (1882–1974),
American film producer (Attributed)

If you mean to keep as well as
possible, the less you think about
your health the better.
OLIVER WENDELL HOLMES, SR
(1809–94), American physician,
professor, and author: *Over the Teacups*

Health is worth more than learning.
THOMAS JEFFERSON (1743–1826),
U.S. statesman and president: *Letter to
John Garland Jefferson*

We are under-exercised as a nation.
We look instead of play. We ride
instead of walk. Our existence
deprives us of the minimum of
physical activity essential for
healthy living.
JOHN FITZGERALD KENNEDY (1917–
63), U.S. statesman and president:
Speech, New York City, 5 December 1961

Of television
A medium, so called because it is
neither rare nor well done.
ERNIE KOVACS (1919–62), American
comedian

How sickness enlarges the dimensions of a man's self to himself! He is his own exclusive object. Supreme selfishness is inculcated upon him as his only duty.
CHARLES (ELIA) LAMB (1775–1834), English essayist: *Last Essays of Elia*

If the nineteenth century was the age of the editorial chair, ours is the century of the psychiatrist's couch.
(HERBERT) MARSHALL McLUHAN (1911–80), Canadian educator, author, and media expert: *Understanding the Media*

Life is not living, but living in health.
MARTIAL (Marcus Valerius Martialis) (?40–?104 AD), Spanish-born epigrammatist and poet: *Epigrams*

Health is better than wealth.
Proverb

By medicine life may be prolonged, yet death
Will seize the doctor too.
WILLIAM SHAKESPEARE (1564–1616), English dramatist and poet: *Cymbeline, Act 5*

STUDY SICKNESS WHILE YOU ARE WELL.

I enjoy convalescence. It is the part that makes the illness worth while.
GEORGE BERNARD SHAW (1856–1950), Irish dramatist and critic: *Back to Methuselah*

Early to rise and early to bed makes a male healthy and wealthy and dead.
JAMES (GROVER) THURBER (1894–1961), American humorist and cartoonist: *Fables for Our Time, 'The Shrike and the Chipmunks'*

Look to your health; and if you have it, praise God, and value it next to a good conscience; for health is the second blessing that we mortals are capable of; a blessing that money cannot buy.
IZAAK WALTON (1593–1683), English writer: *The Compleat Angler*

Lord Illingworth
One knows so well the popular idea of health. The English country gentleman galloping after a fox – the unspeakable in full pursuit of the uneatable.
OSCAR WILDE (1856–1900), Irish poet, dramatist, and wit: *A Woman of No Importance, Act 1*

HONESTY

An honest man's word is as good as his bond.
MIGUEL DE CERVANTES (SAAVEDRA) (1547–1616), Spanish writer: *Don Quixote*

Of Mr Baldwin
It is a fine thing to be honest but it is also very important to be right.
SIR WINSTON LEONARD SPENCER CHURCHILL (1874–1965), English statesman, writer, and prime minister (Attributed)

Would that the simple maxim, that honesty is the best policy, might be laid to heart; that a sense of the true aim of life might elevate the tone of politics and trade till public and private honor became identical.
(SARA) MARGARET MARCHESA OSSOLI FULLER (1810–50), American editor, essayist, poet, and teacher: *Summer on the Lakes*

It is difficult but not impossible to conduct strictly honest business. What is true is that honesty is incompatible with the amassing of a large fortune.
MAHATMA GANDHI (Mohandas Karamchand Gandhi) (1869–1948), Hindu nationalist leader: *Non-Violence in Peace and War*

Do not seek dishonest gains: dishonest gains are losses.
HESIOD (ca. 700 BC), Greek poet: *Works and Days*

It is always the best policy to speak the truth, unless of course you are an exceptionally good liar.
JEROME K(LAPKA) JEROME (1859–1927), English humorous writer: *The Idler*

There is one way to find out if a man is honest – ask him. If he says 'Yes', you know he is crooked.
GROUCHO MARX (1895–1977), American film comedian

Put a rogue in the limelight and he will act like an honest man.
NAPOLEON I (Napoleon Bonaparte) (1769–1821), French emperor and general: *Maxims*

It is annoying to be honest to no purpose.
OVID (Publius Ovidius Naso) (43 BC–?17 AD), Roman poet: *Ex ponto*

Honesty is for the most part less profitable than dishonesty.
PLATO (?427–?347 BC), Greek philosopher: *The Republic*

Honesty is the best policy.
Proverb

You cannot make people honest by Act of Parliament.
Proverb

Verges
I thank God I am as honest as any man living that is an old man and no honester than I.
WILLIAM SHAKESPEARE (1564–1616), English dramatist and poet: *Much Ado about Nothing, Act 3*

It's better to be quotable than to be honest.
TOM STOPPARD (1937–), Czecho-slovakian-born British playwright: *Guardian, 1973*

If you tell the truth you don't have to remember anything.
MARK TWAIN (Samuel Langhorne Clemens) (1835–1910), American novelist and humorist: *Notebook*

It is not the crook in modern business that we fear, but the honest man who does not know what he is doing.
OWEN D. YOUNG (1874–1962), American lawyer and corporation executive

HUMANITARIANISM

It is easy to perform a good action, but not easy to acquire a settled habit of performing such actions.
ARISTOTLE (384–322 BC), Greek philosopher and scientist: *Nicomachean Ethics*

A man of humanity is one who, in seeking to establish himself, finds a foothold for others and who, desiring attainment for himself, helps others to attain.
CONFUCIUS (Kong Zi) (551–479BC), Chinese philosopher: *Analects*

Philanthropy is commendable, but it must not cause the philanthropist to overlook the circumstances of economic injustice which make philanthropy necessary.
MARTIN LUTHER KING, JR (1929–68), American Baptist minister and civil rights leader: *Strength to Love*

There is no higher religion than human service. To work for the common good is the greatest creed.
ALBERT SCHWEITZER (1875–1965), Franco-German medical missionary, organist, and philosopher

Of philanthropy
A good part . . . arises in general from mere vanity and love of distinction, gilded over to others and to themselves with some show of benevolent sentiment.
SIR WALTER SCOTT (1771–1832), Scottish novelist and poet: *Journal, 20 February 1828*

Do not do unto others as you would they should do unto you. Their tastes may not be the same.
GEORGE BERNARD SHAW (1856–1950), Irish dramatist and critic: *Man and Superman, Maxims for Revolutionists*

No benevolent man ever lost altogether the fruits of his benevolence.
ADAM SMITH (1723–90), Scottish economist and philosopher: *The Theory of Moral Sentiments, Part 6*

HUMOUR

The most wasted day is that in which we have not laughed.
SÉBASTIEN ROCH NICOLAS CHAMFORT (1741–94), French writer and wit: *Maximes et pensées*

Wit is so shining a quality that everybody admires it; most people aim at it, all people fear it, and few love it unless in themselves.
LORD CHESTERFIELD, Philip Dormer Stanhope, 4th Earl of (1694–1773), English statesman and writer: *Letters to his godson*

No mind is thoroughly well organized that is deficient in a sense of humour.
SAMUEL TAYLOR COLERIDGE (1772–1834), English poet, philosopher, and critic: *Table Talk*

Total absence of humour renders life impossible.
SIDONIE GABRIELLE CLAUDINE COLETTE (1873–1954), French novelist: *Chance Acquaintances*

There is nothing in which people more betray their character than in what they laugh at.
JOHANN WOLFGANG VON GOETHE (1749–1832), German poet, scientist, and writer: *Elective Affinities*

A jest often decides matters of importance more effectually and happily than seriousness.
HORACE (Quintus Horatius Flaccus) (65–8 BC), Roman poet and satirist: *Satires*

Of Lord Chesterfield
This man I thought had been a Lord among wits; but, I find, he is only a wit among Lords.
SAMUEL JOHNSON (1709–84), English lexicographer, essayist, and poet: Boswell, *Life of Johnson*

Everything is funny, as long as it's happening to somebody else.
WILL(IAM PENN ADAIR) ROGERS (1879–1935), American actor and humorist: *The Illiterate Digest*

IMPARTIALITY

I am free of all prejudice. I hate everyone equally.
WILLIAM CLAUDE FIELDS (William Claude Dukenfield) (1880–1946), American actor and comedian (Attributed)

Neutrality consists in having the same weights and measures for each.
NAPOLEON I (Napoleon Bonaparte) (1769–1821), French emperor and general: *Maxims*

Give credit where credit is due.
Proverb

Justice is impartiality. Only strangers are impartial.
GEORGE BERNARD SHAW (1856–1950), Irish dramatist and critic: *Back to Methuselah*

We all decry prejudice, yet are all prejudiced.
HERBERT SPENCER (1820–1903), English philosopher: *Social Statics*

The man who sees both sides of a question is a man who sees absolutely nothing at all.
OSCAR WILDE (1856–1900), Irish poet, dramatist, and wit: *The Critic as Artist, Part 2*

INTEGRITY

We ought to see far enough into a hypocrite to see even his sincerity.
G(ILBERT) K(EITH) CHESTERTON (1874–1936), English essayist, novelist, poet, and critic: *Heretics, chapter 5*

Perhaps it is better to be irresponsible and right than to be responsible and wrong.
SIR WINSTON LEONARD SPENCER CHURCHILL (1874–1965), English statesman, writer, and prime minister: *Party Political Broadcast, 26 August 1950*

Ethics stays in the prefaces of the average business science book.
PETER F. DRUCKER (1909–   ), American management expert

All truth is not to be told at all times.
THOMAS FULLER (1654–1734), English physician, writer, and compiler: *Gnomologia*

What is moral is what you feel good after and what is immoral is what you feel bad after.
ERNEST HEMINGWAY (1899–1961), American novelist and short-story writer: *Death in the Afternoon*

Integrity without knowledge is weak and useless, and knowledge without integrity is dangerous and dreadful.
SAMUEL JOHNSON (1709–84), English lexicographer, essayist, and poet: *Rasselas*

Integrity is praised, and starves.
JUVENAL (Decimus Junius Juvenalis)
(?60–?140), Roman satirist: *Satires*

**It's a matter of having principles.
It's easy to have principles when
you're rich. The important thing is
to have principles when you're poor.**
RAY A. KROC (1902–84), American fast
food entrepreneur

**The difference between a moral
man and a man of honor is that the
latter regrets a discreditable act,
even when it has worked and he has
not been caught.**
HENRY LOUIS MENCKEN (1880–1956),
American philologist, editor, and satirist:
Prejudices: Fourth Series

**Character is much easier kept than
recovered.**
THOMAS PAINE (1737–1809), English
philosopher and writer: *The American
Crisis*

Polonius
**This above all – to thine own self be
true,
And it must follow, as the night the
day,
Thou canst not then be false to any
man.**
WILLIAM SHAKESPEARE (1564–1616),
English dramatist and poet: *Hamlet, Act 1*

**A little sincerity is a dangerous
thing, and a great deal of it is
absolutely fatal.**
OSCAR WILDE (1856–1900), Irish poet,
dramatist, and wit: *The Critic as Artist*

**In matters of grave importance,
style, not sincerity, is the vital thing.**
OSCAR WILDE, *The Importance of Being
Earnest*

KNOWLEDGE

**The intelligent are to the intel-
ligentsia what a man is to a gent.**
STANLEY BALDWIN, 1st Earl Baldwin of
Bewdley (1867–1947), British statesman (Attributed)

**To know a little of anything gives
neither satisfaction nor credit, but
often brings disgrace or ridicule.**
LORD CHESTERFIELD, Philip Dormer
Stanhope, 4th Earl of (1694–1773),
English statesman and writer: *Letter to
his son, 4 October 1746*

**Knowledge is the only instrument
of production that is not subject to
diminishing returns.**
JOHN MAURICE CLARK (1884–1971),
American economist and professor

**Learn as though you would never be
able to master it; hold it as though
you would be in fear of losing it.**
CONFUCIUS (Kong Zi) (551–479 BC),
Chinese philosopher: *Analects*

**The more extensive a man's
knowledge of what has been done,
the greater will be his power of
knowing what to do.**
BENJAMIN DISRAELI, 1st Earl of
Beaconsfield (1804–81), English
statesman, prime minister, and novelist

The world's great men have not commonly been great scholars, nor its great scholars great men.
OLIVER WENDELL HOLMES, SR (1809–94), American physician, professor, and author: *The Autocrat of the Breakfast Table*

No one can know everything.
HORACE (Quintus Horatius Flaccus) (65–8 BC), Roman poet and satirist: *Carmina*

Knowledge is proportionate to being . . . You know in virtue of what you are.
ALDOUS (LEONARD) HUXLEY (1894–1963), English novelist and essayist: *Time Must Have a Stop, chapter 26*

Knowledge is of two kinds: we know a subject ourselves, or we know where we can find information upon it.
SAMUEL JOHNSON (1709–84), English lexicographer, essayist, and poet: Boswell, *Life of Johnson*

The height of cleverness is to conceal one's cleverness.
FRANÇOIS LA ROCHEFOUCAULD, Duc de La Rochefoucauld (1613–80), French writer: *Maxims*

'Know thyself' is a good saying, but not in all situations. In many it is better to say 'Know others.'
MENANDER (?342–?292 BC), Greek comic dramatist: *Thrasyleon*

Since we cannot be universal and know all that is to be known of everything, we ought to know a little about everything.
BLAISE PASCAL (1623–62), French philosopher, mathematician, and physicist: *Pensées*

A little learning is a dangerous thing.
ALEXANDER POPE (1688–1744), English poet and satirist: *An Essay on Criticism*

Knowledge is power.
Proverb

Knowledge is, in most of those who cultivate it, a species of money, which is valued greatly, but only adds to our well-being in proportion as it is communicated, and is only good in commerce. Take from the wise the pleasure of being listened to, and knowledge would be nothing to them.
JEAN-JACQUES ROUSSEAU (1712–78), Swiss-born French philosopher and writer: *La nouvelle Héloïse*

I know perfectly well that I don't want to do anything; to do something is to create existence – and there's quite enough existence as it is.
JEAN-PAUL SARTRE (1905–80), French philosopher, dramatist, and novelist: *Nausea*

There is only one good, knowledge, and one evil, ignorance.
SOCRATES (?470–399 BC), Athenian philosopher: *Diogenes Laertius*

Science is organized knowledge.
HERBERT SPENCER (1820–1903), English philosopher: *Education, chapter 2*

The desire of knowledge, like the thirst of riches, increases ever with the acquisition of it.
LAURENCE STERNE (1713–68), Irish-born English novelist: *Tristram Shandy*

The things we know best are the things we haven't been taught.
VAUVENARGUES, Marquis de Luc de Clapiers (1715–47), French moralist: *Reflections and Maxims*

LAZINESS

Go to the ant, thou sluggard; consider her ways, and be wise.
The Bible, Authorized (King James) Version, Proverbs 6:6

Idleness is only the refuge of weak minds.
LORD CHESTERFIELD, Philip Dormer Stanhope, 4th Earl of (1694–1773), English statesman and writer: *Letter to his son, 20 July 1749*

He is idle that might be better employed.
THOMAS FULLER (1654–1734), English physician, writer, and compiler: *Gnomologia*

The greatest obstacle to progress is not man's inherited pugnacity, but his incorrigible tendency to parasitism.
WILLIAM RALPH INGE (1860–1954), English theologian: *Outspoken Essays: First Series, 'Patriotism'*

Well, we can't stand around here doing nothing, people will think we're workmen.
SPIKE MILLIGAN (1918–), Irish comedian: *The Goon Show*

The devil finds work for idle hands to do.
Proverb

The hardest work is to go idle.
Proverb

Laziness is often mistaken for patience.
Proverb

One of these days is none of these days.
Proverb

I am happiest when I am idle. I could live for months without performing any kind of labour, and at the expiration of that time I should feel fresh and vigorous enough to go right on in the same way for numerous more months.
ARTEMUS WARD (Charles Farrar Browne) (1834–67), American humorist, editor, and lecturer: *Pyrotechny*

To do nothing at all is the most difficult thing in the world, the most difficult and the most intellectual.
OSCAR WILDE (1856–1900), Irish poet, dramatist, and wit: *Intentions, 'The Critic as Artist'*

LOYALTY

An ounce of loyalty is worth a pound of cleverness.
ELBERT (GREEN) HUBBARD (1856–1915), American businessman, writer, and printer: *The Note Book*

The successful conduct of an industrial enterprise requires two quite distinct qualifications: fidelity and zeal.
JOHN STUART MILL (1806–73), English philosopher and economist: *Principles of Political Economy, book 1*

LUCK

I don't know anything about luck. I've never banked on it, and I'm afraid of people who do. Luck to me is something else: hard work and realizing what is opportunity and what isn't.
LUCILLE BALL (1911–), American actress

We must believe in luck. For how else can we explain the success of those we don't like.
JEAN COCTEAU (1889–1963), French writer and film director

The man who glories in his luck May be overthrown by destiny.
EURIPIDES (?480–406 BC), Greek tragic dramatist: *The Suppliant Women*

He who is not lucky, let him not go a-fishing.
THOMAS FULLER (1654–1734), English physician, writer, and compiler: *Gnomologia*

It is a great piece of skill to know how to guide your luck even while waiting for it.
BALTASAR GRACIÁN (1601–58), Spanish prose writer and Jesuit priest: *The Art of Worldly Wisdom*

Some folk want their luck buttered.
THOMAS HARDY (1840–1928), English novelist and poet: *The Mayor of Caster-bridge*

True luck consists not in holding the best of the cards at the table: Luckiest he who knows just when to rise and go home.
JOHN (MILTON) HAY (1838–1905), American statesman and man of letters: *Distichs*

I am a great believer in luck, and I find the harder I work the more I have of it.
STEPHEN BUTLER LEACOCK (1869–1944), Canadian economist and humorist

It is better to be born lucky than rich.
Proverb

Luck is the residue of diligence.
Saying

MOTIVES

You will find in politics that you are much exposed to the attribution of false motives. Never complain and never explain.
STANLEY BALDWIN, 1st Earl Baldwin of Bewdley (1867–1947), British statesman, quoted in Harold Nicolson, *Diaries and Letters*

We must judge a man's motives from his overt acts.
LORD KENYON, *Judgment in Rex v Waddington*

We should often feel ashamed of our best actions if the world could see all of the motives which produced them.
FRANÇOIS LA ROCHEFOUCAULD, Duc de La Rochefoucauld (1613–80), French writer: *Maxims*

When a stupid man is doing something he is ashamed of, he always declares that it is his duty.
GEORGE BERNARD SHAW (1856–1950), Irish dramatist and critic: *Caesar and Cleopatra, Act 3*

POWER

Power tends to corrupt, and absolute power corrupts absolutely. Great men are almost always bad men . . . There is no worse heresy than that the office sanctifies the holder of it.
JOHN EMERICH EDWARD DALBERG, 1st Baron Acton (1834–1902), English historian: *Letter to Bishop Mandell Creighton, 5 April 1887*

Knowledge is power.
FRANCIS BACON, 1st Baron Verulam, Viscount St Albans (1561–1626), English writer, philosopher, and statesman: *Meditationes Sacrae, 'De Haeresibus'*

Money is economical power.
WALTER BAGEHOT (1826–77), English economist and journalist: *Lombard Street*

Being powerful is like being a lady. If you have to tell people you are, you ain't.
JESSE CARR (1901–), American union leader

Men, such as they are, very naturally seek money or power; and power because it is as good as money.
RALPH WALDO EMERSON (1803–82), American poet, essayist, and philosopher: *The American Scholar*

You shall have joy or you shall have power, said God; you shall not have both.
RALPH WALDO EMERSON, *Journals*

There is always room for a man of force, and he makes room for many.
RALPH WALDO EMERSON, *The Conduct of Life, 'Power'*

Influence those who influence others.
JOHN FAIRCHILD (1927–), American publisher: *Motto*

Men of power have no time to read; yet the men who do not read are unfit for power.
MICHAEL FOOT (1913–), English politician: *Debts of Honour*

There is nothing fortuitous about the tendency for power to beget countervailing power; it is organic. However it does not work evenly. The buttressing of weak bargaining positions has become, as a result, one of the most important of the functions of government.
JOHN KENNETH GALBRAITH (1908–), Canadian-born American economist, diplomat, and writer: *The American Economy: its Substance and Myth*

Under all forms of government the ultimate power lies with the masses. It is not kings nor aristocracies, nor landowners nor capitalists, that anywhere really enslave the people. It is their own ignorance.
HENRY GEORGE (1839–97), American economist: *Protection or Free Trade*, chapter 1

Power is not happiness. Security and peace are more to be desired than a name at which nations tremble.
WILLIAM GODWIN (1756–1836), English political philosopher and novelist: *An Enquiry Concerning Political Justice*

The sole advantage of power is that you can do more good.
BALTASAR GRACIÁN (1601–58), Spanish prose writer and Jesuit priest: *The Art of Worldly Wisdom*

Only he deserves power who every day justifies it.
DAG HAMMARSKJÖLD (1905–61), Swedish statesman and secretary-general of the United Nations: *Markings*

Idealism is the noble toga that political gentlemen drape over their will to power.
ALDOUS (LEONARD) HUXLEY (1894–1963), English novelist and essayist: *New York Herald Tribune, 25 November 1962*

Great power, which incites Great envy, hurls some men to destruction; they are drowned In a long, splendid stream of honors.
JUVENAL (Decimus Junius Juvenalis) (?60–?140), Roman satirist: *Satires*

Power is the ultimate aphrodisiac.
HENRY KISSINGER (1923–), German-born American academic and diplomat, quoted in *Guardian, 28 November 1976*

All life is a game of power. The object of the game is simple enough: to know what you want and get it.
MICHAEL KORDA (1933–), British writer: *Power in the Office*

Nearly all men can stand adversity, but if you want to test a man's character, give him power.
ABRAHAM LINCOLN (1809–65), U.S. statesman and president

Affluence means influence.
JACK LONDON (John Griffith London) (1876–1916), American novelist and adventurer (Attributed)

Power? It's like a dead sea fruit; when you achieve it, there's nothing there.
SIR (MAURICE) HAROLD MACMILLAN, Earl of Stockton (1894–1986), British statesman and prime minister, quoted in Anthony Sampson, *The New Anatomy of Britain*

Economic power is headstrong and vehement, and if it is to prove beneficial to mankind it must be securely curbed and regulated with prudence.
POPE PIUS XI (Achille Ratti) (1857–1939), Italian ecclesiastic and pope: *Quadragesimo anno, 15 May 1931*

Next to enjoying ourselves, the next greatest pleasure consists in preventing others from enjoying themselves, or, more generally, in the acquisition of power.
BERTRAND (ARTHUR WILLIAM) RUSSELL, 3rd Earl Russell, (1872–1970), English philosopher and mathematician: *Sceptical Essays, 'The Recrudescence of Puritanism'*

Power corrupts, but lack of power corrupts absolutely.
ADLAI (EWING) STEVENSON (1900–68), American statesman

Of Lord Northcliffe
He aspired to power instead of influence, and as a result forfeited both.
A(LAN) J(OHN) P(ERCIVALE) TAYLOR (1906–), English historian: *English History 1914–1945*

Men are not corrupted by the exercise of power, or debased by the habit of obedience; but by the exercise of a power which they believe to be illegitimate, and by obedience to a rule which they consider to be usurped and oppressive.
ALEXIS (CHARLES HENRI MAURICE CLÉREL) DE TOCQUEVILLE (1805–59), French politician and political writer: *Democracy in America*

The balance of power.
SIR ROBERT WALPOLE, 1st Earl of Orford (1676–1745), English statesman and prime minister: *Speech, House of Commons, 13 February 1741*

PURPOSE

Ready, fire, aim!
Anon

One should always think of what one is about; when one is learning, one should not think of play; and when one is at play, one should not think of one's learning.
LORD CHESTERFIELD, Philip Dormer Stanhope, 4th Earl of (1694–1773), English statesman and writer: *Letter to his son, 24 July 1739*

First things first, second things never.
SHIRLEY CONRAN, British writer: *Superwoman*

The secret of success is constancy to purpose.
BENJAMIN DISRAELI, 1st Earl of Beaconsfield (1804–81), English statesman, prime minister, and novelist: *Speech, House of Commons, 24 June 1870*

Life, to be worthy of a rational being, must be always in progression; we must always purpose to do more or better than in time past. The mind is enlarged and elevated by mere purposes, though they end as they begin by airy contemplation.
SAMUEL JOHNSON (1709–84), English lexicographer, essayist, and poet: *To Hester Thrale, 29 November 1783*

Year by year we are becoming better equipped to accomplish the things we are striving for. But what are we actually striving for?
BERTRAND DE JOUVENAL (1903–), French writer

If people want a sense of purpose they should get it from their archbishop. They should certainly not get it from their politicians.
SIR (MAURICE) HAROLD MACMILLAN, Earl of Stockton (1894–1986), British statesman and prime minister, quoted in Henry Fairlie, *The Life of Politics*

We set sail within a vast sphere, ever drifting in uncertainty, driven from end to end.
BLAISE PASCAL (1623–62), French philosopher, mathematician, and physicist: *Pensées*

If you don't know where you are going, you will probably end up somewhere else.
DR LAURENCE J. PETER (1919–), Canadian educator and RAYMOND HULL (1919–): *The Peter Principle*

A radical is a man with both feet firmly planted in the air.
FRANKLIN DELANO ROOSEVELT (1882–1945), U.S. statesman and president: *Broadcast, 26 October 1939*

Liberty means responsibility. That is why most men dread it.
GEORGE BERNARD SHAW (1856–1950), Irish dramatist and critic: *Man and Superman, Maxims for Revolutionists*

There are two things to aim at in life: first, to get what you want; and, after that, to enjoy it. Only the wisest of mankind achieve the second.
LOGAN PEARSALL SMITH (1865–1946), American-born English man of letters: *Afterthoughts*

REPUTATION

Have regard for your name, since it will remain for you longer than a great store of gold.
The Apocrypha, Ecclesiasticus 41:12

Work is the price which is paid for reputation.
BALTASAR GRACIÁN (1601–58), Spanish prose writer and Jesuit priest: *The Art of Worldly Wisdom*

A single lie destroys a whole reputation for integrity.
BALTASAR GRACIÁN, *as above*

Worldly wisdom teaches that it is better for the reputation to fail conventionally than to succeed unconventionally.
JOHN MAYNARD KEYNES (1883–1946), English economist: *The General Theory of Employment, Interest and Money*

The world more often rewards the appearances of merit than merit itself.
FRANÇOIS LA ROCHEFOUCAULD, Duc de La Rochefoucauld (1613–80), French writer: *Maxims*

It is generally much more shameful to lose a good reputation than never to have acquired it.
PLINY THE YOUNGER (Gaius Plinius Caecilius Secundus) (?62–?113 AD), Roman writer and administrator: *Letters*

Reputation is often got without merit, and lost without crime.
Proverb

A man's good deeds are known only at home; his bad deeds far away.
Chinese proverb

Cassio
Reputation, reputation, reputation! O, I have lost my reputation! I have lost the immortal part of myself, and what remains is bestial.
WILLIAM SHAKESPEARE (1564–1616), English dramatist and poet: *Othello, Act 2*

One man lies in his work, and gets a bad reputation; another in his manners, and enjoys a good one.
HENRY DAVID THOREAU (1817–62), American essayist and poet: *Journal, 25 June 1852*

Associate yourself with men of good quality if you esteem your own reputation; for 'tis better to be alone than in bad company.
GEORGE WASHINGTON (1732–99), U.S. statesman and president: *Rules of Civility*

One can survive everything nowadays, except death, and live down anything except a good reputation.
OSCAR WILDE (1856–1900), Irish poet, dramatist, and wit: *A Woman of No Importance*

RISK

Uncertainty kills business.
SIR MICHAEL EDWARDES (1930–), British industrialist, quoted in Cary L. Cooper and Peter Hingley, *The Change Makers*

For fools rush in where angels fear to tread.
ALEXANDER POPE (1688–1744), English poet and satirist: *An Essay on Criticism*

Unless you enter the tiger's den you cannot take the cubs.
Japanese proverb

Behold, the fool saith, 'Put not all thine eggs in the one basket' – which is but a manner of saying, 'Scatter your money and your attention', but the wise man saith, 'Put all your eggs in the one basket and – *watch that basket*.'

MARK TWAIN (Samuel Langhorne Clemens) (1835–1910), American novelist and humorist: *Pudd'nhead Wilson, chapter 15*

SELF-INTEREST

'If everybody minded their own business,' the Duchess said in a hoarse growl, 'the world would go

BEHOLD THE FOOL SAITH, 'PUT NOT ALL THINE EGGS IN ONE BASKET' – THE WISE MAN SAITH '... – WATCH THAT BASKET.'

round a deal faster than it does.'
LEWIS CARROLL, (Charles Lutwidge
Dodgson) (1832–98), English writer and
mathematician: *Alice's Adventures in
Wonderland, chapter 6*

**Even wisdom has to yield to
self-interest.**
PINDAR (?518–?438 BC), Greek lyric
poet: *Pythian Odes*

**Every man for himself, and the devil
take the hindmost.**
Proverb

**I know on which side my bread is
buttered.**
Proverb

Look after number one.
Proverb

**We have always known that
heedless self-interest was bad
morals; we now know that it is bad
economics.**
FRANKLIN DELANO ROOSEVELT
(1882–1945), U.S. statesman and
president: *Speech, 1937*

**The world is governed by
self-interest only.**
(JOHANN CHRISTOPH) FRIEDRICH
VON SCHILLER (1759–1805), German
playwright, poet, and historian:
Wallenstein's Death

**Everyone's interest if checked by
everybody else's would in reality
represent the common interest.**

**But when everyone is seeking his
own interest at the expense of
others as well as developing his
own means, it does not always
happen that he is opposed by
equally powerful forces. The strong
thus find it in their interest to seize
and the weak to acquiesce, for the
least evil as well as the greatest
good is a part of the aim of human
policy.**
JEAN CHARLES LÉONARD SIMONDE DE
SISMONDI (1773–1842), Swiss
historian and economist: *Nouveaux
Principes d'Économique politique,
volume 1*

**Every individual . . . generally,
indeed, neither intends to promote
the public interest, nor knows how
much he is promoting it. By
preferring the support of domestic
to that of foreign industry he
intends only his own security; and
by directing that industry in such a
manner as its produce may be of the
greatest value, he intends only his
own gain, and he is in this, as in
many other cases, led by an invisible
hand to promote an end which was
no part of his intention.**
ADAM SMITH (1723–90), Scottish
economist and philosopher: *The Wealth
of Nations, book 4*

**Self-interest is the enemy of all true
affection.**
PUBLIUS CORNELIUS TACITUS (?55–
?120 AD), Roman historian and orator:
History

VISION

Where there is no vision, the people perish.
The Bible, Authorized (King James) Version, Proverbs 29:18

'Men of action,' whose minds are too busy with the day's work to see beyond it. They are essential men, we cannot do without them, and yet we must not allow all our vision to be bound by the limitations of 'men of action.'
PEARL S(YDENSTRIKER) BUCK (1892–1973), American novelist and humanitarian: *What America Means to Me*

Prospect is often better than possession.
THOMAS FULLER (1654–1734), English physician, writer, and compiler: *Gnomologia*

Never look down to test the ground before taking your next step: only he who keeps his eye fixed on the far horizon will find his right road.
DAG HAMMARSKJÖLD (1905–61), Swedish statesman and secretary-general of the United Nations: *Markings*

Visionary people are visionary partly because of the very great many things they don't see.
BERKELEY RICE (1937–), American writer: *The New York Times Magazine, 17 March 1968*

Vision is the art of seeing things invisible.
JONATHAN SWIFT (1667–1745), Anglo-Irish satirist and churchman: *Thoughts on Various Subjects*

INDEX

The index includes themes and authors of quotations in one single listing; themes are shown in CAPITALS.